TEACHING ADULTS

Alan Rogers

Open University Press
Buckingham • Philadelphia

Open University Press
Celtic Court
22 Ballmoor
Buckingham
MK18 1XW

and
1900 Frost Road, Suite 101
Bristol, PA 19007, USA

First edition published 1986
Reprinted 1988, 1989, 1991, 1992, 1993, 1994
First published in this second edition 1996

A catalogue record of this book is available from the British Library

ISBN 0 335 19687 X (hb)   0 335 19623 3 (pb)

Library of Congress Cataloging-in-Publication Data
Rogers, Alan.
     Teaching adults/Alan Rogers. – 2nd ed.
       p.   cm.
     Includes bibliographical references and index.
     ISBN 0–335–19687–X (hardcover). – ISBN 0–335–19623–3 (pbk.)
     1. Adult education.   2. Learning.   I. Title.
   LC5215.R58   1996
   374 – dc20   96–10731
                                                                              CIP

Typeset by Type Study, Scarborough
Printed and bound in Great Britain by Redwood Books, Trowbridge, Wiltshire

CONTENTS

PREFACE AND ACKNOWLEDGEMENTS

This book is about teaching adults in a wide variety of contexts. Most books on adults' learning have tended to concentrate on either non-vocational leisure-type programmes or on vocational, professional and other more formal training courses; a few have addressed themselves to the different forms of community education groups. This book attempts to look at what is common to, and distinctive about, all forms of teaching adults, whether in advanced instructional courses in formal institutions or in informal learning situations, whether taken by lecturers, teachers, tutors, instructors, supervisors, trainers, extension workers, facilitators or other people, whether in the so-called 'developed' countries or in the Third World.

The book has arisen out of courses I have conducted with various groups of teachers of adults in the United Kingdom and abroad. Some were full-time professional teachers of adults; others were part-timers. Several were people who do not see their primary role as educational (for example, clergy and health visitors) but who have come to realise that they spend much of their time teaching adults. The illustrative material used in the book reflects its origins, and is drawn from a wide variety of settings.

Language

The book is intended for all those who find themselves teaching adults. In these circumstances, language is always a problem. I have throughout used the word 'teacher' (sometimes qualified as 'teacher-planner' or 'teacher-agent') for all these people, although I appreciate that many people prefer the term 'tutor' to indicate the informal relationship between teacher and adult student participants. The true role of the teacher – helping the student learners to learn – is no different from that of the tutor. I have also used the form 'student participant' frequently, although it is rather clumsy, to indicate that I do not see the learner as a pupil but as participating in a range of activities that bring about learning.

'Knowledge' too is difficult. A distinction is often drawn between skill-based and knowledge-based courses, between craft, art and literacy on the one hand and politics, economics and literature on the other. The distinction is not entirely valid, for knowledge (in the sense of knowing how to do something) and understanding (seeing the relationships between the different parts of the exercises) underlie all skill-based courses, just as skills (reading, writing, discussing, etc.) underlie such 'knowledge-based' courses. Nevertheless some programmes are aimed *primarily* at the acquisition of skills, others *primarily* at the acquisition of new understandings and insights. This distinction still seems to be useful, so long as 'knowledge' where it is used in this book is seen to relate to skills as much as to other forms of information.

A learning tool

The book has arisen directly out of my teaching. This has caused some problem in ordering the material. In teaching it is often necessary to repeat what has gone before; in a book, such repetition must be avoided as far as possible. I have tried to cut repetition down to a minimum.

A book is a one-way directive medium; but in this case I am using it to discuss what is in many contexts meant to be a non-directive process of self-exploration. At times I have found myself becoming too directive about teaching in a non-directive manner! I have tried to ease this tension wherever possible.

Acknowledgements

I must thank all those who have helped in the preparation of this book. In a number of ways it is a product of the corporate experience built up over many years at Nottingham University's Department of Adult Education, and it reflects the exciting work of former colleagues such as Alan Champion, Gordon Douglas and Sam Lilley, and of Paula Allman, John Daines, David Jones and Karl Mackie, all of whom will see something of themselves in these pages. I wish particularly to thank John Fox and Brian Graham, both of whom read an early draft of the text and offered much encouragement. Above all I must thank my students, who challenged everything and contributed so much.

Acknowledgement is gladly made for permission to print the extract on pages 155–6 from Clyde Reid's book *Groups Alive – Church Alive* (1969), the 'Poem for Everyman' by John Wood from his collection *How Do You Feel? A Guide to Your Emotions* (1974) on pages 62–3 and the poem by R. D. Laing, *Knots* (1972) published by Routledge (Tavistock), on page 65.

Preface to the second edition

A second edition offers the chance to review what was written more than ten years ago in rather stressful conditions in Northern Ireland. I am surprised at how much of this still seems to be valid today. The large amount of writing on adult education both in Europe and in North America over the last years has clearly confirmed much of what was thought; only perhaps in the area of 'learning' have there been substantial revisions.

Nevertheless, every chapter has been amended in one way or another. The section on learning has been completely rewritten, and the chapters on 'Blocks to Learning' and 'Evaluation' have received some additional material.

I have been careful not to include in this book material that I set out in my more recent study *Adults Learning for Development* (Rogers 1992), which deals with other areas of adult education, especially its social change objectives. These matters are not dealt with here.

I am grateful to all those who have helped to make this a better book, not least the reviewers. I hope that many more people will find it useful in their work of helping adults to learn.

BEFORE YOU START

I am assuming that, as a reader of this book, you are a practising teacher of adults, or that you are responsible for organising programmes for adults, or that you hope at some time to teach adults. You bring with you to the reading of this book a good deal of experience and expectation to draw upon. Experience suggests that the best way of relating to the material that follows would be for you to make it concrete for yourself, to apply it to some immediate situation; for this book is not intended to be a theoretical discussion but a practical examination of some of the principles of teaching adults.

I therefore suggest that, before you go any further, you choose an example of a course that you have taught, are going to teach or would like to teach to adults; or for which you have been or are responsible, or have attended as a student participant – any situation, in fact, in which you can envisage yourself in a position of teacher in relation to a group of real or imaginary students. It will, I think, help if you write it out here before you start. You might care to answer the following questions:

What is the subject of the course?

How long is the course and how often will the group meet?

Who and how many are the students?

Where and at what time will the group meet?

You can keep turning back to this page as you read the rest of the book and fill in this outline in more detail.

1

A CONTRACT TO LEARN

How do we come to be here . . . ?

Agreeing to learn together

Teaching adults: a world of difference

People engage in teaching adults in many different contexts and for many different purposes.

Sometimes the *setting* is formal, within the walls of one of our educational institutions. At other times it takes place through an organisation specifically set up to help adults learn – like the Workers' Educational Association (WEA) or an industrial training agency or professional body. Or again it may be within one of a host of informal situations: community and voluntary associations, women's groups, sports and leisure agencies, bodies such as the churches or political parties, museums and libraries, or among members of the rescue and caring professions.

The *forms and contexts* are many. People teach adults formally or informally in prisons and church halls, in colleges and private houses, in sports and leisure centres and factories, in shops and offices, in community centres and military bases, in schools and specialist adult education centres, in health clinics and on university campuses, in training centres and temporary caravans. They teach during the day, in the evening, at weekends and while on holiday.

Sometimes the *process* is a direct one – a course on management or computers or retraining in new techniques of construction, an extension course for farmers, a woodwork class or church confirmation group. Sometimes it is less direct, helping a local history society to mount an exhibition, a residents' group to fight a planning proposal, a choir to sing, a health group to give up smoking, a group of villagers to set up a cooperative.

And it is undertaken for a variety of *purposes*: to lead to a new qualification, or changed personal attitudes, or the development of the community, or new skills for job or hobbies, or the improvement of basic skills, or to open new doors to further learning.

Exercise
Write notes on your chosen course or programme as follows:

- setting:

Would you say that it is formal or informal?

- form and context:

- process:

Would you say that it is direct or indirect?

- purpose:

The field we operate in, the teaching of adults, is a vast one with a myriad of different expressions, confusing because it seems to lack structure and form. Anywhere where two or three people are gathered together to learn something on a systematic basis under supervision, someone is found teaching adults.

It may be helpful to distinguish between three main adult education sectors:

- *formal* – courses and classes run by schools, colleges, universities and other statutory and non-statutory agencies making up the educational system;
- '*extra-formal*' – courses and classes run by formal agencies *outside* the educational system, e.g. government departments, industrial training agencies, trade unions and commercial concerns;
- *non-formal* – educational activities provided by voluntary agencies and informal groups.

The categories partly overlap, since non-formal courses may be provided by formal agencies, for example see Figs. 1 and 2. It would be helpful if you could locate the course(s) you are involved in on these figures, if you can.

There are in addition non-taught self-programming groups of adults, study

Figure 1 The sectors of adult education

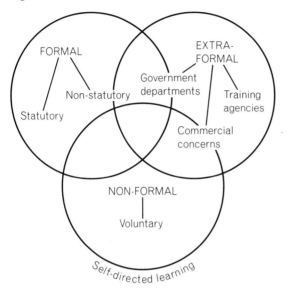

circles without a face-to-face teacher. There is also the area of *self-directed learning*. The latter comprises educational opportunities for individuals provided by bodies like broadcasting organisations, correspondence agencies and publishers of books, journals and magazines. It is not often recognised that one of the most extensive means of adult learning are those newspapers and magazines that mount programmes of study in subjects like cooking, dressmaking, do-it-yourself, woodworking, computing, health and beauty and gardening, all of which attract large audiences. Self-directed learning opportunities are also provided by numerous cultural organisations offering musical and dramatic events, art exhibitions, visits to places of environmental and historic interest and the like – any activity that an adult may choose to take up on his or her own (or with their family) in order to follow a special interest and to achieve a particular accomplishment, whether related to their job or not. But even in this context, there is someone involved in the 'teaching' process, however indirectly: someone who has written the book, planned the learning programme, laid out the sequence of activities or the steps to be followed, or produced the material for study.

A number of different ideologies lie behind these various forms of teaching adults, and they affect the way we as teachers of adults react. The most important of these relate to (1) the objectives of the learning programme and (2) the involvement or non-involvement of the student participants in the planning process. Some programmes are offered with specific objectives, especially those in the training field; others are offered with more open-ended

Figure 2 A possible taxonomy of teaching adults, with examples

	Qualification courses	Vocational courses	Personal growth courses	Basic/access courses	Community development
Formal: statutory bodies, educational • general programmes open to adults, e.g. schools/colleges/universities • special provision for adults, e.g. extramural/Open University/advanced continuing education/industrial training bodies/adult literacy agencies/technical training and validating bodies	School-leaving certs/diplomas/degrees/higher degrees	Short courses and conferences/management/information technology	Non-vocational 'liberal' adult education	New opportunities/return to study	
Extra-formal: courses provided by central or locally administered public bodies and other agencies outside the formal educational system • training agencies/government departments/army/prisons/sports bodies/arts and cultural agencies/museums and libraries • trade unions/firms and businesses/professional associations/mass media	Certificates and other awards	Shop stewards/shopfloor training/farmers' training schemes	Health (smoking)/alcohol/pregnancy/family planning/nutrition/sports and hobbies/cultural		
Non-formal: voluntary bodies • primarily non-educational, e.g. WEA/adult literacy agencies/private colleges/correspondence courses • primarily non-educational, e.g. aid and welfare organisations/churches/community groups/unemployed workers' groups/self-help groups	Some non-professional certificates		Leisure/crafts/do-it-yourself/art Residents' programmes/planning/weight-watchers	Basic education	Women's programmes/unemployed programmes/retirement courses/marriage guidance

goals, such as personal growth. Most programmes lie somewhere between the two extremes. Equally, some programmes are organised with, some without, consultation with the prospective participants; again, each course lies somewhere along the spectrum formed by these two opposites (see Fig. 3). The determination of both of these matters is a question of policy on the part of the providing agency.

> *Exercise*
> Decide for yourself where on Fig. 3 your own course or programme comes.

Figure 3 Organisation of adult education courses

Such issues reflect the distinction that must be drawn in most cases between the *providers* (organisations, institutions or individuals who plan the whole programme and outline the various parts of it) and the *teachers*. The relationship between teacher and provider in adult education is a complex one and varies greatly from place to place. In some parts of the non-formal sector, they may be one and the same person; and in all cases the teacher is a planner of the learning situation as much as (in some cases more than) an instructor. But the interests of provider/organiser and teacher are in many respects different, and it is well to bear this distinction in mind.

Adult education is voluntary and purposeful

Two characteristics are common to virtually all forms of teaching adults. The first is that *the participants are voluntary learners*. Those who come as student participants to the programmes, courses and classes we offer come out of choice, and the teachers who come face to face with them are confronted by people who in most cases have selected their teachers rather than the other way about. There are, it is true, a number of forms of adult learning in which the freedom of the participant is somewhat circumscribed. Programmes of industrial training or staff development provided by firms, for example, are at times less than fully voluntary; pressures may be exerted on some people to come to courses when they would rather be somewhere else; and in several parts of the world financial inducements are offered to encourage participation in developmental programmes of literacy, family planning and agricultural extension education. So it is necessary to keep some qualification in mind when we speak of the voluntary nature of the adult student. Nevertheless the adult nature of the student participants means that they are attending programmes of education because they have determined for one reason or another to be there and not to be elsewhere; they have *decided* to be there.

And *they have come with an intention*, in most cases to achieve a learning goal. Again we need to bear in mind some qualification to this general statement. Those who are there because they have been told to come may have less clear intentions than the others. Some will have come more for social reasons than for the immediate learning, while others may not always know clearly what they want or may want one thing and in fact find achievement in something different. Nevertheless they all come for a purpose – and if they don't get it, sooner or later they will stop coming. There are, it is true, many known cases of adults staying in courses from which they are getting little for long periods out of politeness or a sense of loyalty, but in the end they almost always drop out.

Two conclusions follow:

- The provider and the teacher in programmes for adults need to *attract* participants into their programmes. The keyword in all the many varied fields of adult education is 'offer'. The providing agency offers a learning opportunity, and the adult student participant determines whether to accept the offer.
- This means that a *bargain* is thought to have been struck. An agreement is concluded between the provider/teacher and the learner: that the one will offer the learning opportunity and that the other will work to achieve some goal or other, whether this be literacy or some advanced-level engineering technique or increased confidence or the skill of making furniture. This is true not only of those cases where the content and format of the programme have been negotiated between the provider (and/or the teacher) and the potential participants, when the terms of the engagement may be set out in some detail; it is also true when the organisers devise the programme on their own. The terms of the bargain may not be spelled out in full, but the agreement is there nonetheless.

A contract to learn

An agreement exists, then, in all forms of adult learning, wherever adults come voluntarily to learn. There are major divergences amongst those who teach adults concerning the nature of adult education and its goals and

objectives. Some providers and teachers see their main function as imparting skills or knowledge; they instruct their students. Some see their aim as
the development of awareness, comprehension and understanding; they
engage their students in discussion and other exercises. Others see their
purpose in more general terms as influencing attitudes and, through this,
behaviour; they pursue a more active engagement with the student participants in simulation exercises and other activities. Yet others see their role in
a less directive fashion as providing opportunities for the participants to
learn what they want to learn in their own way, to grow and develop, to
explore for themselves, to come to their own conclusions, to finish up in a
place determined not by the teacher but by the learner.

These differences do not negate the proposition that an agreement has been
struck. It takes a different form for each type of teaching–learning context;
but what will not be in doubt is the willingness of the teacher-agent to set up
the learning environment and programme, and the agreement of the participant to engage in a series of learning activities in order to achieve certain outcomes. (The phrase 'learning contract' has recently been used to describe a
particular form of educational encounter, but I am using the word 'contract'
here in a more general sense as applying to all forms of teaching adults.)

Assumptions

Such an agreement is based on assumptions made by both teacher and adult
student participant even before the two have met. Neither teachers nor learners start with a blank sheet. The teachers begin with a set of ideas about who
and what they will be teaching, and the adult student participants have some
idea of what they want and what they are going to get. These assumptions
have been created in part by calling into play views developed over many
years, in part by interpreting the description of the particular programme on
offer.

Many of these assumptions are unspoken, even when a lengthy process of
consultation with prospective student participants has been engaged in or
when the learning programme is set out in detail; for on both sides there are
hidden presuppositions about the process in which they are engaged. The
assumptions may or may not be true, but to a large extent they determine
the effectiveness of the learning process. We need therefore to explore the
process by which these assumptions are created.

The information provided

The assumptions of the potential participant are based on the information
given about the course or programme. This varies widely. At its minimum it
gives some indication of the subject (usually a title to the course), format

(frequency of meeting and length of time involved), location and timing, and institution or organisation under whose umbrella the programme is being provided; there is sometimes a 'blurb' containing details about the content of the programme of study. The following examples reveal something of the range of information offered to potential student participants.

A field studies centre:

May 9–13 **Understanding the Countryside**. A four-day environmental studies course for primary schools at a specially reduced rate.

May 27–29 **Insects**. A weekend course on the identification and ecology of insects. Particularly suitable for beginners. Tutor: A. S— PhD.

July 27–August 3 **Understanding Rocks**. For all interested.

From an adult education programme leaflet:

Course	Day	Commencement date
Beekeeping	EC	October
French – Beginners	Mondays	October
Leaving Cert. English Language	Tuesdays	*
Ballroom Dancing	EC	*

(Details of the abbreviations, dates and locations are provided elsewhere in this local authority leaflet.)

Sometimes more detail is provided:

The Earth beneath Us H — B — Mondays 7.45 p.m. This course is designed to be suitable for beginners as well as those who have some knowledge of geology. It will primarily be concerned with the earth, structures, mineral locations and the development of scenery.

Coping with Crises D — J — Wednesdays 7.45 p.m. We all meet crises in our lives and deal with them in our own way. This course will look at some of the most common problems that arise. It will be of interest to everyone, especially parents and those working in a voluntary capacity with various agencies. Among the areas covered will be relationships, separation, bereavement, communicating with adolescents, divorce and living with elderly dependants.

Elsewhere the details are more explicit:

Philosophy and Philosophers I
Tutor: A. J. D — Mondays at 7.30 p.m. from 1 October 199–.

Topics covered in this course will include: the nature of philosophy; the nature of reasoning and in particular philosophical reasoning; important concepts used in philosophy; the central problems of philosophy; the history of philosophy and the ideas of some of the great philosophers; the main 'isms' and 'ologies' within philosophy (positivism, existentialism, phenomenology, etc.); and the relationships between philosophy and other disciplines.

The course is designed in three parts, each free-standing but interrelated. Each part consists of ten sessions and the second part, *Philosophy and Philosophers II*, will be offered, subject to demand, in the Spring Term.

Fee: £16.00

Secretarial Development: Building Personal Effectiveness

Course outline
This is an important course for secretaries who wish to build confidence and to bring more authority, understanding and conviction to their positions.

Role-play exercises and discussion are used extensively within a workshop format to develop a greater understanding of ourselves and our relationships with others. The objective is to learn to handle ourselves more effectively, so that we deal with colleagues and superiors with greater sensitivity and authority.

The workshop includes short sessions aimed at developing skills which are of particular importance to secretaries. These include:

- clear thinking;
- handling difficult situations;
- self-analysis and self-protection;
- understanding the behaviour and reactions of others.

Duration: Two days

For whom: Secretarial staff in third-level education who wish to develop skills in relating effectively to others.

Course leader: E — M —

Date: Thurs. 14 to Fri. 15. March 199–

Fee: £150.00

Such information, however brief, immediately creates a set of expectations. For example, the implication of

---

Keep Fit: Tuesdays

---

in an adult and community education service programme is clear; a course of meetings will be held on each Tuesday evening for the next ten or so weeks in a suitable (designated) building, open to anyone of either sex who wishes to attend (however unfit he or she may be) and who pays the relevant fee. A series of exercises, some painful and some relaxing, will be undertaken, the net outcome of which (apart from a number of unexpected outcomes like sickness or divorce) will be in most cases a 'fitter' person. All this and more can be read into those three words viewed in the context of the rest of the leaflet.

Publicity versus the learning contract

The information provided for potential participants about the contract on offer is often very limited. It is argued by some providers that this is due to the lack of money available to adult education agencies for publicity; but frequently it is because organisers do not see the necessity of giving more detail. The material produced is primarily issued as publicity for the programme rather than as a description of the learning agreement. Its main aim is to persuade the readers to join the course.

This desire to attract participants into our programmes leaves much unsaid. We dare not say too much of what is involved in our programmes in case we 'put people off'. The publicity aspect normally predominates, and the search for striking phrases sometimes outweighs the informative content.

Some adult education programmes offered to the public consist of little more than a list of titles:

Welding	Mondays
Upholstery	Mondays
Restoration of Antiques	Tuesdays
Car Maintenance	Tuesdays
Beehive Construction	Wednesdays
Traditional Music	Wednesdays
Creative Dance	Thursdays
Bridge	Thursdays

All classes will commence in the week beginning 1 October, will run from 7.30 p.m. to 9.00 p.m., and will last for nine weeks. Cost £35 per course; special discounts for OAPs and the unemployed.

What more, it is urged, is needed? The potential learners do not need to know the name of the teacher or what the course is about; it is enough (so the argument goes) for them to know that if they turn up on Wednesday evenings in the place and at the time specified, pay the stated fee and do the work (unspecified), they will be taught how to make a beehive.

But such a list is not adequate. There is no indication of the level of work intended, of the demands to be made upon the learners, of the entry requirements for each course, and so on. The organiser tends to assume that all these items of information are already known by the reader. But they may not be; is the beehive construction course intended for the expert carpenter but novice apiarist or for the expert apiarist and novice woodworker – or for both?

The omission of all matter other than the title of the course and particulars of its length, time and duration of meeting, location and cost reveals much about the assumptions of the organisers. In many cases they are relying on the reputation of the providing agency for the credibility of what they offer. They are looking mainly to previous student participants rather than to breaking new ground, attracting hitherto untouched groups of learners. The fact that the programme is run by such-and-such university, local authority, college, voluntary body, development agency or training organisation is to them enough indication and guarantee of the kind and quality of the courses offered (see Exercise on the next page).

But whether it is enough to persuade new participants to join in our programmes must be doubted. Potential student participants need to have enough information if they are to formulate in their own minds and to accept a contract of learning: what the course is all about, what is expected of them and what they themselves might expect to gain from the experience. These lists, unless backed up by other information, will not be very effective in attracting people who have never before been in an adult or continuing education course; they will result in a good deal of uncertainty on the part of those participants who do decide to come, and it will take some time once the course has commenced to resolve this uncertainty.

Books and blurbs

We can illustrate all of this by looking at books. Books are often a form of adult learning opportunity; they offer the chance to their readers to pursue a course of activity (reading, and in some cases undertaking exercises) that will lead to some more or less concrete result (greater understanding or more developed skills, etc.). They thus make a bargain with their readers, a contract.

This book is itself an example of such a learning contract. It is intended for those who know or wish to know something about teaching adults. It sets out to suggest that, if you read it and if you experiment on the basis of it, then you will have an opportunity to reassess your teaching of adults and to examine possible alternative approaches. You can use the book entirely

Keep Fit and Leisure Activities

Course	Day	Commencement dates
Badminton – Advanced	Monday	*
Badminton – Beginners	Monday	*
Bridge – Beginners	Monday	*
Bridge – Advanced	Monday	
Swimming – Continuation	Monday & Tuesday	6 sessions Mon. & Tues. over 3 weeks
Ladies' Keep Fit to Music	Tuesday	
Keep Fit – Men	Wednesday	*
Keep Fit/Weight Lifting – Men	Wednesday	*
Swimming – Beginners	Wednesday	6 sessions Wed. & Fri. over 3 weeks
Badminton	Thursday	*
Keep Fit	Friday	*
From Walking to Rock & Mountain Climbing	Monday	4 weeks & weekend outings

Building

Production Techniques in Pre-cast Concrete
Duration: 1 afternoon and evening.
Date: 11 October 199–.
Location: ---

Civil Engineering
Site Supervision
Duration: 3 days.
Dates: November–December 199–.
Location: ---

Construction Planning and Programming
Duration: 3 days.
Dates: January–February 199–.
Location: ---

Computer Programming in BASIC for Engineers
Duration: 1 evening per week for 6 weeks.
Dates: January–February 199–.
Location: ---

Seminars for the Professional Interview of the Institution of Civil Engineers
Duration: 1 evening per week for 6 weeks.
Dates: 5 February–12 March 199–.
Location: ---

as you please, reading some bits and skipping others; you can use it to achieve your own purposes. It is a tool of your own self-directed learning; in fact this is its main aim, to become a resource for you to reflect critically on your own work in teaching adults. This is the contract the book offers.

The contracts offered by books are usually drawn up unilaterally by the publisher and/or the author; there can rarely be any process of consultation, and there is little the reader can do to change the terms of the contract. Sometimes the terms of the offer are expressed in the title and the name of the author without further detail. To take an example at random from my shelves, Konrad Elsdon's classic study *Training for Adult Education* (1975) has nothing other than the title and the name of the series in which it appears (Nottingham Studies in the Theory and Practice of the Education of Adults) to indicate what the book is all about. But more often a blurb on the dust-jacket or cover serves as both publicity to sell the book and as information sheet. In many cases the contract is set out in more detail in the introduction, indicating what the book is about, how it came to be written and who it is intended for. But however it is presented, the prospective purchasers in each case must make up their mind on the basis of the information provided (including the appearance of the book, its illustrations, format, length and price), what sort of opportunity is being offered and whether to accept it or not.

Two examples: the first comes from *I'm OK – You're OK* (Harris 1973) (originally published, less successfully, under the title *The Book of Choice*). The contract in this case is: 'If you read this book you will learn how to cope better.'

> I'm not OK – You're OK . . . I'm not OK – You're not OK . . . I'm OK – You're not OK . . . **I'M OK – YOU'RE OK**
>   This practical guide to Transactional Analysis is a unique approach to your problems.
>   Hundreds of thousands of people have found this phenomenal breakthrough in psychotherapy a turning point in their lives.
>   In sensible, non-technical language Thomas Harris explains how to gain control of yourself, your relationships and your future – *no matter what has happened in the past.*
>   Originally published by Jonathan Cape Ltd as *The Book of Choice.*

I'm OK – You're OK is intended to be popular and non-selective in its readership. Other books aim at a particular audience. A second example, the cover copy of *Live and Learn* (Claxton 1984), is more highbrow in tone. It achieves this partly by its title, which although general and brief is qualified by a longer subtitle, and partly by the language it uses. The references to named psychologists indicate that the book is intended for those who already know something about the subject:

Live and Learn: An Introduction to the Psychology of Growth and Change in Everyday Life

This is an introduction to the psychology of learning which takes a fresh approach. It sees learning in the context of everyday experience, and looks at the kinds of things people learn, how they learn them and what makes it easier or more difficult for learning to take place. It points to the opportunities that arise for learning in the course of everyday existence, and shows how people deal with these opportunities or get in the way of their own learning. The book tells a coherent 'story' of learning in which the psychology of Skinner, Rogers, Bruner, Kelly and Piaget each has its place. Rather than recapitulating these theories, the book aims to show how they enhance, illuminate and complement each other.

'This is a most stimulating and readable book, based at all points on an excellent and comprehensive knowledge of psychology, and breaking much in the way of new ground ... It is a poor look-out for psychology if a book like this does not sell, and does not stimulate a great deal in the way of new thinking.' David Fontana

Guy Claxton lectures at London University on the psychology of education

A similar situation exists in teaching adults. The information needed to attract them into our programmes and to set out for them the terms of the learning contract is much the same: a title, a statement of the format of the programme, a note of the teacher and of the cost of the course. In addition some description of the content of the course is necessary if potential participants are to have enough material – an indication of the market at which the programme is aimed and the intended outcomes of the experience:

Painting for Beginners L — McC — Mondays 7.30 p.m. It will not matter if you have never painted in your life before as these classes are intended to acquaint the beginner with how to prepare materials and how to use different styles for different effects.

French for Beginners J — M — Mondays 7.30 p.m. This course is designed for those who have no knowledge of French or who have forgotten what they have learnt at school.

What is Politics? K — S — Mondays 7.30 p.m. A course intended for those who want to know more about current affairs but who are interested in major political theories such as liberalism, capitalism, socialism, etc.

Creating the contract

All three parties to the adult learning experience – the organiser or providing agency; the teacher; and the potential student participants – are actively involved in drawing up the contract (Fig. 4).

Providing agency

The organiser establishes the parameters to the learning opportunity – the framework, including the rest of the programme within which the course is set; the subject of the course; the format (location, number of meetings, time and duration of each meeting); the modes of publicity. They may do all of this on their own, or in association with the teacher and/or after discussion with a prospective student group. Where a professional association, residents' group, local history society or similar body exists, it is relatively easy to discuss in advance what they want to learn and in what way, and increasingly adult teaching bodies are discussing future programmes with firms and

Figure 4 Drawing up the learning contract

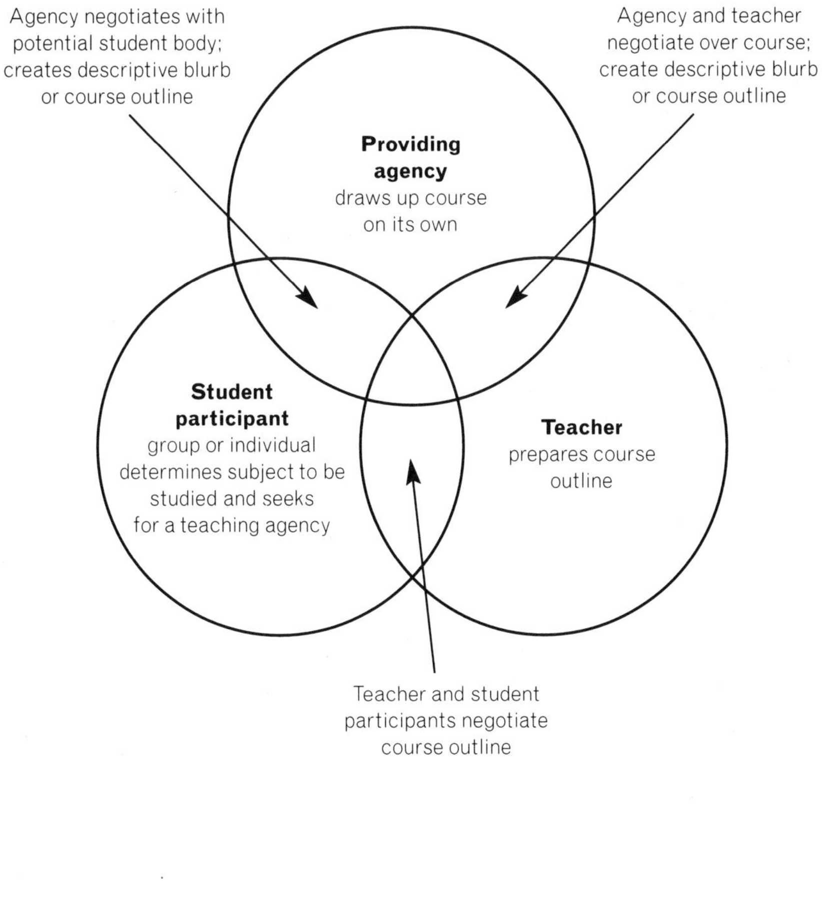

Agency negotiates with
potential student body;
creates descriptive blurb
or course outline

Agency and teacher
negotiate over course;
create descriptive blurb
or course outline

**Providing
agency**
draws up course
on its own

**Student
participant**
group or individual
determines subject to be
studied and seeks
for a teaching agency

Teacher
prepares course
outline

Teacher and student
participants negotiate
course outline

other potential 'customers'. But on other occasions such opportunities, even where they clearly exist, are not taken. The organisers determine by themselves or in discussion with their teachers what they think the potential student participants should learn and how.

Teacher

There are occasions when the teacher is excluded from the discussion. The organisers build up a course outline and set out to find someone to teach 'their' programme. In these cases the teachers take over a contract already created and fit their work to that. If, for example, we are asked to take a ten-meeting course for beginners on upholstery, the parameters have already been set, irrespective of whether we feel that ten meetings constitute an appropriate length of time for beginners to master anything meaningful about upholstery or not.

But more usually the teacher is a party to the construction of the learning opportunity. This is often our first task, to determine what is to be taught, how much can be covered in the time available and at what level, how it should be taught, to whom and to what purpose. Again, like the organiser, we may do it on our own, or in association with the providing agency or in consultation with prospective learners.

Teacher and participants

The programme devised by the teacher is constructed for the student participants. The contract to learn is made with them, not between the teacher and the providing agency (a different contract may be in force there). The organisers will usually be keen to see what we have in mind to teach; in most cases they will be able to offer advice based on practical experience on matters of both publicity and course content. It is thus well worth our while to discuss the course outline with the providing agency; but the contract is not written for that body. Nor is it written for other teachers, examining boards, professional associations, local education committees or academic colleagues. The contract is made directly with the potential student participants; it is the first point of contact between teacher and learner.

In most cases what we have to offer is drawn up *before* we meet the potential student participants, even before we know who the learners will be. This problem is often a severe one. One answer that has been proposed, probably the worst of all possible worlds, is to do no planning at all, to wait until we meet the learners for the first time. But normally this is impractical. We need to establish the subject of the course just to call together the prospective student participants. Where a group already exists, it is possible for us to meet them and to determine the outlines of the programme of learning jointly; but even here our expertise as teacher or group leader and our experience in this type of programme are called upon to indicate the realistic limits of what can be achieved in any given length of time and to set out practical proposals for a programme of work. The task of planning the course normally falls to the teacher, however much we may negotiate with the potential student participants in the process.

Limitations on the teacher

We are not completely free in drawing up our proposals. First, we are limited by the context within which we are teaching. The format of the course has usually been set already – by custom, by the organiser or by negotiation with the learners – and this may impose restrictions on what can be done. Many aspects may already have been fixed for us when planning our course:

- the *timing of the course* (still too often determined by traditional school terms even outside the formal adult education sector, although courses other than the 'one-term' or 'twenty-meeting' variety are now appearing, determined by the time the learners have available or the time needed to master some skill or branch of study);
- its *frequency of meeting* (still usually once a week, although again other formats are becoming more common);
- the *duration of the class meeting* (usually one and a half or two hours, which experience suggests is appropriate to adult learning groups in most contexts);
- and its *location*.

Exercise

You might care to indicate in connection with your own course or programme described above whether these areas of planning were undertaken by yourself or whether they were 'given' to you or whether you agreed them jointly with the planner and whether the students determined any of them:

	Planner	*Teacher*	*Jointly*	*Students*
The time of the course				
The frequency of meeting				
The duration of the class session				
The location of the course/programme				

Secondly, we are limited by our view of the prospective students. Consciously or unconsciously, we make a range of decisions about who they are, how much they already know about the subject, what they want to learn, how much work they will expect to do, what sort of activity they will be prepared to engage in. We may be wrong in all of this. They may not be willing to play games, hand in written work, bring floral specimens for classwork; but in our planning we make assumptions on all these matters. The programme we draw up is not a matter of what we as teachers alone want; using our experience, we produce a balance between what we have to offer and what we assume the student participants may or may not be looking for or what they may or may not be willing and able to do.

The parts to the contract

A book cover usually describes several aspects of the book; it includes a title, a note of the book's theme and subject, and the name (or a fuller description)

Adult Learners, Adult Education and the Community
by Stephen Brookfield

Adults are continually learning outside of conventional educational frameworks (evening classes, etc.) – acquiring new skills and knowledge in the family, in leisure pursuits, at work, and in a range of other community settings. Stephen Brookfield discusses this informal independent learning and explores:

• The extent and quality of this informal, independent learning.
• The learning which goes on in various groups in the community –
  across a spectrum from hobby clubs to activist groups (from
  beekeeping societies to tenants' associations).
• The ways in which adult educators can work with independent
  adult learners to support and enhance their learning.

He draws upon historical and contemporary examples from Britain and North America in providing an analytical and comprehensive exploration of adult education, community education and their essential interconnections.

Stephen Brookfield was formerly a Lecturer/Organiser at an adult education centre, a Professor of Adult Education at the University of British Colombia, and a Research Officer for the Advisory Council for Adult and Continuing Education in England. He is now Assistant Professor of Adult and Continuing Education at Teachers College.

Open University Press

---

of the author, as the book blurb example illustrates. And much the same is true of the offers made in adult education programmes. The different parts of the statement concerning the learning programme need further discussion.

First there is the *title* of the course (or at the least some indication of the subject). As with some books, these are on occasion chosen more for their euphony or intended striking qualities than for the light they throw on the subject-matter. This may be adequate for those student-learners who come back year after year to the same sort of programme and who have grown accustomed to the stylistic habits of the organiser, but it does not always help to draw new people into our programmes. 'Men under Masters', without any further elaboration, is not exactly indicative that a study of local history in a nineteenth-century industrial Midlands town is intended.

Few publishers would think of issuing a book without the name of the author; but many organisers issue adult education programmes without the name of the *teacher*. Those who are considering whether or not to accept the learning contract we offer have the right to know who the teachers are and what expertise and experience they possess. On occasions it is assumed that the teachers will be well known to potential participants from their other activities and thus only their names are given; sometimes a programme is offered simply on the reputation of someone as 'a good teacher'. In these cases recruitment is largely confined to those who know of the teacher and their immediate circle. At other times the teachers will be endorsed by the qualifications or position they hold or by the experience they can bring to the task.

Usually there is a *description* outlining the subject-matter of the course. These are normally short and uninformative. We expect the learners to have some idea about the subject they want to learn before they come to our

---

Management for the 1990s
Mr J. A. T— BA MSc. IPFA DMA MBIM. Six lectures commencing 3 October 199–, 7–9 p.m. Fee: £15.00 Old Hall Centre, High Street, ---

The course will explore the range of techniques, skills and behavioural styles available to the modern manager including decision-making techniques; leadership and motivation; communications; personnel and the management of change. It is intended to meet participants' needs as far as possible and will use discussion groups, practical exercises and consciousness-raising techniques.

Course texts: P. F. Drucker (1982) *The Practice of Management* (Pan Books), T. Lupton (1979) *Management and the Social Sciences*.

classes. A full description of our course would take up too much space, but the prospective participant is entitled to know something of what the programme of work will be about, what sort of learning is expected to take place, what the purpose of the exercise is, at what level and for how long the programme will continue, who the course is intended for and what sort of activity they may expect to be engaged in.

Selecting the participants

At times it may be necessary to spell out the target group or level of commitment, experience or ability that the programme calls for from the participants, particularly any pre-requirements set by the teacher. This is sometimes done in the title. A school-leaving certificate course provided for adults, such as 'O-level Biology: Tuesdays 7–9 p.m. starting 17 October', makes this clear, as do programmes listed as:

Typewriting – Beginners	Monday
Shorthand – Continuation	Monday

or 'Drug Therapy Update for GPs'. Or this can be done in the descriptive blurb: 'This introductory course . . .' or 'This advanced language course . . .'. However, even then we leave it to the readers to decide for themselves whether the levels *they* have in mind are the same as ours.

At other times more indirect methods are employed – the selective use of language, for example – to indicate the level of the course and to select the participants. A two-day course on 'Personal Construct Theory in the Assessment and Treatment of Dysfluency' is clearly intended for specialists, just as a one-day 'Makaton Vocabulary Workshop' will appeal only to those who know what Makaton applies to. Courses entitled 'Assertiveness: Never Say Yes When You Mean No' (six meetings), 'The First Five Years: Mother and Child Relationships' (20 meetings), 'Return to Study' (one-year course), 'Bookkeeping for Small Businesses' (four-day block course) and 'Law for the Householder' (ten meetings) all select their own audience and indicate the level by the choice of words in the title.

Language may be used in the description even more pointedly to select some and to exclude others. The inclusion of specialist names and the presence of long or technical terms are calculated to put off anyone not already acquainted with the subject. Carefully chosen language is sometimes employed in this way to direct the publicity towards the kind of participant who can benefit most from the learning opportunity being offered (see Fig. 5).

Elsewhere, the language used in titles and descriptions is careless and inconsistent. A ten-meeting course entitled 'Cybernetics' (without further explanation) in a liberal education programme is unlikely to be seen by many

Figure 5 A learning contract designed to deter the novice from attending

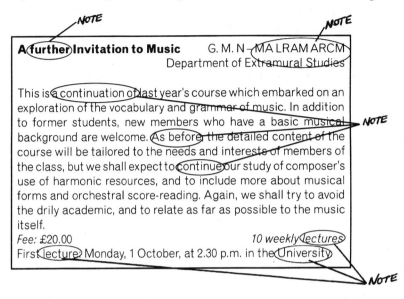

people as a purely introductory programme on robotics; it will tend to attract only participants with a good deal of knowledge already. Similarly, courses entitled 'Peace as an Ecumenical Imperative' and 'The Methodology of Consumerism' may well put off precisely those for whom they are intended. On occasion the blurb can contradict itself. The class on child psychology which states that it is designed to appeal to mothers who have no prior knowledge of child development will nevertheless discourage precisely this same group by sprinkling the blurb with names like Pavlov, Skinner, Laing, Bruner, Maslow and Piaget, as if the teacher wished even before the classes have started to show how much he or she knew. Such unthinking internal contradictions occur time and again in the programmes we offer to adults.

The learner and the contract

Perhaps the most important aspect of the course description is that, although the terms of the offer are initially drawn up by the provider and/or the teacher, the potential student participants are nevertheless active in interpreting what they read. They are the third party to the contract. They do not passively accept or reject what is on offer, but read the material presented to them in the light of their existing knowledge and experience. They assess, often unconsciously, the language in which the programme is set out. They weigh up the context in which the course is being provided; this, as they see it, will 'control' the class or at least give it its orientation. They will bear in mind the building in which it is located, the title of the body that has organised it, what they know about the teacher, and so on. And they will decide on the basis of what they see and what they assume whether to go to a programme or not.

Potential students have to work with what they are given. In some cases they can deduce from the title or description that the course is introductory or more advanced. More often they have to fall back in interpreting the contract on what they know about the institution providing the programme.

The population at large has fairly fixed expectations of what each of the main providing bodies offers in the way of adult programmes. For example, courses organised by local educational authorities and their constituent centres are often (rightly or wrongly) judged to be more directive and practical in nature, while those provided by voluntary bodies are seen to be more participatory and with a measure of social concern lacking in local authority courses. Programmes offered by further education colleges are in general felt to be more technical, those offered by universities more academic. WEA-type classes are frequently assumed to be introductory in level, university extramural programmes to be more advanced, appealing to those who already have some educational attainments. Programmes offered by voluntary agencies will, it is thought, be informal rather than formal in teaching–learning styles (all except the churches, interestingly, which are frequently felt to be more formal in their approach to such matters); those organised by industrial and other training bodies are considered more intensive and exclusively vocational (even narrow) in content; and university 'continuing education' programmes are thought of as confined to professional and other highly qualified individuals who require these courses for their career advancement.

None of this is strictly true, but these views influence behaviour. Thus some people attend courses offered by an advanced training institution because of their expectations of what will happen to them and of how useful the programme will be, while these same people will not go near exactly similar classes offered by a voluntary body such as the WEA – and vice versa. However much one may wish to change the image of the body concerned, it is difficult to do so.

Understandings and misunderstandings

The prospective learners are, then, active participants in the process of creating the contract; they interpret what they read. Frequently those who prepare courses for adults do little to help them. A church-run course established by the minister as a Bible study group, adult confirmation class or pre-marriage course, is sometimes offered without any details of what is expected; those who plan it assume more often than not that the prospective participants know what to expect. But what may be in the mind of the minister when he announces to the congregation that there will be a group led by himself for the next eight Thursday evenings in the church hall (or parsonage lounge) on 'The Letters of St Paul' may not be the same as the expectations that such an announcement will create in the minds of his hearers. Some of them will not come, clear perhaps that they could not cope with the work required; others will attend out of loyalty to person or institution. A number will come in anticipation of getting something out of the programme, but will not be sure what it is they are expected to get. The minister may well not have clarified for himself whether he hopes the outcome will be a greater understanding of that part of the New Testament, or a greater liking of reading the Bible in general, or changed moral attitudes leading to changed patterns of behaviour. A contract exists but it is vague because much of it has been left unformulated; the participants may come to the wrong conclusion because they have so little information to go on.

Although there are three active partners in the process of creating the contract to learn, the exact nature of what is being offered is often unspecified; much is presumed (Fig. 6). There is a range of assumptions in the mind of the organiser: about the subject, about the purpose of the programme, about the student participants, about the teacher. There is a series of expectations and objectives in the mind of the teacher: about what the providing agency wishes, and what the student participants want or are able to do. The process of publicising the course and recruiting voluntary adult participants arouses a set of anticipations in the minds of the potential students. With so much unstated, to expect any real match between these three sets of assumptions is asking too much. The potential for uncertainty, for misunderstanding, for hindrances to learning and even for conflict, when the basic premises of all parties have been so ill-stated, is great. Effective learning calls for the contract to be spelled out more clearly and if possible agreed by all sides.

Figure 6 The contract to learn – hidden assumptions

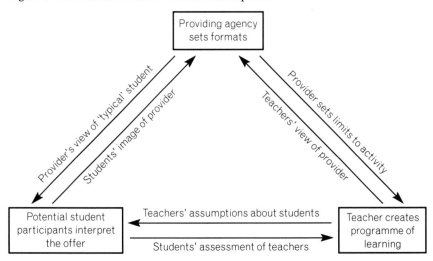

The schedule of learning

Once the group has met, the teacher and learners can together explore the nature of the bargain they have made. It is useful for the teacher of any group of adults to try to discover at the start what sort of contract each of the group members has drawn up in their own mind from the publicity material, what their expectations are. We as teachers also need to set out more fully our own expectations. This can be done through a course outline, presented to the student participants for discussion. Such a procedure enables us to test the assumptions we have made and to amend the proposed schedule of work in the light of this reassessment; and it enables the participants to alter the pattern of work proposed, to adjust their expectations if necessary and to decide whether to renew or cancel their commitment to the programme on offer. Although like the descriptive blurb the more detailed course outline is drawn up by the teacher, it differs from the description in that it is not offered on a take-it-or-leave-it basis; it is put up for amendment and even perhaps for scrapping altogether.

What this book is all about

We can illustrate this last point by setting out in more detail what this book – as an example of an adult learning opportunity – aims to do, what it contains, who it is for and how it came to be written. As the title indicates, the book is about teaching adults. It is not intended to be a theoretical work, however, or a textbook (although there is something of this in it). Nor is it a book of handy tips for teachers, a manual on how to cope (although again there is something of this in it). Instead it occupies the middle ground. It aims to explore some of the basic principles that I have come to believe teachers of adults will find it helpful to know.

The book has arisen out of my own experience. During the last 35 years I have been both organising and providing courses for adults and teaching adults. Most of this work has been done in the context of community-based Workers' Educational Association and university extramural programmes. My own teaching of history (especially local history) to groups of adult students widened to help others (particularly those who taught in my programmes) to teach in similar classes, both local historical studies and other subjects. This then widened again to engage with other groups of teachers of adults – clergy, some industrial tutors, teachers of practical subjects and so on; and I have been involved in planning programmes of training for part-time teachers and extension workers both in the United Kingdom and abroad.

The pattern of the book follows the themes of the courses for such tutors that I have taught with a number of colleagues over the last few years. Chapter 2 defines the terms 'adult', 'education' and 'adult education'. This is followed by an examination of the different elements of the teaching–learning encounter: the adult student (Chapter 3), the nature and objectives of learning (Chapters 4 and 5), the learning group (Chapter 6), the roles of the teacher and the participants in the group (Chapter 7), and the methods used in teaching adults (Chapter 8). There is some discussion of blocks to learning (Chapter 9) and of the necessity for constant evaluation (Chapter 10). The book is rounded off with a plea for greater student participation in all parts of what is really their own process of learning (Chapter 11).

I have tried to make the exercise as practical as possible. The book has been written directly out of a teaching–learning experience with a group of part-time teachers who have worked through every section of the material presented here. It may then be of value not merely to teachers of adults but also to those engaged in tutor training. The material presented in box form represents the hand-outs I have used with my own part-time teachers, which may be useful to others.

The core of the book focuses on the basic attitudes involved in teaching adults. The question is often asked whether there are differences between teaching adult students and teaching younger people in other branches of the educational service. The answer to that question is not simple, because two things tend to get mixed up: what is good teaching practice in any circumstances and what is special to the teaching of adults. It is not always easy to distinguish between these, and in general I have not attempted to do so. What will concern us will be good teaching of adults and the criteria by which we can judge this.

The book is based on the premise that as teachers of adults we have much to learn about our craft; teachers need to learn how to teach. I have been under pressure to call the book some variation on *Adults Learning* rather than *Teaching Adults* in order to stress that all adult education is student-centred, that teachers of adults should be more concerned with what their students are doing than with what the teachers as teachers are doing. While I agree with the basic concern being expressed, I want to resist this pressure. Teaching is an activity that calls for a range of attitudes, skills, knowledge and understanding on the part of the teacher, and all of these have to be learned. This book is about learning to teach; it aims to provide a learning opportunity for the teacher of adults – not just to discuss how adult learners learn but how the teacher can so plan and act as to help them to learn more effectively.

I am conscious that to adopt this attitude may seem to be too directive. Some will feel that the book allows inadequate scope for choice on the part of its readers, that it may seem to be too concerned with 'right' attitudes, 'right' practice, and not enough concerned with personal growth. I hope this is not true, that its concentration on basic principles rather than specific methods will allow for the maximum individual interpretation. But a book is by nature a partial tool of adult education. It cannot establish that two-way learning process lying at the heart of all good adult education; it can build on the experience of the reader only to a limited extent.

Nevertheless, used properly it can do something. It is important that you, the reader-learner, constantly relate the material discussed to your own experience and use it to reflect critically on your experience in your own way. A series of exercises have been designed and located at appropriate points to help you to do this, but you can ignore these and devise your own means of active involvement with the subject-matter in these pages. Without some activity relating the material to your own situation, the discussions will remain remote from real life. This section, on the learning contract, for instance, must be drawn out from what you already know. Much of the book will be concerned with matter with which you are familiar; it attempts to provide you with an opportunity to make conscious what you are doing or planning to do, to explore it more fully for yourself and to systematise it.

Writing a learning contract

We must therefore draw together this discussion and relate it to the task you have undertaken. In teaching adults, we assume that our student participants choose to come to our programmes because they understand what it is we are offering them. We are on occasion surprised to find that they have something different in mind when they come. Frequently we put the blame on to them; we allege that they have not read the course description carefully enough. But we as teachers rarely make any effort to make the contract explicit. It would be a valuable exercise both for our own sakes and for the sake of the student participants to set it all out clearly:

- if you do this (what?)
- under my supervision (why?)
- you will be able to . . . (what?).

The main medium for setting this out is the publicity issued for the course. On the whole, the teacher is not concerned with the programme in which the course is set, and the more detailed course outline comes most usefully when the teacher and learners meet for the first time. It may thus be a useful exercise to look at the description, if one exists, for the course that you proposed for yourself on page xi; if one does not exist, you could try to write one now.

The description, then, needs to be examined in the light of what we have been saying in this Introduction. What does it say, not merely as a piece of publicity but as a learning contract? Whom will it attract as potential voluntary participants and whom will it deter? What image will they gain from it of the course or programme on offer? How much will they be able to deduce from the notice and how much from the context in which the course is being offered? Will there be contradictions, confusions, or will blurb and context complement each other?

It is then possible to proceed to a fuller version of our learning contract. In this, we will need to be much clearer as to the objectives we wish to achieve and the steps to be taken in order to achieve them. The contract is not with our colleagues or our employing agency; it is with the potential student participants even if we have never seen them. The contract will need to address itself at least to the following items:

- What is the course all about? What is its subject? What will it cover and at what level?
- What is the format of the course? How long will it last, and what is the frequency and duration of the meetings? What work will it call for between group meetings?
- Who is the course for? What preliminary knowledge or experience is required? How will you make sure that the right kind of student participant gets to know about the course and is persuaded to join it?
- What will the programme of work be? What sort of learning do we expect to take place?
- What is the purpose of the exercise? In what ways will the learners be different at the end of the programme of work?

(If you are currently teaching a group of adult students, you could invite them to do the same exercise and see if there is any mismatch between their understanding of the learning contract and yours; at least you can get them to discuss the course outline you have prepared in this way.)

Such a statement is not final. Once we have met the participants, once we and they have embarked on the process of learning together, we will find it necessary to renegotiate the contract, sometimes more than once as the course progresses. This is part of the creative process of teaching adults. But the fact that the contract to learn has to be renegotiated in this way is not a reason to refuse to think about it from the start, to leave it until later. Because our students have chosen to study with us, to accept our package out of all those on offer, we need to make sure that both we and they are clear what that package is.

Further reading

Costello, N. and Richardson, M. (eds) (1982) *Continuing Education for the Post-industrial Society*. Milton Keynes: Open University Press.

Faure, E. *et al.* (1972) *Learning to Be: The World of Education Today and Tomorrow*. Paris: UNESCO.

Legge, D. (1982) *Education of Adults in Britain*. Milton Keynes: Open University Press.

Lowe, J. (1982) *The Education of Adults: A Worldwide Perspective*. Toronto: OISE Press.

McGivney, V. (1993) Participation and non-participation: a review of the literature, in R. Edwards *et al. Adult Learners, Education and Training*. Milton Keynes: Open University Press.

Rogers, J. (1989) *Adults Learning*. Milton Keynes: Open University Press.

Russell Report (1973) *Adult Education: Plan for Development*. London: HMSO.

Stephens, M. D. (1990) *Adult Education*. London: Cassell.

Thompson, J. L. (ed.) (1980) *Adult Education for a Change*. London: Hutchinson.

Tight, M. (1983) *Education for Adults*. Vol. 2: Opportunities for Adult Education. Beckenham: Croom Helm.

2
DEFINITIONS
What do we mean by . . . ?

The search for understanding

The area of definitions in adult education is one of considerable difficulty. More ink has been spilt on trying to determine what we mean by these words than on any other aspect of the subject, but there is still much confusion. Despite the fact that the practice of adult and continuing education is becoming increasingly important in the public eye, a good deal of uncertainty exists as to what it really is. As K. P. Cross (1981), speaking of 'lifelong learning' (one of the phrases sometimes used to amplify or even to avoid using the term 'adult education') says to her United States readers.

> It is quite possible that lifelong learning now outranks motherhood, apple pie and the flag as a universal good. Almost everyone is in favour of lifelong learning, despite mounting confusion over the meaning of the term.

In spite of the problems it is worth persevering with trying to understand the concepts that lie at the heart of what we want to do, to teach adults.

A number of different terms have been coined in an attempt to overcome some of the problems seen to be inherent in the expression 'adult education', each of them conveying some additional information or idea. It is important to remember that the different terms used represent different ideologies and that the meanings and value systems they indicate change over time.

- *'Continuing education'* – this term has changed its meaning from its emergence in the 1960s. Then it stressed the unity of education, for children and for adults – 'from the cradle to the grave'; education continues throughout life. Gradually however it came to have a more limited meaning: education which is planned for adults who are returning to the formal educational system of schools and colleges, people who in America are called 'non-traditional students' and who form a major focus of interest in adult education at the moment (Davies 1995). And even more narrowly, the term 'continuing education' is often used to mean professional and vocationally oriented training programmes at an advanced level for adults who have already received a good deal of education. 'Education' is thus increasingly being seen in narrower, not wider terms.

- *'Recurrent education'* is another such phrase. It embraces schooling as well as adult education, and stresses the right of individuals to enter, leave and re-enter the educational world at will. In particular, it calls for the reform of the formal schooling system to accommodate the needs of new groups of learners. Particular concern has been shown by many of those who advocate 'recurrent education' for older-aged student participants, for whom a number of special learning programmes such as the University of the Third Age have been devised.
- *'Lifelong learning'* and the French term *education permanente* are also used, with slightly different meanings, but both seeing education as built into the process of living rather than as separated into a range of special classroom and study activities.
- *'Non-formal education'* describes all out-of-school education for any group of any age. It refers not merely to the format of this education but also to the contents, which are seen to be more life-related than the traditional school curriculum, and to the processes which are more interactive and participatory than directive.

Part of the reason for the lack of agreement is the search for a definition that will cover the very diverse educational cultures of (for example) Ireland, Indonesia and Indiana, so that the practice of adult education in all countries can be compared. Some people hope that an overriding conceptual framework can be devised to cover what is one of the most culture-bound of all activities. As a result of this concern, international statements defining adult education have become longer and increasingly involved in an attempt to suit all places and all conditions. The OECD, for example, has indicated its belief that

> adult education refers to any learning activity or programme deliberately designed by a providing agent to satisfy any training need or interest that may be experienced at any stage in his or her life by a person that is over the statutory school-leaving age and whose principal activity is no longer in education. Its ambit thus spans non-vocational, vocational, general, formal and non-formal studies as well as education with a collective social purpose.
>
> (OECD 1977)

UNESCO, concerned for the Third World as well as the West, has a wider view of the scope of adult education:

organised programmes of education provided for the benefit of and adapted to the needs of persons not in the regular school and university system and generally older than 15 . . . organised and sustained instruction designed to communicate a combination of knowledge, skills and understanding valuable for all the activities of life.

(UNESCO 1975a: 4)

It thus uses the term 'adult education' to include the

entire body of educational processes, whatever the content, level or method, whether formal or otherwise, whether they prolong or replace initial education in schools, colleges and universities, as well as apprenticeship, whereby persons regarded as adult by the society to which they belong develop their abilities, enrich their knowledge, improve their technical or professional qualifications, or turn them in a new direction and bring about changes in their attitudes or behaviour in the twofold perspective of full personal development and participation in balanced and independent social, economic and cultural development.

(UNESCO 1976)

Perhaps the broadest definition of adult education is that of the (then) National Institute of Adult Education (now NIACE), England and Wales:

any kind of education for people who are old enough to work, vote, fight and marry and who have completed the cycle of continuous education commenced in childhood. They may want to make up for limited schooling, to pass examinations, to learn basic skills of trade and profession or to master new working processes. They may turn to it because they want to understand themselves and their world better and to act in the light of their understanding, or they may go to classes for the pleasure they can get from developing talents and skills – intellectual, aesthetic, physical or practical. They may not even 'go to classes'; they may find what they want from books or broadcasts or take guidance by post from a tutor they never meet. They may find education without a label by sharing in common pursuits with like-minded people.

(NIACE 1970: 10)

There is, then, no easy answer to what is meant by 'adult education'. A discussion of the finer points of each definition will be unlikely to help us in teaching adults.

Post-initial education

The term 'post-initial education' has lately come to command a good deal of support as a description of adult education. It is implicit in the NIA(C)E statement of 1970, and the term is used in the Nairobi declaration (UNESCO 1976), while a number of reports have relied heavily on the idea, if not the term itself. The Advisory Council for Adult and Continuing Education (ACACE) wrote that understanding the term 'adult education' would be assisted

> if a major distinction was made between 'initial' and 'post-initial' education. This is a more basic distinction than such kinds of administrative divisions as 'compulsory' and 'post-compulsory'. The initial education stage would obviously include going to school, including nursery school, but it could go on full- or part-time into the mid-20s. After compulsory schooling, initial education takes a wide variety of forms: full-time study in sixth form, university, college, polytechnic, medical school, military academy and so on; part-time day-release; evening classes and correspondence courses; on-the-job training in the factory.
>
> (ACACE 1979: 9–10)

All education after this is post-initial – that is, adult education. The Alexander Report for Scotland used the term 'initial education' to mean all educational experiences undertaken by a person prior to the time of taking up a first full-time career post (which today may be long delayed). On this basis, initial education includes

> all school-based or compulsory education and also the education of those who go straight from school to university or college in pursuit of higher qualifications. In addition we regard those whose immediate post-school employment involves vocational day-release or sandwich courses or apprenticeship training schemes as still undergoing initial education. All educational experience which an individual undergoes subsequent to or additional to this initial education we term continuing education [the phrase Alexander preferred to 'adult education'].
>
> (Alexander 1975)

In Northern Ireland, (adult or) continuing education is seen in similar terms:

> Continuing education is regarded as any education which adults voluntarily undertake, excepting that which they pursue full-time or part-time directly following the period of their compulsory education.
>
> (Strategy Report 1980: 10)

The report of the Adult Education Commission for the Republic of Ireland (Department of Education, Ireland 1984) used a definition that is only slightly different:

> Adult education includes all systematic learning by adults which contributes to their development as individuals and as members of the community and of society apart from full-time instruction received by persons as part of their uninterrupted initial education and training.
>
> (p. 9)

Figure 7 Initial and post-initial education in the lifespan of the population

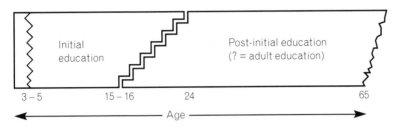

The idea thus implies that an individual engages in a preliminary period of initial education starting at the age of 3, 4, 5 or 6 in most countries, and ending at some age usually between 12 and 24 according to whether they leave school at the earliest possible moment or stay on to college, university, professional and even post-graduate studies. At the end of this period, after a gap, all people of whatever age who 'return' to education are engaged in 'adult education' (see Fig. 7).

System or process

There are however several difficulties with such a definition. First, applying this concept to those countries where a considerable number of people receive no initial education at all, or where there is a high drop-out rate at various ages between 6 and 16, is not easy. Even in the West the distinction between the end of initial education and the beginning of adult education is not always straightforward, especially as new forms of initial education are emerging. Does adult education cover those many young people who nowadays leave initial education for a short period and then return to it in the form of apprenticeships, day-release or block-release programmes, part-time courses, youth training schemes and other activities where they may join older persons in search of some means of qualifying themselves for a job? What about those compulsory training programmes that some people are required to take during their first years in post under their contract of employment (in the banks, for instance)? Are graduates who take further full-time training courses to make themselves more attractive to a prospective employer still in initial education or in post-initial education? What about the person who does one or two years' social work and then goes back to college for professional training?

More important than all of these from the teacher's point of view is the decision as to what courses and programmes constitute 'post-initial' education. Is a training course or school-leaving certificate course (for example, in a college of further education) attended by both school-leavers *and* returning adults (a 'mixed economy' course) initial or post-initial education? This is a matter of considerable import to the teacher.

> **Exercise**
> Is the course that you are teaching
>
> • initial education or
>
> • post-initial education?

A definition of adult education which sees it in terms of post-initial education – that is, as part of the *structures* of a hierarchical educational system ranging from primary (or pre-primary) through secondary and third-level education, all of which comprise initial education and are followed sequentially by post-initial or adult education – would seem to be unsatisfactory. Rather than see our work as forming a separate part of a universal system, a better way forward is to see the distinctiveness of education for adults as lying in its *process*. To understand this process, we need to look in more detail at the meaning of the terms 'adult', 'education' and 'adult education'.

Adult

A wide range of concepts is invoked when we use the term 'adult'. The word can refer to a *stage* in the life cycle of the individual; he or she is first a child, then a youth, then an adult. It can refer to *status*, an acceptance by society that the person concerned has completed his or her novitiate and is now incorporated fully into the community. It can refer to a social *sub-set*: adults as distinct from children. Or it can include a set of *ideals and values*: adulthood.

Most people tend to think of 'adult' in terms of age. But no single age can define an adult even within one society, let alone on a comparative basis, because legal and social liabilities come into play at different ages. We have only to think of voting, getting married, fighting for one's country, holding property, buying a drink or cigarettes, being sued, incurring sentences, obtaining credit, driving a vehicle, engaging in paid labour or attending various forms of entertainment, all of which have age-related restrictions applied to them, to see that we cannot say an individual becomes fully adult at any specific age. There are many who feel hesitant about using the legal school-leaving age, which varies from country to country, even in the West; and the legal age of majority is lower than the end of initial education for many people. The problem of defining an adult – and a non-adult – is so great that at times those bodies with greatest experience of making such definitions give up. UNESCO in 1976 determined that adults are those people whom their own society deems to be adult. An adult is both self-recognising and recognised by others.

A more satisfactory approach may be to identify some of those characteristics inherent within the concept of adulthood. This approach, rather than the socio-legal one, will be of greater value to teachers of adults. We all have

Figure 8 The adult and aspiring adulthood

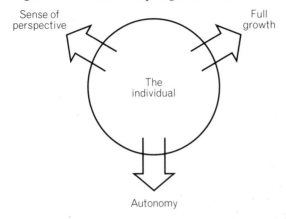

in our minds a series of expectations about those who claim (and whom we recognise) to be adults, though these will vary from person to person and from culture to culture. Characteristics such as far-sightedness, self-control, established and acceptable values, security, experience and autonomy are amongst the most common ones advanced, although not all of us would claim that to be an adult anyone needs to possess all these traits.

Three main clusters of ideas lie within any view of adulthood (see Fig. 8). First, the term is used in the sense of being *fully grown*. An overriding concept behind the word 'adult' is that of maturity. In the natural world, we speak of a mature tree or mature cheese as being fully developed, at the peak of growth. Maturity is not just a state (though we can recognise the characteristics of a mature person) but also an ideal to be aimed at rather than achieved in full. Thus when applied to human beings, the word bears stronger overtones than it does in respect of the natural world. Nevertheless it still includes the idea of *full development*, personal growth, the expansion and utilisation of all the individual's talents; and the process of moving towards ever greater maturity is one we all acknowledge as being associated with adulthood.

The other two clusters of ideas linked with adulthood may be seen most clearly by looking at its opposite, childishness. There are occasions when an older person is regarded as behaving 'childishly', in a non-adult fashion. Such childishness may consist of the individual seeing themselves as either being more important than they are seen by others to be, or conversely as less important than they really are. The former throws a tantrum, acts petulantly, makes a fuss and is frequently further infuriated by the accusation of childish behaviour; the latter withdraws, sulks or submits passively, normally accepting the charge of childishness with less hostility. In both cases we expect 'adults' to behave with a greater sense of *perspective* than is being shown, a perspective that will lead to sounder judgements about themselves and about others. We expect them to have accumulated experience that, if drawn upon, will help them achieve a more balanced approach to life and to society, to be more mature, more developed in their thinking in relation to others.

Associated with this is the third element of adulthood, responsibility. One of the key concepts of being adult and not being childish is that of being responsible for oneself, for one's own deeds and development. Frequently the adult is responsible for others as well, but at the very least he or she is responsible for their own actions and reactions. The adult can decide not to be responsible in some respect or other, but this surrender of self-reference is one of the characteristics of childishness, a denial of adulthood. Adulthood implies some measure of *autonomy*, responsible decision-making, voluntariness rather than involuntariness.

Adulthood, then, in each of these three aspects is seen by many people as an ideal to which each person is striving – never fully attained but always more or less clearly set out before us. Adults continue to strive to become more mature, more 'balanced' and more responsible.

Adulthood and education

These three characteristics – full development, perspective and autonomy – are traits that mark off the adult from the non-adult in almost all societies. They carry profound implications for us as teachers. They help to establish both the aims and the curriculum of the education we provide for adults (Fig. 9). Our programmes and courses, if they are to confirm and promote the adulthood of our student participants,

- should seek to promote *personal growth*, the full exploitation of the talents of the individual;
- should seek to encourage the development of a sense of *perspective*;
- should seek to foster confidence, the power of choice and action, to increase *responsibility* rather than to deny it.

Figure 9 Adulthood and education

Adulthood/ maturity	'Childishness'	Implications for goals of education
Personal growth/ fully developed	Lack of perceived talents, interests	Personal development and exploitation of talents and interests
Perspective/mature judgements about others and self	Lack of perspective: • over-important • too humble	Development of sense of perspective
Autonomy/self-reference/ decision-making	Flight from responsibility	Development of confidence/practice of responsibility

If the content and the material of the classes or other learning groups we conduct and the methods we employ in them do not tend to help our student participants to become more mature, to be less childish, to be more self-determining, then we are denying the adult nature of those we are teaching.

Exercise
In what ways does the class we have specified

- encourage the *full development* of each of our student participants?
- help to develop their sense of *perspective*?
- help to develop confidence, *responsibility*, choice?

Adulthood, then, in each of these three aspects is seen by many people as an ideal to which each person is striving – never fully attained but always more or less clearly set out before us. Adults continue to strive to become more mature, more 'balanced' and more responsible.

Education

Education and learning

The term 'education' is often used loosely. It is not uncommon to hear people say that an activity such as watching a television programme, travel, going to a sports event or to a nightclub can be an education in itself. What they mean is that they learned a lot from the experience. But education is not simply the same as learning, though it includes learning. Learning is an activity in which we take part all the time throughout life. Any concept of education based on the view that initial education can provide all the learning needed for life in all of its aspects is inadequate. As Sir Richard Livingstone once put it, those who work on that assumption

> behave like people who would try to give their children in a week all the food they require for a year: a method which might seem to save time and trouble but would not improve digestion, efficiency or health.
>
> (cited in Rogers 1980: 11)

Throughout our lives we face situations in our work, in our domestic settings and in our wider relationships that were not conceived of when we were at school or college, and they all call for new learning.

Areas of change

Such continued learning is an informal natural process, performed as we

- enter new social roles;
- work at our various occupations;
- develop new personal interests;
- prepare for more learning.

We need to learn as we enter new *social roles* – as wage earner, house-holder, as spouse, parent and grandparent, as voter and member of a local political community. What is more, society is constantly revising its interpretation of those roles; today's parents adopt postures towards their children and towards the rest of society often very different from the postures adopted by their parents. How we relate to other people is one area that calls for constant new learning.

We need to learn to meet the changing demands of our various *occupations*, whether heart surgeon, historian or handicrafts. All the tasks we engage in, whether they comprise paid employment or work in the home, call for new knowledge, new skills and new attitudes at various stages. There are some senior posts (e.g. in government and the churches, education and commerce) for which there is no form of initial education and which therefore have to be learned 'on the job'. Some occupations make constant calls for readjustment and new learning, while others require considerably fewer changes. Even those who are unemployed find themselves engaged in a series of tasks that demand new learning.

As we change and grow older, there are corresponding changes in our personal interests, ambitions and desires, as our opportunities for learning change. The need to learn as part of our individual development, for our *self-fulfilment*, is a major element in these lifelong learning activities. As some skills decline, new ones are learned; new interests replace earlier ones. Marbles give way to antiques, outdoor pursuits to less energetic ones.

These three main areas – social roles, occupational or vocational activities and self-fulfilment – are not of course entirely discrete. Learning in relation to our job may also be part of self-fulfilment and personal growth; so too may social role learning. But they do provide a general guide to the main groups of changes with which learning adaptations are designed to cope.

Incidental learning
In most cases, we learn incidentally, from many new kinds of experience and perceptions; for example, from advertisements, news items, chance meetings and accidents. All of these provide us with learning opportunities (usually unintended) which we may seize upon or pass over as we feel inclined. All leave marks on us, some more and some less permanent. This natural learning is part of the process of living.

But such incidental learning that occurs at random throughout life is not 'education'. Education must include learning, which is its essential ingredient, as flour is of bread. Nevertheless flour on its own is not bread; learning on its own is not education. The OECD definition of adult education as 'learning opportunities for adults' is not adequate, for such learning opportunities exist in a haphazard fashion all around us, whereas education occurs at specific times. There are times when we are not engaged in education, even though we may still be learning; something more is needed to make learning into education.

Education is planned learning

Education is an artificial creation, unlike the natural learning processes. Harold Wiltshire draws a distinction between the two when he describes education as being

> planned processes of learning undertaken by intent, the sort of thing that commonly (though not by any means always) goes on in classrooms and that involves some who are teachers and some who are taught. . . . In much discussion of adult 'education', the word is used much more loosely. Thus in much French writing about *'education populaire'* it seems to be used so as to include the whole range and apparatus of leisure-time activities – cinemas, libraries, television and sports clubs – on the grounds that these exert an educative influence on people who use them and are therefore aspects of education. Certainly there is a sense in which anything that happens to us, from getting drunk to listening to Beethoven, may be said to be 'quite an education'; and certainly we learn (living tissue can hardly help doing so) from our experiences, including those of our leisure. But such learning is unplanned and largely unintended: we do not go into either the pub or the concert-hall with a primary intention of learning. If we intend to learn we behave differently: we join a class or buy an instruction manual; we adopt the role of student and submit ourselves to a planned process of tuition.
>
> (Wiltshire in Rogers 1977: 136–7)

Education, then, is planned learning, contrived and purposeful learning opportunities. Words like 'structured', 'development', 'cumulative', 'sequential' and 'progress' are associated with the concept of education. To take just one example, the UNESCO report on *Educational Radio and Television* (1975) stated that 'educational' broadcasts are marked off from other programmes by the fact that

- their purpose is to contribute to *systematic* growth;
- they form a *continuum* of provision;
- they are so planned that their effect is *cumulative*.

(In addition, UNESCO asserted that educational broadcasts were to be reinforced with other material so as to make sure that the learning was effective and long-lasting, and that some machinery for feedback was to be created to evaluate whether the desired learning was taking place. Some modern broadcasters in their desire to widen the scope of 'educational' programmes have doubted this definition, but it still seems to be the most satisfactory one.)

The aim of all this planning, preparation and review is to promote and to direct learning. Education may therefore be seen as the provision of organised conditions for learning to take place, a means of providing learner support. It is aimed at maximising effective learning.

Education involves at least two parties. There is first of all the agent (for example, a formal educational body, a firm or business, a voluntary organisation or church, a publisher, editor or correspondence-course writer) or the teacher, or both. They plan the learning opportunity and intend certain outcomes to spring from their planning, even though in the process they will themselves come to learn much. Secondly there are the student participants. They too intend certain outcomes from the activities in which they are engaged; they are motivated by an intention and a willingness to engage in a range of activities in order to achieve a particular goal. There is in education purpose and planning on both sides.

Much has been written in recent years about 'self-directed learning'. In this process (which is described in more detail under the heading of 'learning episodes' – see pages 84–7), the learner takes the initiative and to some extent plans his/her own structured learning process. But in most (though not all) of these cases, there is some outside planner as well – someone who wrote the textbook or manual, who planned the sequence of articles in the magazines or journals used by the learner. Without such an element of planning (on the part of some teacher-agent or the student-learner), it may be doubted if the experience can be called 'education' at all.

Educational episodes

Three other characteristics may be identified as inherent within these planned and purposeful learning activities.

- The process is *sequential and cumulative*. It is not just a number of un-related 'magazine' items, individual parts without any interconnection. Rather it builds up piece by piece, making relationships between the diverse elements of the learning process.
- The process addresses itself in some form or other to *general principles*. It does not consist of the anecdotal, the one-off episode, miscellaneous facts, but draws from these some conclusions that may be applicable elsewhere. Consumer education, for example, is not a matter of identifying an individual product or supplier of which particular consumers should be wary; rather it uses those incidents in such a way that the consumers can make judgements for themselves in a wider range of instances. The result of the learning that takes place in education is that the learner can apply the new skills, knowledge and understanding acquired in different situations and not just in the classroom.
- The process is also in some sense *complete*. However open-ended the educational process may be, there is some 'rounding off' of the material dealt with, some form of fulfilment, of meeting the goals, so that the student participants do not feel left high and dry, incomplete, unsatisfied. There is, however, a sense in which education is never complete; it consists of

opening doors, leading on to the next stages of the sequence. Nevertheless, each stage has some completeness in itself, some sense of achievement, even of satisfaction and pleasure.

The elements of education

Education, then, is a planned learning opportunity which one party provides for another in relation to an agreed objective. There are four main elements to education, which may be seen to be in close relationship to each other (Fig. 10):

- the *teacher-agent* (TA), who may be at programme level the institution, organisation or association that provides the learning opportunity, and at class level the teacher/tutor;
- the *student participant* (SP), the individual or group who put themselves intentionally into the learning situation;
- the intended *goals and objectives* (GO), however loosely or closely defined;
- and the sequence of events that will enable the student participants to learn, the steps towards the intended goals; that collection of *methods/content* (M/C) lying at the heart of the planned learning process.

The relationship between these elements may be illustrated as in Fig. 10, although this representation is too static for what is one of the most dynamic of human situations. All elements of the planned learning opportunity undergo change, and each goal leads on to new developments and to new goals.

The role of the *teacher-agent*, whether organiser or teacher, in this process is crucial. It is the teacher-agent who sets up the learning situation, even though the student participants may come increasingly to take control of the learning process. The teacher-agent assesses the needs of the prospective learners, establishes the goals (see Chapter 5) and constructs the programme of methods and contents, the course of action that will enable the student

Figure 10 The educational process

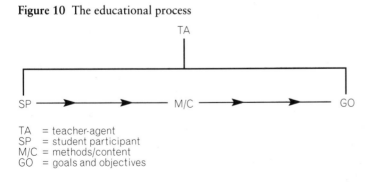

TA   = teacher-agent
SP   = student participant
M/C = methods/content
GO = goals and objectives

participants to 'learn' their way towards the agreed goals. The teacher-agent is the planner – at least in the first instance.

The *student participants* too are active in the planning process. They intend to learn, to achieve their own goals. They, like the agent, have certain outcomes in mind; they come to the learning situation with a set of intentions (often unformulated) and actively set about fulfilling these.

Education as encounter

In determining the *goals* of the learning process, the planning agent (teacher-provider) has in mind certain *expected outcomes*, the results that will flow from the learning undertaken in changed attitudes and behaviour (see Chapter 5). However, most of the student participants come with their own intentions, which may or may not be the same as those set out by the agent; they will use the learning opportunity for their own purposes, to achieve their own outcomes. Each of these sets of purposes influences the other. The teacher's intended outcomes help to shape the learners' expectations, and the learners' intentions and hopes should affect the formulation of the teacher's intentions.

Both sets of proposed outcomes may well be different yet again from the *effective outcomes* of the educational process. Since those being taught consist of a mixed group of learners, each of whom responds to the learning in a different way, there will always be a series of unexpected outcomes. The teacher-agent needs to keep these differences in mind when planning the learning encounter.

Some would argue that, even with this caveat, what we have proposed is too mechanical a notion of education. Instead they see education as an encounter without prior determination of the outcomes. They lay stress on the fact that each student participant reacts uniquely to the material they are meeting for the first time or are perceiving anew, and that in any case the outcomes may not reveal themselves until some time after the course has ended. They emphasise the open-ended nature of the encounter between learner, teacher and material, and the unpredictability of learning. In fact, they urge, learning may not take place at all; and in the nature of the encounter, the teacher may learn as much as the student.

All of this is true, but a teaching–learning situation still calls for a *conscious decision* to create such an encounter, even when that decision is accompanied by a desire for open-endedness – perhaps for undirected personal growth or development on the part of the learners. There is still a *purpose* behind the encounter. It still calls for a process of *planning*, of selection of the material to be used as the basis of the encounter. Equally, such a view of education as encounter calls for an *intention* on the part of the participants, a willingness to engage in the encounter. The outcomes of our teaching may be different from those we plan for or anticipate, but some element of planning is essential.

Figure 11 Goals in relation to methods/content – the continuum

Goal	Achievement, externally moderated	Personal growth, internally moderated
Teacher's role	Teacher introduces student to subject-matter	Encounter between student and teacher
Student's role	Student more passive	Student participant dominant
Content	Discipline of subject-matter limited choice	Open-endedness subject-matter less important than activities
Methods	Directive	Autonomous and interactive

The nature of the goals that we set in the planning process will bring in its train a range of implications for the role of the teacher. If we have a narrow objective, aiming at some specific competency or externally moderated achievement, we will tend to lay greater stress on the part played by the teacher than on the learners' activities. If, on the other hand, we set our sights more on the growth of the individual, then the emphasis of our programme will be more learner-centred than teacher-centred (see Fig. 11).

Methods/content

Thus the nature of the goals we set helps to determine whether the emphasis of our programme of work lies more towards content or towards method. We cannot easily separate methods from content; the two are closely related. But the balance between them varies. Programmes with narrowly prescribed objectives tend to concentrate more on content than on methods; an adult class leading to a school-leaving certificate in English literature, for instance, or a course on new legislation relating to industrial relations, define for themselves more or less precisely the content of the teaching–learning encounter. The teachers of such programmes will feel it necessary for the student participants to come face to face with a set amount of material. This decision in its turn affects the methods employed; they will tend to be directive rather than participatory. Both teacher and taught expect a specified content to be 'covered'.

On the other hand, programmes aimed more at personal growth, confidence building, assertiveness – courses on public speaking, management and the like – are less rigidly controlled. Their impulse lies more in the field of the processes involved in the teaching–learning encounter. In these cases, we may feel it more important to engage in particular activities – participative learning methods – than to cover a set amount of material.

Whatever our decisions, which may well change as the course progresses and as we reassess the needs of the learners with their help, methods and content are integrally related in the planning of an educational experience. They cannot be discussed apart, and neither is more important than the other.

Dynamic education

The dynamic relationship between all the elements within education is not confined to the initial planning of the learning programme. It becomes clearer as the process goes on. The teacher-agent is active all the time, reassessing the student participants, evaluating progress made, amending and redefining the goals, reconstructing the methods and content, and learning all the time from the participants. The learners too are active, clarifying their intentions and changing their objectives. A course once set and never altered, directed towards unchanging goals, can only with difficulty be called 'education'; for education is a process of change in which teacher and learner join together in relation to a third element, a series of agreed but changing goals.

Education, training and indoctrination

Our definition of education as a planned and interactive learning opportunity is not enough unless we also consider whether the term carries with it a value judgement or not. Are *all* planned learning situations 'education'? Agencies may provide planned learning experiences for a variety of purposes. A terrorist organisation's programme of field training will be seen by most people as very different from the local conservation society's series of outings or a women's group's acting workshop, although all three may be motivated by a desire to change attitudes and thus behaviour and ultimately systems in society at large. So we are forced to ask whether, for education to be education, the goals must be 'good'. On the one hand, education as a concept may be value-free; it may cover all planned learning programmes. On the other hand, the term may be confined to those planned learning activities, and only those, intended to have 'good' outcomes.

The problem is an old one: how to define 'good' in this context. 'Socially acceptable' may in some circumstances not be adequate to describe the good that education is intended to do, for many of us wish to use our learning opportunities to encourage some form of change in society, and change is not always 'socially acceptable' (think, for example, of the early women's movement). Those of us who have been brought up to think in terms of traditional liberalism will conceive of the good that education can bring as increased freedom. Others may assume that an increased ability to generate wealth (either for oneself or for society at large) is the good that education should achieve, while yet others will talk of the rectification of social inequalities or the increase of cultural richness and harmony or environmental balance.

Rather than pursue this line of thought here (it is discussed further in Chapter 5), perhaps the most useful approach to this question is in terms of 'wide' and 'narrow' goals. In this sense all structured learning opportunities can be seen once again as forming part of a continuum. At one end are those planned teaching–learning programmes with narrow goals, the aim of which is to demonstrate that there is a 'right' way to do something or other. These are largely in the skills area but not entirely so; some people are taught that there are 'right' ways of understanding, of behaving and even of learning. Choice is strictly limited and not encouraged. This is what we usually mean when we speak of *training*. At the other end are all those activities that set out to convince us that there is a 'right' way of thinking and feeling. Once again there is a limitation, even a denial, of choice; there is only one way to think, one set of values and attitudes to hold. This is essentially *indoctrination*. Between these two extremes is that large area of education where the goals are wider: to demonstrate that there are many different ways of thinking and doing, to encourage the development of choice and self-determination (see Fig. 12).

Our question, then – whether 'education' may refer to *all* planned learning opportunities or only to those for which the goals are 'good' – is a matter of personal choice. We can call all learning activities specifically created by one agency for another group of people 'education', in which case we can talk of 'bad' education as well as 'good' education, of using education for good or bad ends. Or we can define 'education' as consisting only of those programmes and courses with wide rather than narrow goals, thus cutting off training and indoctrination from the world of education. It is a question of semantics.

On the whole this is more a matter of concern to the organiser of programmes than to the teacher. Nevertheless we as teachers have to decide for ourselves whether our goals are wide or narrow, whether we are engaged in education, training and/or indoctrination. Probably elements of all these will

Figure 12 Training, education and indoctrination

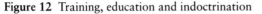

| Narrow goals; the 'right' way to do; no choice | Wide goals: many ways of thinking and doing; development of choice | Narrow goals; only one way of thinking |

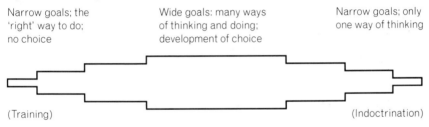

(Training)   (Indoctrination)

come into our teaching at different times, arising from our commitment to our students and to our subject.

> **Exercise**
> Are the goals of your course
>
> • wide?
> • narrow?
>
> Does your course consist more of
>
> • training: the right way to do something?
> • indoctrination: the right way to think?
> • education: the increase of choice?

Adult education

Is adult education simply the addition of our definition of 'adult' to our definition of 'education', the provision of planned learning opportunities for those persons whom society deems to be adults, or does the phrase imply something more? Is there a distinction to be drawn between 'the education of adults' and 'adult education'?

Some people have argued that the difference between these two concepts lies in terms of the *contents* of the programmes. Thus they see the 'education of adults' as referring to all forms of education for those over the age of 16 (or 18 or 20), whatever is being studied. It thus includes some subjects (both skills and knowledge) better learned at a younger age (for example playing a musical instrument). On the other hand they would restrict the term 'adult education' to what can be learned or best learned only as adults, because they rely on experience (politics, say, or interpersonal relationships, or spirituality) or because they relate to adult roles (parenthood, say, or management). Thus, it is suggested, the 'education of adults' covers all programmes for adults, while 'adult education' is confined to 'adult' subjects.

> **Exercise**
> Is the subject of your course
>
> • especially appropriate to adults?
> • more appropriate to younger persons?
> • equally relevant to both groups?

Such a definition however would exclude from 'adult education' a great deal that belongs to it. Literacy and basic skills, for example, typewriting, sports, languages, woodworking and computing are all better learned while young, but they feature in most programmes of recognisable adult education. And there are some subjects – art, for instance – which experience shows do not have age-related criteria for learning.

The difference between what may properly be termed 'adult education' and the 'education of adults' lies less in *what* is being learned (although some subjects are especially appropriate to adults) than in the *approach* to adult learning. A distinction can be drawn between those programmes that teach adults as adults and those that teach them in ways more appropriate to younger learners. The 'education of adults' can then be seen to cover all forms of education (planned learning opportunities) for those over the age of 16 (or whatever), whether the student participants are treated as adults or whether they are treated as if they were younger learners – taught, that is, as if they were largely or completely ignorant of the subject being studied, without relevant experience, unable to be relied upon to control their own learning, having little or nothing to contribute to the learning process. 'Adult education', by contrast, consists of all those forms of education that treat the student participants as adults – capable, experienced, responsible, mature and balanced people.

We have suggested above that all forms of teaching adults should respect and enhance the adulthood of those who have voluntarily become our students. This makes any approach to the education of adults that does not possess the characteristics of 'adult education' inappropriate. To deny the adult students' adulthood is not just to create unnecessary barriers to effective learning, to deprive ourselves of the most useful resource we have for the learning task; it is to insult them with our own arrogance.

This approach creates tensions for ourselves as teachers of adults. For one thing some of our students may express a wish to be taught in ways that deny their adulthood (see page 36); they want to go back to school, to surrender their autonomy in order to learn some new thing. At the same time, our concern for the subject-matter to which we have submitted ourselves and to which we hope our students will submit themselves pulls against this concern for the adulthood of the student participants. The primacy of the goal of greater adulthood over all other goals is one of the main problems faced by those of us who teach adults.

Two patterns of education

This distinction between treating participants as adults ('adult education') and failing to do so (what we may call 'adult schooling') reflects a tension deep within education itself. The tension is felt in all sectors but is at its most acute in the teaching of adults. It reflects two contrasting attitudes towards the task in hand and to all elements of that task. The tension can be expressed in a series of polarities:

- between education as content and education as process;
- between education as 'teaching a subject' and education as 'teaching people';
- between education as preparing for life and education as a part of living;
- between education as discipline, conformity to an external standard and education as liberation for the student.

A useful (though in places overdrawn) summary of these two approaches can be seen in Fig. 13.

Exercise

Are the course we teach and the methods we adopt closer to

- the conformist end, or
- the liberation end

of the continuum?

It would be a mistake to suggest that one of these models is correct and the other is wrong. Rather they represent a tension that is never resolved. This tension impinges on both the teacher and the student participant. Education is both in part a preparation for life and in part an integral element in the process of living; it seeks both to change the student participants towards a predetermined goal and yet at the same time to make them independent. It is both training and education, both discipline and free growth. In education the teacher helps the learner to become free, but within the limits of a field of study or expertise; we seek to bring the student participants into contact with the primary material and leave them free to use it for themselves.

The teacher too is torn – between the desire to help the students develop into something they have already indicated they want to become (a painter, a local historian, a more confident person, a more efficient professional, a more skilled technician or trade union official, etc.) and the desire to respect and encourage the autonomy of the adult. We are torn between the clear vision we have of our subject and our willingness to encourage our students to see it for themselves in different ways. The teacher – and the teacher alone, at least at first – is aware that there is such a thing as the 'bad' use of literature, bad dressmaking, bad gardening practice, bad history and so on; that there are standards, in fact. Although we may be conscious of the limitations of our own judgements, nevertheless we believe that there are agreed criteria in our discipline to which we ourselves seek to conform and to which we hope our student participants will wish to conform. Yet we want our students to grow in independence, not in dependency on ourselves as teachers.

Figure 13 Two approaches to teaching

'Conformist'	'Liberation'
Make student participant (S) like teacher (T)	*Make student participant (S) independent of teacher (T)*
1 There is an external reality towards which S must fit (subject discipline). Truth is known.	1 There is no externally 'right' way of behaving. Truth is not known.
2 S can't be trusted to pursue own learning; T takes initiative.	2 Human beings have a natural potential for learning; S takes self-initiative.
3 Presentation = learning.	3 Most significant learning acquired through doing.
4 Material exists on its own, independent of both T and S.	4 Significant learning takes place when subject-matter is perceived by S as having relevance for his or her own purpose.
5 T must transfer knowledge to S – S cannot obtain knowledge by him/herself.	5 Knowledge cannot be transferred; all knowledge is created by S for him/herself.
6 Process of education is to accumulate brick upon brick of factual knowledge – progression of subject is externally set.	6 There is no set sequence of learning; S engages with material in his or her own way and in own sequence.
7 Constructive and creative citizens develop from passive learners.	7 Creativity in learning depends on direct active involvement in learning process; S participates responsibly in learning process.
8 Evaluation by T of S's progress is a necessary part of learning.	8 Learning is best achieved when self-criticism and self-evaluation are primary; evaluation by others is of secondary importance.
9 Cognitive learning can take place without affecting rest of person.	9 Learning that involves the whole person – feelings as well as intellect – is most pervasive and lasting.
10 Learning is a once-off experience and need not be repeated.	10 The most useful learning in the modern world is learning how to learn; a continuing openness to experience and an incorporation of the process of change into oneself are necessary goals of education.

There are times, in the ordering of the material that the student participant handles in order to move towards the agreed goals, when the discipline side predominates; times when the training aspect – the right way to do things – is most prominent, when the teacher's role is to point out the good and the bad (the process of evaluation, as we shall see, depends on *values*). Even here however the ideal is for the participants not just to accept the judgements of the teacher but to come to make their own judgements, to accept the discipline of the subject for themselves. But education cannot consist of this alone; there are other times when the freedom, the self-determination of the student participant, the autonomy of the adult, has full play.

It is not just a question of getting the right balance between these two aspects of education. The tension is inherent within the whole process of planning for learning. The introduction of a purpose, a goal, as a third element into the relationship between the teacher-planner and the learner creates the tension. For this goal is independent; it exists in its own right and makes its own demands on both the teacher and the learner. It directs both the material and the methods used in the learning process. The teacher who has a goal is not totally free, any more than the learner who desires to achieve a goal can be completely free; freedom in this respect comes from accepting discipline.

The purpose of the educational encounter is to achieve a series of mutually agreed objectives, and this purpose imposes discipline on both the teacher and the taught. Both, but particularly the teacher, will feel the tension between the discipline that education is and the freedom that it seeks to promote. There is no right solution to the problem. We all have to live with both sides of the equation.

Further reading

ACACE (1979) *Towards Continuing Education*. Leicester: ACACE.

Brookfield, S. (1983) *Adult Learners, Adult Education and the Community*. Milton Keynes: Open University Press.

Jarvis, P. (1983) *Adult and Continuing Education: Theory and Practice*. Beckenham: Croom Helm.

Lawson, K. H. (1980) *Philosophical Concepts and Values in Adult Education*. Milton Keynes: Open University Press.

Newman, M. (1979) *The Poor Cousin: a Study of Adult Education*. London: Allen and Unwin.

3

ADULT STUDENTS

Who are they . . . ?

A profile

Much attention has been given in recent writings on adult education to the adult learner. Whole books have been devoted to the topic, and most general studies of adult education, based on the premise that all forms of teaching adults ought to be student-centred rather than teacher-centred, contain sections dealing with the way adults learn.

Drawing a profile

One feature of this discussion has been the compilation of lists of general characteristics of the adult student. Their aim is to help teachers of adults to become more conscious of what they are doing when they draw up a profile of their students, to test out the items specified to see which do not apply to their particular group and to identify other characteristics specific to their teaching context. One of the more helpful of these lists is that compiled by Harold Wiltshire (1977), but like so many it is limited in its application in that it is directed more towards the traditional student in non-vocational liberal adult education of an academic orientation than to basic education, practical skill-based courses or professional development programmes.

In many of these descriptions there are a number of myths about the adult student participant. Large generalisations are frequently made. It has been suggested at various times that adult students are people well beyond school-days, full of a mixture of regret, determination, guilt and ambition, but dogged by lack of confidence and self-belief, harrassed by noise and diversions, facing problems of time and space to study, tiredness and opposition and mockery from spouses and friends. (These descriptions have all come from a number of recent writings purporting to describe the general principles on which adult education is predicated.) But clearly these do not describe all (or even perhaps many) adult students. Each such description needs to be drawn up with a proper regard to the individual group in question.

We all draw some picture of who our student participants are going to be. We do this as an integral part of the process of planning the programme and the course. Most of us can rely on past experience to help us, but new teachers of adults cannot do this; they may turn to other more experienced teachers to assist them, but even this is not always possible.

The process of compiling such a profile is often unconscious. We rarely make explicit the views we hold about the prospective learners, their abilities and motivations, what we can and cannot expect from them. Even in those programmes where the goals are negotiated with the potential learners, the teacher-planner still makes several assumptions: for example, that the participants want to join in, that they are willing to entertain the notion of change and that they are capable of engaging in the processes put before them.

We thus fall into unquestioned and possibly false presuppositions about our prospective student participants. We may on occasion assume that the learners are at the opposite extreme from our goals: that they possess no skills at all, if our goals relate to the acquisition of skills; that they are completely ignorant of the subject in hand, if our goals are knowledge-related; that they hold negative attitudes, if our goals are attitude change; that they have not yet begun to comprehend, if our goals are concerned with understanding; that they lack all forms of confidence, if our goal is confidence-building. None of this may be true. Indeed, it is most unlikely to be true. Those who come on a bird-watching course are already more likely than not to know something about the subject; those who attend car-maintenance classes will invariably have had some experience of a car; those who wish to learn about women in literature are most likely to have done some reading in this field already and will have views on the subject; those who come to family-planning classes often know more than their teachers allow for. Unless we make conscious what we believe about our potential student participants, we are in danger of presupposing falsehoods.

Testing the profile

Having compiled a list of apparent characteristics of our potential learners, it is necessary to test these assumptions at the earliest possible moment. In some forms of teaching adults – correspondence courses, for example, or the educational programmes offered by the media, and the self-directed learning materials prepared by many agencies – the teacher-planners never meet the learners, so that the assumptions made cannot easily be assessed to see whether they are right or wrong. But in most other cases it will quickly become apparent whether we have judged correctly what the prospective student participants are able to do, what they are willing to do and what they want to do. Sometimes we will get it all wrong, so that there is nothing to be done after the first meeting with the participants other than to redesign the whole learning package. As with most skills of teaching, however, we can improve with practice; but even after long experience, because every group of adult learners is different, we must still test whether the presuppositions we have made about our student participants are correct or not, so that the programme of work can be revised or amplified as necessary.

Teachers are sometimes reluctant to do this in their first encounter with the student participants. It may be that they are hesitant to expose themselves from the start of their relationship with the learners, to give the impression that they are in any way uncertain. Or, having prepared something for the first meeting, they may be anxious to go ahead and give it. These teachers sometimes justify this on the grounds that the participants who have turned up want to have something 'meaty' at the first session so as to judge better the content, level and pace of learning involved in the course, that some prospective participants would find a first meeting devoted to a general discussion about the course an unsatisfying experience. Or the teacher accepts at face value the student participants' assessment of their own ignorance of the subject, their inability to contribute anything useful towards setting the goals and constructing the programme of work. There are many reasons for not opening up the assumptions we have made about the participants to challenge.

Despite all of this, it might be better to spend at least part of the first meeting with any group of adult student participants listening rather than talking, assessing whether the assumptions we have made about their interests and abilities are right or not. Even if we do not do this at the first meeting, the task will have to be done at some stage during the course. It should be done as early as possible so that there is no lengthy gap between bringing together their expectations as learners and our expectations as teachers.

The range is wide

In order to test out these presuppositions, we need to undertake the process consciously rather than subconsciously. It is useful to write down our description of the potential student participants, and here we run into the biggest problem of all. Most of us teach in groups, and the wide range of those who join such groups, even small groups, may hinder us from making realistic judgements about what we can in general expect from our student-learners.

Let us take one example as illustration. It is now thought that intelligence is not a fixed inherent ability that cannot be improved after the end of formal schooling, or a range of abilities that grow and decline along mathematical curves. Rather it is seen as being 'plastic'; it rises to peaks or falls into troughs

throughout adulthood, largely governed by whether the activities engaged in
and the environmental factors are stimulating and encouraging or whether
they are damaging and inhibiting. Particularly the development of intelligence seems to be dependent as much on the amount of educational experience one has received and on the subsequent use of learning skills in one's
occupations as it is on the basic learning ability developed when young.
People who have had a good deal of education and who have been engaged
in tasks calling for considerable and regular amounts of new learning will be
'more intelligent' at 50 than they were at 25; conversely, those who have been
employed in occupations that have not required them to engage in new learning are likely not to have developed their intelligence to the same extent. Thus
in any group of adults engaged in a learning programme, the range of learning ability, even among people of roughly the same age and same initial education, is likely to be considerably wider than in a comparable group of
children.

Lifespan studies

It may be useful at this point to outline the general conclusions of what have
been called 'lifespan studies' in relation to adult learning; for if learning is a
process of personal changes made in adapting to changed situations and
experiences, the study of different patterns of life is likely to throw light on
such learning.

In the 1970s and 1980s, a general view of lifespan development emerged
based on ideas about the major points of meaningful change that occur
during adulthood. This was thought to give teachers a useful basis for this
process of drawing a profile of their student participants. Although it is given
less credence today, it is still worth reviewing this field. What follows is not
intended to be a comprehensive guide to this area of study but an introduction. Teachers who want to pursue the subject further are referred to the
books listed at the end of the chapter.

The terms 'growth', 'change' and 'development' are used in a variety of
senses. Some educational writers see 'change' as quantitative accumulations
to the content of thought, and 'development' as a qualitative transformation
of one's thinking structures; but these distinctions omit any reference to
intention and purpose. A more satisfactory definition sees 'change' as value-
free, indicating an undirected process, whereas 'development' implies purposeful change, directed towards the achievement of some goal.

A number of writers see adult progression as growth, the gradual and
natural increase of maturity. Others see it as development, i.e. goal achievement. For writers like Piaget and Kohlberg, the goal is one of 'rational autonomy'; for others there is the increasing sense of perspective as well. Viewed
in goal-achievement terms, it is possible to determine stages of progress. On

the other hand, some writers have rejected the concept of 'development' and replaced it with a more or less value-free view of change throughout adult life.

General considerations

It seems to be accepted that there are, for the adult, few (if any) age-related changes. Unlike the child and the adolescent, whose different stages are recognised (even if not universally agreed), adults change and develop more by experience and by the exercise of abilities than by mere age. There are physical changes that occur with increasing age, but none of these is related to any specific age, and the changes that take place differ for each individual.

Additionally there is in the West a strong emphasis on the physical elements in human make-up. Thus ageing is seen as a phenomenon to be resisted, something to be overcome rather than welcomed and valued for the wisdom and status it brings.

Adult development has several other dimensions. On the one hand, there are the changes that occur within each person as the years advance. On the other hand, there are those changes within the social and cultural context of the individual which call for new responses. We are dealing with a changing person in a changing world. Change, not stability, is the norm.

Among those many changes are variations in perspectives, including the view of the ageing process itself. Traditionally in Western societies, youth has been seen in positive terms while ageing has been regarded more negatively. But in recent years, views in relation to older persons have shown significant changes, with growing positive attitudes towards older age groups and rather more negative attitudes towards younger people, perhaps a result of the increasing number of older persons in society as a whole. In many developing countries on the other hand, influenced by Western cultural patterns, the reverse would seem to be happening, despite the increasing number of older persons in various forms of adult education. Society is not only imposing roles on individuals but is constantly reinterpreting those roles – and all these changes will call for learning on the part of every adult.

Ages of man and woman

Most of us are acquainted with Shakespeare's 'seven ages of man': the infant, the schoolboy, the lover, the soldier, the justice, the 'lean and slipper'd pantaloon', and finally second childhood. Since Shakespeare's time there have been many attempts to better this description of adult changes. Some are very general: Whitehead's successive phases of romance, precision and rationalization, or Egan's romantic stage, philosophic stage and eirenic or fulfilled stage. Some still display the so-called 'plateau effect' of Shakespeare: growth, maturity and decline. The very title of the University of the Third Age perpetuates the outdated concept of a three-stage life consisting of growth, performance and 'completion'.

Recently it has been recognised that some of the earlier schemata relating to adult development were too closely tied to successive stages, and attempts have been made to break away from this. There is however still a tendency to see adults in too great an isolation from the social and physical environment in which they are located, to see society as static while the individual changes, to underestimate the effect of changes in social structures and values on the adult. Equally there is an underestimate of the effect that different educational and cultural backgrounds and different experiences can have on adults.

Dominant concerns

The most influential group of lifespan theories are those that see changes during the adult phase of life in terms of dominant concerns. Havighurst (1952) suggested that the individual passes through eight main stages; after the two periods of childhood and adolescence comes adulthood, a 'developmental period in about as complete a sense as childhood and adolescence are developmental periods'. From 18 to 30, adults are focusing their life; there is a concern for self-image. Self is a major preoccupation, not society (voting and civic duties are less frequent at this period). This is a period of experimentation, of settling into jobs and love affairs. Education tends to be turned to by some as an instrument for occupational advancement. From 30 to 40, adults are collecting their energies; this is a period of stability and relatively less introspection, less self-doubt. The job is now most important, with child-rearing a close second. Involvement in education now tends towards the expressive rather than the instrumental. The decade from 40 to 50 is a period of self-exertion and assertion. This is the peak of the life cycle. Public and civic activities are more prominent, whereas participation in educational programmes tends to decline. This stage is characterised by a turning out towards society from oneself, the family and the job. 'Action' is the means of dealing with the world, and this emphasis on action brings about the first consciousness of physical deterioration.

From 50 to 60, adults maintain their position and at the same time change roles; educational involvement is for expressive rather than instrumental purposes. There is increasing evidence of physical deterioration (sight and hearing), and larger amounts of energy have to be exerted to avoid losing ground. Often it is asserted that the adult is more passive and deferential, with a sagging sense of self-assurance. 'Thought' rather than 'action' is the means of dealing with the world, and there is more concentration on short-term rather than long-term achievements. The adult spends the years between 60 and 70 deciding whether and how to disengage. This is often the period of the death of friends and relatives, of less social concern, of less active preoccupations and more short-term gratifications. From 70 onwards is the period of making the most of disengagement. Healthy adults are not too preoccupied with the past, are self-accepting and relatively content with the outcomes of their life, but often the period is characterised by poor health, reduced means and dependence on others.

Havighurst's views, as set out above, are frequently cited by adult educators. They are almost the only ones that relate such changes directly to educational activities. But they are too simplistic, too rigidly tied to ages, and they are based on Western male-dominated concepts of a successful work career. Major changes in social structure have rendered such a neat analysis suspect.

These considerations have led to a more sequential approach without tying each stage too closely to ages. Neugarten (1977) speaks of adulthood as representing a 'movement from an active, combative, outer-world orientation to . . . an adaptive, conforming inner-world orientation'. Three stages are identified: a period of expressiveness, expansiveness and extroversion, of autonomy and competence (up to about the age of 30); an intermediate period of reorientation; and a third stage of change from active to passive modes of relating to the environment with greater introversion.

Tensions

Erikson (1965) sees the stages of human development in terms of different tensions. There is the general and continuing tension between 'the inner wishes . . . and the demands to conform to other people's standards and requirements', which all people experience and which leads to compromises if the adult is 'to maintain the integrity of his [sic] personality'. In addition there are a series of developmental tensions; in puberty and adolescence, there is the tension between identity and role confusion; in young adulthood, intimacy versus isolation; in adulthood, generativity versus stagnation; and in 'maturity', the integrity of the self versus despair. The educational implications of each stage are delineated: initial education for the child and adolescent, vocational education for the young adult, social and community education for the adult, and philosophical and creative education for the mature. Boshier (1989) similarly speaks of tensions (incongruence); he draws upon the work of Carl Rogers (1974) to depict the individual as having

> two problems; maintaining inner harmony with himself [sic] and with the environment. Incongruence is developed within the person (intra-self) and between the person and other-than-self experiences (self/other). . . . The research of life-cycle psychologists supports the notion that younger [adults] manifest more intra-self and self/other incongruence than older, more mature [people].
>
> (Boshier 1989: 147–50)

Time perspectives

Lifespan changes may be seen in terms of how time is viewed. Some writers have suggested that the child sees the future as far away; for the adolescent, the future is rosy; for the adult, time is finite, while the mature adult feels that time is running out. Friedman elaborated this version of the 'plateau' theory of lifespan changes, being particularly conscious that successive stages do not correlate with ages. He thus overlapped some stages:

- The *entry stage* (say 18–25): orientation is to the future – the future will be better than the present; change is good.
- *Career development* (say, 20–50): orientation is increasingly more to the present than to the future; away from interest in promotion towards an interest in the intrinsic value of work, together with participation and achievement in non-work areas.
- *Plateau* (say, 35–55): the main time-focus moves from the present to a feeling that time is running out; there is increasing neuroticism, especially among the lower socio-economic groups, who cope less well than professionals and managers (!).

After 55 comes a period of decline.

Sex and class factors

As these examples show, there is considerable sex and class bias in such analyses. This indicates the origin of most of the studies – amongst American white professional males, those who on the whole predominate in continuing education programmes in the United States. The sexual bias is surprising; all of these theories relate to male careers despite the fact that women predominate in most forms of non-vocational adult education. The women's movement has been seeking to redress the balance, exploring the cycle of adulthood for women. Similarly, it is likely that the lifespan stages and expectations of blacks are different from those listed above.

The class bias has received less attention. Almost all the above descriptions rely upon doubtful assumptions concerning the social and educational background of the participants; they relate to the educated, the professionally employed and the ambitious. One attempt to redress this balance towards the working class (by Guy Hunter, quoted in Stephens and Roderick 1971) suggests that

> there is a rough sequence in a working life which the intellectual is too apt to forget. After the first period of school and pure technical training, the worker, for the ten years from 15 to 25, is pitchforked into practical life – finding and holding a job after marriage and founding a home on small resources . . . between 25 and 35, as the worker approaches a more responsible job, education should broaden his ideas

of the nature of authority, of the social and human implications of any new job, of the deeper purposes of society. Once this broadening process has been started, it may well lead on into history, literature and art. . . . It means at 21 bread and butter and the wage packet. At 30 it may include ideas of status, leisure, civic responsibility; and at 40 and thereafter it may deepen into a concept of the good life.

(p. 195)

Roles and crisis points

This attempt to draw up an alternative lifespan sequence to that of the male professional still assumes a working life. Long-term unemployment on a large scale and changes in attitudes to work and retirement have thrown doubt on much of the existing research. These changes and the patronising air that surrounds such efforts to define working-class life stages have led to a number of different approaches, some of which concentrate on the pattern of family life and/or lifestyles. Others seek not so much for the variations between separate groups of adults but for a comprehensive view of development common to all adults. A way forward is found in concentrating on the changing *roles* of the adult or on the crisis points that occur in the life of most adults of a particular generation, whether male or female, working class or middle class, black or white – although reactions to these new roles and crisis points vary considerably according to experience and the culture of the individual.

The most common roles and crisis points identified (Sheehy 1976) usually relate to the first job, marriage, parenthood, the departure of children from the home, bereavement (especially the loss of parents and spouse), separation and divorce, loss of a job or other role, retirement and (less sequential and more occasional) moving house (a major period of stress in the lives of many people). Amongst these writers, a common crisis point is seen to occur somewhere about the age of 40 in both males and females.

Summary

The search for the stages of man or woman is still under way. From our point of view as teachers, it is wise to remember that adults age; and that, with ageing,

- physical changes occur, to a greater extent for some people than for others and in different ways;
- roles change, all calling for new learning, and there may on occasion be difficulties in adapting to new roles or to new perceptions of roles;
- various crisis points are passed, sometimes easily, sometimes with difficulty.

The mixed group that most teachers of adults face will not only possess a wide range of ability; they will also be at different ages and at different stages of development, and will in any case react in different ways to the very varied changes each one is experiencing in their own life.

General characteristics of adult student-learners

Despite the wide variations that exist between the members of our learning group, however, it is still possible to identify some of the common characteristics of adult student participants. What follows is my list; you may find it helpful to decide for yourself how far each of the categories is appropriate in your own circumstances. I have selected seven characteristics that seem to me to be true of the large majority of adult learners, whatever their situation or stage of development, although cultural settings may modify these to some extent:

- The student participants are adult by definition.
- They are in a continuing process of growth, not at the start of a process.
- They bring with them a package of experience and values.
- They come to education with intentions.
- They bring expectations about the learning process.
- They have competing interests.
- They already have their own set of patterns of learning.

---

1 They all are adults by definition

We have seen that adulthood is an ideal, never fully achieved. The concept implies movement, progress towards the fulfilment of the individual's potential, the development of balanced judgements about themselves and others, and increasing independence. Our student participants are people who are becoming more mature, and the way we teach adults should encourage this development in self-fulfilment, perspective and autonomy.

The most visible way in which the adult learners exercise their adulthood in relation to our programme of work is by voluntarily choosing to come to our classes. Adult student participants are not dependent in the way children are. Malcolm Knowles, who has written one of the more perceptive accounts of the subject (*The Adult Learner*, 1990), suggests that adulthood is attained at the point at which individuals perceive themselves to be essentially self-directing (although this may not be for many persons a single point). He points out that there is a natural process of maturation leading organically towards autonomy, but that this is limited by what the social culture permits.

In many societies the culture does not encourage the development in some groups of people (women, for instance, especially married women, in many parts of the world) of those abilities needed for self-direction. Self-directedness then is often partial; it may not extend to all parts of life (including to education). Knowles points to the gap or tension that exists in these cases between the drive and the ability to be self-directing.

Some people will feel more strongly than others this compulsion, this urge to take control of their own lives, to be involved increasingly in the decision-making processes affecting their life choices. But it is there in virtually all adults nonetheless. The educational process for adults, to be effective, should coincide with this process of maturation. A situation that reverses the trend, treating the developing adult as a child, will find itself faced on most occasions with major blocks to learning. Our programme must adapt itself to this increasing sense of self-determination if it is to maximise learning.

Against this must be set the fact that some adults, re-entering education after some time away from school, expect to be treated as children. The expectations of 'being taught' are sometimes strong, and if these expectations are not met in some way or other, once again learning is hindered. Experience suggests however that even the most docile group of adult students, happy for much of the time to be passive learners as if they were back in school again, will at the right time rebel against their teachers when the affront to their adulthood becomes too great. It can be a great help to provoke such a situation when we feel the time has come to break up the more formal atmosphere and secure greater participation by the students in their own learning process.

2 They are all engaged in a continuing process of growth

Contrary to some assumptions, adult student participants have not stopped growing or developing. They are not at a static period in their lives, a plateau between the growth stages of youth and the declining stage of old age; they are still people on the move. Whatever our view about the way adults develop (see pages 34–7), the key issue is that growth and change are occurring in all aspects of our student participant's life – in the physical arena, in the intellectual sphere, in the emotions, in the world of relationships, in the patterns of cultural interests. This is true of all participants in all types of adult learning. The pace and direction of these changes vary from person to person; but that it is happening cannot be called into question.

The teacher should take this pattern of change seriously. The people we are trying to help to learn are not passive individuals; they are actively engaged in a dynamic process. And they are in the middle of this process, not at the start. They may be at the start of a new stage of the process, but this stage will draw upon past changes and will in turn contribute to the whole programme of development and growth. It is a process that, although continual, is not continuous; it usually proceeds in spurts, triggered off by new experiences (such as the adult class itself) or new perceptions.

We are normally aware of this process of change within ourselves; indeed, coping with teaching adults itself forms part of the changing pattern of our lives. But we are sometimes reluctant to accept that such a process occurs within the student participants, that they are in the midst of a series of changes when they come to us. It is not practical for us to know all our student participants intimately enough to assess accurately the position each of them has reached and the way by which they have got there. But we can be aware that the process is in every case still continuing. Sensitivity to this fact, and to the fact that the educational experience we offer forms part of this ongoing change process, helps a great deal in creating our responses to the varying demands the students make upon us.

3 They all bring a package of experience and values

Each of the learners brings a range of experience and knowledge more or less relevant to the task in hand. New students are not new people; they possess a set of values, established prejudices and attitudes in which they have a great deal of emotional investment. These are based on their past experience. Knowles (1990) suggests that, for children, experience is something that happens to them; for adults, experience serves to determine who they are, to create their sense of self-identity. When this experience is devalued or ignored by the teacher, this implies a rejection of the person, not just the experience.

This is true in all fields of teaching adults, even in the formal technical and higher educational programmes, but it becomes particularly important for the adult teacher in those contexts where personal growth forms the major objective of the educational programme. The tensions and concerns of both the learner and the teacher in these contexts have been particularly well described by John Wood in his 'Poem for Everyman' (1974).

Poem for Everyman

I will present you
parts
of
my
self
slowly
if you are patient and tender.
I will open drawers
that mostly stay closed
and bring out places and people and things
sounds and smells, loves and frustrations, hopes and sadnesses,

bits and pieces of three decades of life
that have been grabbed off
in chunks
and found lying in my hands
they have eaten
their way into my memory
carved their way into my
heart
altogether – you or i will never see them –
they are me.
if you regard them lightly
deny that they are important
or worse, judge them
i will quietly, slowly
begin to wrap them up,
in small pieces of velvet,
like worn silver and gold jewelry,
tuck them away
in a small wooden chest of drawers

and close.

Such sentiments are not characteristic of all adult student participants. Far from being reticent, some are confident, and a few positively push their views and experiences at the group and at the teacher. But it is perhaps true of more adults in learning situations than we are aware of. The teacher of adults needs to be sensitive to the situation whenever it arises, and it often occurs in the most unlikely of settings and in every class, whether it is a closed group brought together for a specific training purpose, an open-recruitment general-interest course, a highly structured formal class or a community education or development group.

What are the implications of students' prior experience, knowledge and values for our approach to teaching?

First this 'package' determines what messages are received by the learner. The student participants see all new material they encounter through the lens of their existing experience and knowledge (just as the teacher does), and this may distort the messages. Constant feedback from the participants is essential if the teacher is to remain alive to exactly what the student is learning.

Secondly, in those cases where the student participants do not believe that they possess any relevant experience or knowledge, where they insist that they 'know nothing at all about the subject', it is possible to help them to become aware that they do in fact possess relevant material. For unless the new learning is related to this existing reservoir of experience and knowledge, it cannot be fully absorbed into the person; it will sit uneasily with the rest of the individual's make-up, it will be compartmentalised from the rest of their being and will thus not fully affect their attitudes and behaviour. It is not a difficult skill for the teacher to acquire to explore with the participants something of what they already know about the matter in hand: words and phrases relating to the subject of the course, collected from the participants and listed on a blackboard or otherwise, can demonstrate to them that they are able to contribute towards the programme of learning (see page 207). It is usually necessary only for the teacher to make a beginning; once the process has begun, the participants will normally be able to continue the exploration for themselves and find new ways of relating the content of the course to different parts of their own experience and knowledge. The start of the process is the most difficult step for some of the student participants to take, but it is an essential one before deep and permanent learning can take place.

Thirdly, not all of this set of values, experience and knowledge is correct or helpful to the required learning. What is correct and helpful needs to be confirmed and reinforced; what is not correct needs unlearning. Experience of teaching adults reveals that there is often as much unlearning to be done as new learning, and because of the emotional investment in the existing patterns of experience and knowledge, the unlearning process is one of the more difficult tasks facing the teachers of adults (see Chapter 9).

Fourthly, this experience and knowledge (some of it unique to the individual participant and therefore new to the teacher) is a major resource for learning and can be harnessed into the work of the class to the enrichment of the whole group. Much new material can be drawn out from the student participants rather than be presented by the teacher to the taught. Theoretically, we should all start from where the student participants themselves are; but since we usually teach in groups this is not often possible except where the contract to learn has ensured that a more or less homogeneous group has been created. But the utilisation of the varied experience and knowledge of all the members of the group is essential not only to ensure effective learning at a personal level; it will help to bind together the group and make all of its members richer.

4 They usually come to education with set intentions

It is often argued that adult students come to adult education because of a sense of need. We shall look at this area of needs in adult education in more detail later (pages 86–7), but here we must note one or two points. First, it is not always strictly true that the members of our classes are motivated by needs; some job-related programmes, for instance, contain participants who have little or no sense of need. Perhaps it is more useful to talk of all adult student participants as having a set of 'intentions', which for many of them can imply the meeting of a felt need.

Secondly, for those who do come out of a want or need, it is on occasion a confused area. Sometimes the participant is imbued with a vague sense of unease and dissatisfaction. The reason for attending that they give to others and even on occasion to themselves is not the true reason; sometimes the reason is not related to learning at all but more towards social contact or getting out of the house or to please some third person (some research suggests that there is a high correlation between attending some forms of adult education and problems within the marriage relationship, to take but one example). Even when this sense of need is related to learning, there is at times an uncertainty as to what it is that they should be learning. R. D. Laing has expressed something of this in his poem 'Knots' (from the 1972 book of the same title):

Knots

There is something I don't know
     that I am supposed to know.
I don't know *what* it is I don't know
     and yet am supposed to know,
and I feel I look stupid
     if I seem both not to know it
          and not know *what* it is I don't know.
Therefore I pretend I know it.
     This is nerve-racking
     since I don't know what I must pretend to know.
Therefore I pretend to know everything.

I feel you know what I am supposed to know
but you can't tell me what it is
because you don't know that I don't know what it is.

You may know what I don't know, but not
     that I don't know it,
and I can't tell you. So you will have to tell me everything.

At one end of the spectrum of student intentions then is the satisfying of some vague and ill-articulated sense of need. At the other end are those who are present out of a desire to solve a clearly identified problem or to undertake a particular learning task which they feel is required for the performance of their social or vocational roles – for example, to learn a language for their next holiday; to acquire mastery over a computer for job or leisure fulfilment; to understand the development processes of very young children to help them cope at home; or to come to a knowledge of one of the systems of government to enable them to play a more effective role in their local community. In the course of their own continuing development, these people find that they need a specific skill or knowledge or understanding to enable them to fit more easily into some existing or new situation. Even those who come to adult education classes in search of 'a piece of paper', a qualification, rather than new learning may be there for different motives. For some, it is the necessary preliminary to securing promotion or access to more education; for others, it is part of their pursuit of self-affirmation, a need to achieve a goal for themselves. A number come to seek reassurance, confirmation of their ability to achieve the goal. There is a wide range of such wants and intentions. These purposes, often perceived clearly, are almost always concrete and meaningful to their immediate concerns, though on occasion the learning is intended for longer-term future application.

These are the two extremes to this spectrum of adult intentions: those who come to achieve a particular piece of learning related to their present pattern of life, and those who come for social and/or personal reasons or out of some general indeterminate sense of urgency. In the middle are the many who come to learn a 'subject'. Here are those who wish to learn history or cooking or painting or bird-watching, material that is specific enough but not directly related to the solution of an immediate problem. For them it is a matter of interest, of adding to the richness of their present way of life.

Often no clear-cut distinction may be drawn between these three groups. Nevertheless, they may be more or less equated with what C. O. Houle, in his classic work *The Inquiring Mind* (1961), has identified as the three main orientations of the adult learner. In any adult learning situation, he claims, some of the student participants are *goal-oriented*. They wish to use education to achieve some external objective such as a certificate or promotion or to solve an immediate problem facing them. For them the learning experience tends to come to an end once the objective (often separate from the learning process) has been achieved.

A second group is described as *activity-oriented*. They like the atmosphere of the adult class, they find in the circumstances of the learning a meaning for themselves independent of the content or of the announced purpose of the activity. They attend because they get something out of the group apart from the subject-matter involved; it meets a range of needs that are mainly personal and/or social. These people frequently seek the continuance of the activity even though the content of the learning may well change; they may pass from one class to another, searching for satisfaction in the activity itself.

The third group is described as *learning-oriented*. They desire the knowledge or skill for its own sake. They pursue the subject out of interest and will continue to pursue it even without the assistance of a formal programme of adult learning (see Fig. 14).

The implications for the teacher of the different intentions of each of these three groups (and of the many who occupy places on the spectrum between

Figure 14 Orientations of learning

Orientation	Intentions	Learning process	Continuation at end of programme?
Goal-oriented; end product	Achievement; problem-solving/ attainment	Learning most in certain specific areas	Process ceases on 'successful' completion of course
Learning-oriented	Interest in subject	Learning in all parts of subject-matter	Continued learning in same or related subject area
Activity-oriented	Social or personal growth needs; often indeterminate	Find in activities satisfactions to needs	A new situation or activity is sought

these three positions) are considerable. The responses of each group to the demands of the learning programme will vary. Those participants who are motivated to attend courses out of some sense of internal need may on occasion exhibit anxiety, sometimes mixed with hesitation and uncertainty; for the concept of need is threatening, demeaning both to oneself and to others. Such anxiety can be a useful thing – it can promote learning provided it is not too great (see pages 211–14). A gentle encouragement of the sense of need and particularly an attempt to focus it upon particular learning objectives that may help towards meeting the needs often bring about greater readiness to learn. The development of a clearer conception of the nature of the learning task and of the relevance of the material to the immediate concerns of the participant is an essential preliminary to the use of the learning programme to satisfy such needs. On the other hand, those whose motivation is to achieve some external goal (to pass an examination, for instance) will often reveal a great keenness. Here too, the clearer the awareness of purpose and of the relevance of the task to meet this purpose, the greater the motivation to learn.

5 They bring certain expectations about education itself

Adult student participants come to their learning programmes with a range of expectations about the learning process, a series of attitudes towards education in general. These are usually based on their experience of schooling and of education since leaving school (if any). The conception of what education is and what it is for varies widely. Some people enjoyed their years in school; others did not. A number of our student participants assume that adult education will be like school. They expect to be taught everything by a teacher who 'knows everything'; they expect to be put back *in statu pupillari*, which is what education and learning imply for them. On the other hand, some are more confident, willing to engage for themselves directly with the material being handled. For some of them the joy of the adult class is that it is unlike school. Even for many of those who enjoyed their schooldays, the value of adult education is often that the contents and the methods employed are different from those experienced in the formal education system (Figure 15).

Figure 15 Student expectations of adult education

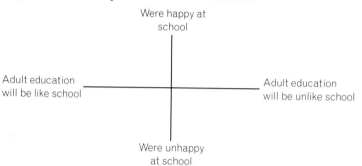

These expectations have different results on the attitudes of the participants towards the work of the group. Some tend more towards conformism, while others seek for a measure of independent learning. Some see, in the formal structure of an adult education class, support for themselves, feeling more at home with 'being taught' – though they may still be anxious as to whether their skills of learning are adequate for the purpose or not. They may feel that their ability to learn has declined since they were last in education (and this may be true; on occasion we may have to spend some time with our student participants boosting their confidence and, even in some advanced courses, strengthening their skills of formal learning). Some of those who have had experience of education over a longer time may look for a less formal structure or become impatient, wishing to push on faster; they feel able to deal with the material easily.

In particular, both kinds of student participant bring with them a set of *self-horizons* relating to the sort of material they can or cannot master. Most of us believe that there is some subject or other that we can never learn, that is just not compatible with our range of inherent abilities and interests. It is odd that so many voluntary adult students still find themselves in classes containing a good deal of material that from the start they are adamant they will never be able to learn. Students attend courses in religion and yet say they cannot cope with 'theology'; students join art classes with a firm belief that they can never learn to draw. Learning in parts of these fields is not for them;

they confine themselves to the role of 'looker-on', as presumably they were at times in school. They may plead age, using this as an excuse to avoid causes of failing for other reasons. By contrast there will be those who see the entering of new areas as a challenge, difficult but not beyond the learning resources they can call upon.

We need to explore these views, about schooling, learning and what is expected in education, from an early stage in the learning programme. The worst thing we can do is treat all the participants alike, teaching one course to them all. The problem of the teacher of adults faced with a mixed group of student participants, encouraging those with low self-horizons and keeping the more self-reliant satisfied with their own progress, is one of constantly making choices between alternatives, of balancing between the needs of one sub-group and those of another while maintaining loyalty to the subject-matter of the course and the group as a whole.

6 They all have competing interests

Apart from those adults, still too few, who are for a relatively short period engaged in full-time courses, adult students are part-time. Education for them is a matter of secondary interest; it is not their prime concern. It is constantly overshadowed by the 'realities' of life: their job or lack of job, their family situation, their social life, other competing issues.

The adults who come to join us in the learning enterprise come from a complete social environment. They all have relationships such as parents, partners, workmates and friends, as well as being students. Adult learners should not be divorced from their background if their learning is to be relevant and thus effective. We need to take seriously the whole of the context within which our student participants live and where they use the new learning they have acquired. Students in other parts of the educational world may be taken out of their life situation to concentrate on their learning, but part-time adult learners continue to live within their world and to apply what they learn in that world.

Within that background there are factors supporting the learning endeavours as well as some militating against these same endeavours. Not all of the competing concerns that the participants bring with them to our programmes are hindrances. Some are supportive. Indeed, periods of intensive study can hardly be carried through without the identification of the support networks existing all around the adult learner, and it is to the advantage of both teacher and student participant to encourage the full exploitation of these supporting factors. This is particularly true where the class is a one-off episode, not backed up by other studies as it is at school or college. A short course, taken part-time and on its own, assumes in the life of many student participants rather less significance than it has for the teacher. We must not be surprised if our students' attention is at times distracted towards the more urgent problems of the family's health, or the omission to fulfil some promised errand, or problems at work.

7 They all possess set patterns of learning

Adults are engaged in a continuing process of lifelong learning, and they have already acquired ways of coping with this. They often fail to see this as 'learning' in the educational sense, but it exists all the same. We shall look in more detail at the special features of the adult learning process (pages 94–5), but here we must note two points: that each of the participants has developed such a style already; and that the styles that exist in our adult groups are varied.

Over the years, each of our adult student participants has developed their own strategies and patterns of learning, which they have found help them to learn most easily, most quickly and most effectively. Learning changes are not brought about without effort, and the process can be painful; it takes an investment of time and emotions, and, once done, no one wants to do it again. We all thus seek ways to ease the pain, shorten the time taken to master the necessary new material, and make the gains acquired more permanent. Experience has taught us what strategies we can adopt to achieve these ends.

Each of us learns in our own way, according to our particular aptitudes and experience. Some handle figures more easily than others. Some have fostered different methods for memorising facts (addresses, telephone numbers, etc.). Some need to see the written page in order to comprehend more fully rather than rely on the spoken word. Languages particularly throw up differences of approach in this respect. Some learners need a book and practise sounds from written words, finding it hard to react to spoken words, while others respond easily to oral tuition; both are valid methods of learning languages, and we should not try to force any learner into adopting a particular style because we prefer it to any other. We must thus remember that our student participants all have their own ways of dealing with learning needs, and opportunities to exercise these have to be created if new learning is to take place.

The pace of learning of each student participant also varies. In general, in those areas where the participants can call upon a good deal of experience – social relationships and roles, for instance – or where they may have direct experience of the subject-matter, they tend to learn fast, a good deal faster than young people, provided that the new material does not conflict with existing knowledge. But where they have less experience on which to fasten the new material – languages, for example, or computer studies – especially if it calls for extensive memorising, they tend to learn more slowly and have greater difficulty in mastering the material than their younger counterparts.

Such matters are central to our concerns as teachers. There is a wide range of learning styles within any group of adult learners, and we need to devise methods that give each of the participants full scope for exercising their own particular learning method, and as far as possible not impose our own upon them.

Implications for the teacher of adults

We can see, then, that teachers of adults, especially those who teach in groups, are faced with a difficult task from the start. Unless the group is narrowly conceived (as in some forms of industrial training), our student participants will consist of a wide variety of people all bringing their own advantages and disadvantages to the learning situation.

- Some are more adult than others; some are still searching in education for dependency, others for autonomy.
- All are growing and developing, but in different directions and at a different pace.
- Some bring a good deal of experience and knowledge, others bring less; and there are varying degrees of willingness to use this material to help the learning process.
- They have a wide range of intentions and needs, some specific, some more general and related to the subject-matter under discussion, and others unknown even to themselves.
- They are all at different points in the continuum between those who require be taught everything and those who wish to find out everything for themselves; and they each have some consciousness of what they can and cannot do in the way of learning.
- They all have competing interests of greater importance than their learning.
- And they have all by now acquired their own ways of learning, which vary considerably the one from the other.

It is easy to view all of this in negative terms, to see most of what we have discussed as hindrances to learning. The pressure from competing interests, the worry and anxiety especially about their learning abilities, based as they often are on misconceptions as to what education involves, the problem of coping with unlearning and the attack on the personality that this can at times imply – all of these may seem to make the task of the teacher of adults particularly difficult. We must not be surprised if some of the student participants do not move as fast as we would wish them to; if they have difficulty in grasping some of the material that *we* find so easy and have so carefully constructed for them; if they show a lack of responsiveness to all our promptings to engage more wholeheartedly with the subject-matter of the class. We must not be put off if some of the learners require us to demonstrate or lecture when we would rather that they practise for themselves or discuss.

But there are many aspects of this discussion that give cause for hope. Within the group is a well of resources that we can use. Some of these can be quickly identified: the wealth of knowledge, skills and experience gathered together in one room; the fact that all the student participants, whether they know it or not, are already engaged in some form of learning; the awareness, however dim, of purpose and need; the greater use of reasoning powers, and the fact that adult students, when provoked, 'accept' the teacher's word less readily (those of us who prefer to demonstrate and to lecture, to perform rather than to watch, to listen to our own voice rather than to the voice of the learners, will not see this as a resource); the desire of many of the learners to apply what they learn one day to their lives the very next day and the fact that (unlike full-time students) they are in a position to do so. All these factors can be seen as combining to form a powerful aid to learning.

We need to try to identify both those factors that prevent us from being fully effective in the teaching–learning process and those resources that we can bring into play in order to overcome the obstacles. In adult education, our students are not there just to be taught; they are our greatest resource in the learning process.

Application

It should be important to you, as you look through this material, to relate it to your own experience. You may find it helpful to write down what assumptions you made about the potential student participants for the course you have chosen as your own, what characteristics they will bring with them to your course. It may be possible for you, if you actually ran a course, to test this against the group that materialised so that you can assess how accurate your first thoughts were.

A second useful exercise at this stage is to set out for yourself the range of helps and hindrances that you think your students will bring with them to the programme of study. Most of us do this without being fully conscious of it; to make it a deliberate process will help to bring into focus those whom we hope to help to learn.

Further reading

Allman, P. (1983) The nature and process of adult development, in M. Tight (ed.) *Education for Adults*. Beckenham: Croom Helm.

Chickering, A. W. (1977) *Experience and Learning: An Introduction to Experiential Learning*. New Rochelle, NY: Change Magazine Press.

Chickering, A. W. and Havighurst, R. W. (1981) The life cycle, in A. W. Chickering (ed.) *The Modern American College: Responding to the New Realities of Diverse Students and a Changing Society*. San Francisco, CA: Jossey Bass.

Cross, K. P. (1981) *Adults as Learners: Increasing Participation and Facilitating Learning*. San Francisco, CA: Jossey Bass.

Evans, P. (1975) *Motivation*. London: Methuen.

Giles, K. (1981) *Personal Change in Adults*. Milton Keynes: Open University Press.

Jarvis, P. (1987) *Adult Education in its Social Context*. Beckenham: Croom Helm.

Keeting, M. T. (ed.) (1976) *Experiential Learning: Rationale, Characteristics and Assessment*. San Francisco, CA: Jossey Bass.

Kidd, J. R. (1973) *How Adults Learn*. New York: Association Press.

Knowles, M. S. (1990) *The Adult Learner: a Neglected Species*. Houston, TX: Gulf.

Knox, A. (1977) *Adult Development and Learning*. San Francisco, CA: Jossey Bass.

Levinson, D. (1978) *The Seasons of a Man's Life*. New York: Knopf.

Levinson, D. (1986) *The Season of a Woman's Life*. New York: Knopf.

Miller, H. L. (1964) *Teaching and Learning in Adult Education*. London: Macmillan.

Pressey, S. and Kuhlen, R. (1957) *Psychological Development through the Lifespan*. New York: Harper.

Rayner, E. (1971) *Human Development: an Introduction to the Psychodynamics of Growth, Maturity and Ageing*. London: Allen and Unwin.

Rogers, J. (1989) *Adults Learning*. Milton Keynes: Open University Press.

Sheehy, C. T. (1976) *Passages: Predictable Crises of Adult Life*. New York: Dutton.

4

THE NATURE OF LEARNING

What is it . . . ?

Introduction

Some readers may understandably be tempted to give this chapter a miss. The world of educational psychology is full of division and uncertainty, and it is not always clear how a consideration of the various learning theories can help us as teachers of adults in the practice of our craft.

Nevertheless, it is always useful to stand back from what we are doing and look at it in terms of general principles. On the one hand, it is surely necessary that the overall theories should be pressed into service to assist concretely the teaching process; there is otherwise little point in all the speculation. This is beginning to happen: although relatively few of those who research into learning processes have devoted time and space to considering the relevance of their studies to the activity of teaching, there is a small but growing interest in the application of this type of theory to practice.

From the point of view of the teacher of adults, then, an examination of theory is important. For how we view learning affects how we teach. Teaching is concerned with the promotion of learning, and we therefore need to understand what it is that we are promoting. In particular, part of our task is to help our adult student participants to 'learn how to learn', or rather to learn how to learn more effectively. To be able to do this properly, we need to be aware of what is involved in the process of learning.

The distinctiveness of adult learning

And here we run immediately into an issue which has been debated widely among educators and adult educators particularly. For the first question that needs to be addressed is whether the differences which characterise adult learning are so great that they call for a different view of learning from that applicable to younger age groups. The issue is whether the learning – and thus the education built upon it – that occurs throughout the whole of life in both youth and adulthood is essentially the same or whether adult learning – and thus the education of adults – is distinctive. Is there any justification for discussing *adult* education at all or are we just talking about education in general and 'good' (i.e. effective) education in particular?

In many ways this is the most crucial question facing teachers of adults. We have to decide whether we believe that teaching adults is different from teaching children or younger persons or not; whether the same strategies by which we were taught as young people, and which we may already be using in other settings, are appropriate for the groups of adults now under our supervision. It is not just a question as to whether the adult student participant – the mother, the worker on the farm or in the factory, shop or office, the trainee or manager, the churchgoer, the local resident, the interested member of the public, the keen sportsman or -woman – whether they all *expect* all education to be the same, whether they expect or wish to be taught in the same way they were taught at school or college. The question is rather how we as teachers of adults see our student participants.

Those who teach adults are divided in their approach to this question. Many – indeed, I think an increasing number – argue that there is only one activity, 'education', and that adult education is essentially the same as teaching younger persons. The education of adults is for them merely one branch of the whole field. But others point out that within this field of education, we already draw distinctions; we distinguish between the various branches in one way or another. The education of primary children, of secondary pupils and of students in further, advanced or higher education all call upon different teaching–learning processes. We may at times use similar methods with all of these groups, but the basic approach in each case is varied. We cannot teach an 18-year-old in the same way as an 8-year-old. We assume that each level of student can cope with distinct learning tasks and that they are motivated to learn most efficiently through the adoption of teaching–learning styles appropriate to the stage of development they have reached.

We have in part then answered the question. Even if there is only one general activity, education, there are variations between groups of learners. The question thus becomes: in what ways does the teaching of adults differ from the teaching of younger students? It is the difference in degree that is at issue.

At the same time, by concentrating on various strategies appropriate to different levels of student learners, taking into account their motivations, their experience, skills of learning and the development of their capabilities, we have immediately created another problem. For we have noticed that adults are enormously varied, far more varied than any school class or college year. Some have much wider ranges of (relevant and irrelevant) experience to draw upon than others; and among those with a wide range of experience, some are apparently more willing and more able to learn from this experience than others (some studies of soldiers returning from active campaigning have shown this). The range of motivations will be very wide indeed. And some adults have been away from education for a long time and in some cases have never developed the range of their formal educational skills greatly, while others have continued to use on a regular basis and in a structured way the talents for learning they have acquired. Do we treat the former like primary and/or secondary pupils and the latter in a more 'advanced' way, using sophisticated techniques of learning and more complex conceptual materials? Or is there a common way in which all adults learn that can form the basis for our adult teaching?

Both of these seem to be true. It is necessary to adapt our methods of teaching adults to the range of educational skills they possess. Those with the least developed skills, either because they never fully mastered them during their initial education or because the formal learning skills they once possessed have fallen into disarray, will need to be helped in building up these skills as well as coping with the task of the moment. Those who are accustomed to learning may often be left with the activity to work at on their own. Both formal and non-formal strategies may be appropriate at different times, with different groups and at different stages of each learning task. But at the same time, there are ways in which the learning processes of adults in general are distinctive, and we will best serve our student participants if we can understand these processes and build our educational programmes upon them.

This is a huge field, fraught with dangers and complexities. Whole books have been written about learning theories or about small parts of one particular theory. The language is often abstruse, and there is no agreement as to the 'true' models; polemics fly. Particularly there is a call by some writers today for a complete transformation of the relations between teacher and taught, and between all members of the learning group (including the teacher) and knowledge, authority and expertise. There is no general consensus yet among adult educationalists, although there are signs of some growing together. To attempt to sum all this up within the compass of two chapters may seem to be courting disaster.

To assist you with finding your way through this section, it may be helpful to set out here its structure. It will look in turn at the following topics:

- what do we mean by 'learning'?
- when do we learn?
- adult learning: the natural 'learning episode';
- why do we learn?

- how do we learn?
- learning styles;
- and finally, the implications of this discussion for the teacher of adults.

What is learning?

In common parlance the word 'learning' carries at least two meanings. There is first a general one of some kind of change, often in knowledge but also in behaviour. 'I met Mr X today and learned that he had lost his job.' 'Today, a new bus timetable was introduced. A spokesman for the council said that he believed the public would soon learn to use the new routes.' But there is also a more intense sense of the verb 'to learn' meaning to memorise, learn by heart: 'Take this poem home and learn it.'

We may leave on one side the meaning of the word as 'memorising' and concentrate instead on the 'learning as change' meaning. To say that 'learning is change' is too simple. First, not all change is learning. The changes brought about by ageing or other physical processes can hardly be described as 'learning changes', though they may in their turn bring about learning changes. Secondly, some forms of learning are confirmation rather than changes of existing patterns of knowledge and behaviour. Since the knowledge is more strongly held or the behaviour more intensely engaged in after the learning has taken place, it can still perhaps be said that learning is change, but on these occasions the changes are directed more towards reinforcement than to alteration of patterns of knowledge and behaviour.

Learning as change takes two main forms. There are those more or less automatic responses to new information, perceptions or experiences that result in change; and secondly there are those structured purposeful changes aimed at achieving mastery. There is a difference in meaning between the use of the word in contexts such as: 'He burned his fingers. He learned not to do that again', and 'I had some trouble with the machine but I learned how to manage it.' The second implies both purpose and effort which the first, being unintended and involuntary, lacks.

What we usually mean by 'learning' are those more or less permanent changes brought about voluntarily in one's patterns of acting, thinking and/or feeling. There is a widely held (and even more widely practised) view of learning which says that it is the receipt of knowledge and skills from outside. But recent work on learning indicates that

- learning is active, not the passive receipt of knowledge and skills;
- learning is personal, individual: we can learn from and in association with others, but in the end, all learning changes are made individually;
- learning is voluntary, we do it ourselves; it is not compulsory.

There are then two models of learning, traditional and modern:

Traditional/input	Modern/action
passive	active
receipt	search
fill a deficit	seek for satisfaction
responsive to outside stimulus	initiated by inner drive
keywords: 'give, impart'	keywords: 'discover, create'
transfer of knowledge/skills	problem-solving
need for teacher	self-learning

Areas of change (learning domains)

There have been several attempts to describe the different areas of learning change. Many of these are overlaid with philosophical assumptions about human nature and the nature of knowledge that are difficult to test. Sometimes they are seen to be hierarchical – that is, some areas of learning are viewed as being of a higher order than others, though not necessarily dependent on prior learning.

The main and traditional distinction has of course been between learning knowledge and learning skills; but others have elaborated on this. Several have pointed to the need to include the learning of attitudes as a third area of learning. In the field of learning objectives, knowledge, skills and attitudes (KSA) is a well-worn path. Bloom (1965) drew a clear distinction between learning in the cognitive domain and learning in the affective domain. Kurt Lewin (1935) suggested that learning changes occur in skills, in cognitive patterns (knowledge and understanding), in motivation and interest, and in ideology (fundamental beliefs). Gagné (1972) identified five 'domains' of learning:

- *motor skills* which require practice;
- *verbal information* – facts, principles and generalisations which, when organised into larger bodies of information, become knowledge: 'the major requirement for learning and retaining verbal information appears to be its presentation within an organised, meaningful context';
- *intellectual skills* – the skills of using knowledge; those 'discriminations, concepts and rules' that characterise both elementary and more advanced cognitive learning in a way that motor skills and verbal information do not;
- *cognitive strategies* – the way knowledge is used; the way the individual learns, remembers and thinks; the self-managed skills needed to define and solve problems. These require practice and are constantly being refined;
- and *attitudes*.

Learning then takes place in a number of different spheres. We may categorise these using the mnemonic KUSAB:

1 We may learn new *knowledge* as we collect information that is largely memorised.
2 Such knowledge may be held uncomprehendingly. We thus need to learn to relate our new material in ways that lead to new *understanding*, that process of organising and reorganising knowledge to create new patterns of relationships.
3 We may learn new *skills* or develop existing skills further; not just physical skills, our ability to do certain things, but also skills of thinking and of learning, skills of coping and solving problems and survival strategies.
4 Further, since we can learn new knowledge, new understanding and new skills without necessarily changing our attitudes, the learning of *attitudes* is a distinct sphere of learning.
5 Finally, it is possible for learning changes to be brought about in all four of these areas without accompanying alterations in our way of life, our pattern of behaviour. It is therefore necessary to learn to apply our newly learned material to what we do and how we live, to carry out our new learning into changed ways of *behaving*: what some people would call to learn 'wisdom', in short.

The way these five areas of learning change relate to each other is complex. Changes in attitude rely to a large extent on changes in knowledge and understanding, and behavioural changes can hardly take place without accompanying changes in one or more of the other areas. But the relationship between changes in knowledge and attitude or between new knowledge and changed behaviour is idiosyncratic and uncertain. When new knowledge (e.g. 'smoking can damage your health') meets contrary behaviour (the habit of smoking), one of a number of different reactions may occur. The information may be decried, ignored or rejected ('It's all very exaggerated', or 'I know but I don't care'); the new knowledge may be accepted but rationalised away by other knowledge ('Less than 30 per cent of smokers die of cancer caused by smoking and I'll be one of the lucky ones', or 'It is more dangerous to cross the roads than to smoke'); or the new knowledge can be accepted and the way of life adapted to fit in with it. The way any individual reacts to learning changes in any one domain seems to depend on personality and situational factors.

From the teacher's point of view, it is useful to keep the distinctions between these different areas of learning in mind during the preparation of the learning programme. We will find it helpful to ask ourselves whether our teaching is *primarily* in the area of skills or knowledge or understanding or attitudes or behaviour. For this will influence the practices we adopt in the programme of learning. Most of our teaching will cover several different areas of learning, probably all of them. It is doubtful whether they can be kept apart. Nevertheless, while bearing in mind that teaching which concentrates primarily on one of these areas (e.g. skills) inevitably involves learning in other areas (knowledge, understanding, attitudes and behaviour) as well, we need to ask ourselves precisely what sort of learning change we and our student participants are attempting to deal with at this particular stage of the learning programme.

When do we learn?

Learning is not of course confined to the classroom.

It is strange how many people who know a lot about adult education and lifelong learning use language very loosely. They talk about 'motivating people to learn', they urge that we need 'to get people into learning' – by which they mean that they wish to persuade people to come to classes, thereby implying that there is no learning going on outside of the classes. They use the word 'learners' to mean those people who are in the classes, as if those who are not inside their classes are not learners. 'Learning' and 'education' thus very frequently get mixed up. Even experienced adult educators use the term 'lifelong learning' and speak about adult education as existing 'to provide opportunities for lifelong learning' when they really mean 'lifelong education', that the function of adult education is to provide structured programmes of directed learning, often classes, which are open to people of any age. They do not realise that 'lifelong learning' is simply that, learning which goes on more or less all the time without any help from adult educators, that 'opportunities for lifelong learning' exist around us every day and in everything we do. But as we have already seen, there is a distinction to be drawn between learning and education. All education must involve learning; but not all learning is education.

We do therefore need to stress very clearly that learning is quite independent of the classroom. People are learning all the time, whatever they are doing.

Learning is part of living

Learning comes from experience. It is closely related to the way in which individuals develop in relation to their social and physical environment. And since experience is continuous, so too learning is continuous. It occurs throughout life, from start to finish. Nearly everything we do has been learned and is constantly being relearned.

And this means that learning is individual. It is not a collective activity. 'Each individual is processing the experience uniquely for personal use. . . . In learning, the individual is the agent, even though the agent may be subject to the social pressures of the group' (Brookfield 1983: 1–4). Learning is affected and may even to some extent be controlled by society or other collectives, but the learning activity itself – introducing learning changes – is personal.

Learning desires

Learning, then, is natural, as natural as breathing. It is the continual process of adapting to the various changes which we all face, changes in our social and cultural contexts, changes in our own social roles, the daily tasks we perform, our own personal growth and development.

But it goes deeper than this. Within every individual there is a bundle of learning desires. In part they spring from the drive towards adulthood which we have already seen, the urge towards more maturity, the search for meaning, the drive towards more responsibility and autonomy. In part they spring from half-finished earlier learning activities. In part they spring from our own interests and experiences, an earlier spoken or written word or a glimpse of something having aroused unsatisfied curiosity.

Some of these learning desires are very pressing, arising from or reinforced by urgent matters. But most of them lie dormant, overlaid by more immediate concerns, awaiting either a suitable learning opportunity or an increased sense of need to bring them to life (this is the 'I've always wanted to learn something about this or that' syndrome). For some people, these desires for more learning have been damaged or buried deep by other experiences (often by formal education, especially at secondary levels where discovery learning methods are sometimes less frequently used than at primary level), but they still exist and can in appropriate circumstances be awakened.

Intentional and unintentional learning

Much of our learning – perhaps most of it – is unintended. A good deal is very casual: it comes from chance happenings (roadside posters, snatches of overheard conversation, newspaper reading or television watching, meeting people: 'adventitious learning [which] springs from accidental encounters with unintentional sources' (Lucas 1983: 2–3). There are however some 'sources of learning' who intend learning to take place – through mass campaigns, advertisements, political persuasion, social propaganda, etc. – even though the learner has no intention of engaging in learning.

But beyond this, there are occasions when we engage in some more purposeful learning activity, some structured process of mastering a situation – learning to deal with a new piece of equipment, for instance, or to adjust to new bus timetables or to cope with a new baby. At certain times throughout their lives, all adults will bend their energies and attention to achieving some learning task directed towards a set goal. Some of these occasions may call for formal methods of learning (learning to drive a car is probably the biggest

Figure 16 Learning matrix

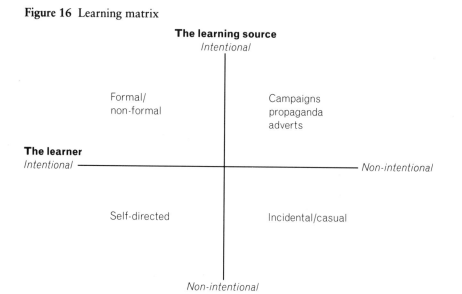

formal programme of teaching adults in many countries) but with most of them we cope more informally (see Fig. 16).

Learning episodes

Such 'learning episodes', as we may call these intended purposeful learning activities, are usually voluntary and are always purposeful. Some of course come from external requirements: a new task set for us by our employers, for example, or changes in legislation which call for changes in our working practices; learning called for by some of the welcome or unwelcome changes that may come in our personal circumstances, and so on. Many an adult has had to learn about new financial matters through divorce or separation. But the majority are undertaken voluntarily and with some measure of enthusiasm and commitment. And they are always purposeful: they are designed to achieve a particular goal which the learners set for themselves. Learning episodes are therefore distinct from the incidental and unintended learning which characterises the majority of our learning experiences.

Such learning episodes arise from a perceived need or challenge – from those changes in our social relationships, in our occupations (however widely defined that term may be used), in our personal development or in preparation for further learning which we wish to pursue, as we have noted above (pages 37–8). It is therefore clear that such learning episodes are closely related to the lifespan development of each one of us, however that lifespan development is defined.

Learning objectives or 'clearing up messes'?

These learning episodes are voluntary, intentional, purposeful; the adult learner is seen to be active, struggling with reality, rather than responsive to stimuli. And this would seem to suggest that they are directed by clearly perceived learning objectives.

To some extent, this is true. When we set out to learn to meet some need or to increase our expertise in some field of interest, there will be occasions when we will be able to focus our efforts on defined learning objectives, when we can see what it is that we are trying to achieve. When deciding to learn to drive a car, for example, we can set for ourselves a clear goal, and we can see relatively plainly whether we are making progress towards the achievement of this goal. We can clear our mind of all that will block the way and set out to achieve the mastery we require of ourselves.

But in other cases, the situation is not so clear. Ackoff (1978) (talking about managers) has pointed out that we are often in a more confused situation: we

> are not confronted with problems that are independent of each other but with dynamic situations that consist of complex systems of changing problems that interact with each other. I call such situations 'messes'. Problems are extracted from 'messes' by analysis; they are to messes as atoms are to tables and chairs . . . [We] do not solve problems, [we] manage messes.

This would seem to be particularly true of many learning episodes which we undertake throughout our lives – for example, coping with a new baby. Our task in these cases is not straightforward, simply meeting a need. Rather, it is to unravel a tangle, to sort out a mess.

In these circumstances, how and what we learn depends on how we define the situation we are facing. We analyse the issue, determine what the problem looks like so far as we can see it, and try to solve it. How we do that depends on how much and what kind of experience we can bring to the 'mess'. That will determine the way we look at the problem and the language in which we express it. Learning is a haphazard process of trial and error and we often get it wrong. As Donald Schön puts it in regard to his chosen professionals:

> Problems must be constructed from the materials of problematic situations which are puzzling, troubling and uncertain . . . [We] are frequently embroiled in conflicts of values, goals, purposes and interests . . . the effective use of specialised knowledge to well-defined tasks depends on a prior structuring of situations that are complex and uncertain.
>
> (Schön 1983)

Learning episodes and the teaching of adults

These structured and purposeful learning episodes may be undertaken by the learners on their own or they may invoke the assistance of some helper. And it is here that they can be seen to be of considerable significance for teachers of adults. For our purpose is to create one or a number of such learning episodes for our adult student participants.

Not only this but, since they are intended and purposeful, these natural learning episodes reveal more about the sort of learning opportunity that we as teachers of adults seek to construct than do the more ubiquitous, haphazard and largely unintentional learning activities that spring from the constant interaction of the individual with the environment. The way adults learn purposefully on their own will tell us much about the way they will learn in our programmes.

Some adult educators are hesitant about using these natural learning episodes as the basis for building a theory of adult learning. They point out that each of us engages with the environment in ways limited by our experience and existing learning abilities, and that this social environment itself controls our learning. They suggest that what is needed is to break free from such restraints. Nevertheless, these episodes show us something of the way adults learn and the special features of adult learning as distinct from the processes of schooling. They can form a guide as we construct learning opportunities for those who come to our programmes.

Characteristics of learning episodes

There are three characteristics about these self-directed learning activities that are relevant to our discussion.

First, *they are usually episodic in character, not continuous*. They come in short bursts of relatively intensive activity, absorbing the attention, and they usually come to an end as soon as the immediate purpose has been felt to be achieved. There are some, particularly in the self-fulfilment area, that spring from long-term interests (gardening, for instance, or following trends in modern or classical music); but even within these overall patterns of persistent learning, there come more intensive short-term episodes of learning directed towards the achievement of some immediate goal. We cannot keep this sort of pressure up for long; we need to be motivated by an achievable purpose; and when that is over, there may come a rest or a slower pace of learning before the next episode occurs. (How far this episodic character is part of our way of life in a modern Western society rather than an inherent adult process is not clear, but it would seem to be of more general application than confined to just one form of social structure and culture.)

Secondly, *the goal that is set is usually some concrete task, some immediate problem that seems important*. Such learning episodes, self-directed or otherwise, are in general aimed at the solution of a particular problem. The situations they are designed to meet are concrete rather than theoretical. We need to decorate this room, to master the relationship between these stamps, to cope with this particular change in the family circle, to understand a new procedure at home or at work, and so on. Even when the learning is part of a long-term and developing interest (chess, say, or cooking), the individual episode of learning is directed towards a particular goal to be achieved.

There are several implications flowing from this:

- We do not on the whole approach any situation academically. To decorate a room, we do not study design as such. To cope with a family issue, we do not take a course on interpersonal relations or psychology – although we might well consult books on the subject. We are not concerned so much with a subject as to resolve a one-off concrete situation.
- This means that the learning task is rarely pursued in a systematic way. It is limited learning, limited to the task in hand. Adult learners do not often pull down a textbook and start at the beginning, with a general introduction to the field of study, nor do they pursue it from A to Z in sequence to the end. It is only with those who have had extensive experience of formal education, who have developed and maintained advanced study skills, that a systematic exploration of a field of knowledge becomes at all common. This is a replication in private of the formal systems of learning that characterise schooling and is thus confined to relatively few, and to a few occasions in their lives. They too will also engage in the more limited goal-oriented episodes of learning at other times. Most of us most of the time use only those parts of any subject that help us to meet our immediate task.
- The learners do not start with the simple and move on to the more difficult. They tackle the problem with which they have to deal at the level at which it occurs in their lives. They cope with quite difficult language and terms from the start so long as these are of direct relevance to the learning process.
- The learners do not on the whole draw on compartmentalised knowledge such as was learned at school, history separated from geography or maths from physics. They bring all that they know from all sorts of fields to bear upon the particular instance. Such an academic compartmentalised approach may occur on occasion, especially in the self-directed learning activities noted above (pages 81–2); but even here there is often a particular need to be met that leads to the use of knowledge from different fields of study rather than a restricted compartmentalised approach to knowledge.
- Such episodes are aimed at immediate rather than future application. There are, it is true, some learning episodes which are intended as a preparation before embarking on a course of action: religious preparation classes, pre-marriage groups, holiday language courses, pre-retirement

programmes are examples of these. But on the whole, most learning episodes are undertaken in the process of doing a particular task or meeting a situation. The material, as it is mastered, is applied at once. We learn how to use a new washing machine by using it; we learn a new bus timetable as we use the service; we learn how to cope with a baby by coping with a baby.

Thirdly, since most of these learning episodes are directed towards specific goals, *there is relatively little interest in overall principles*. Few attempts are made by the learner to draw general conclusions from the particular instance being learned. Once the immediate situation has been resolved, the goal attained or the problem solved, the adult learner normally brings the process of investigation to a close, storing away the learning gained for another day. What is stored is the way to cope with the particular situation, not general principles. Learning to use a new washing machine will be concentrated on the specific instrument in hand, not on washing machines in general. The learning needed to cope with a new bus timetable will deal not with the entire transport system but with the one or two routes needed to make a particular journey. Learning a new craft or industrial technique will be confined to what is needed for the moment, not to wider applications. All of these situations may arouse in our minds wider issues of obsolescence and modern technology, or public and private transport provision or the demands of new processes as a whole; but these will occur mainly as spasmodic thoughts and grumbles, usually quickly pushed away and forgotten. The efforts are centred on the immediate and the particular, not on the long-term and the general.

Why do we engage in these learning episodes?

There is a very large literature which suggests that all learning (certainly all purposeful learning) comes from a sense of need.

> Learning is something which takes place within the learner and is personal to him [*sic*]; it is an essential part of his development, for it is always the whole person who is learning. Learning takes place when an individual feels a need, puts forth an effort to meet that need, and experiences satisfaction with the result of his effort.
>
> (Leagans 1971)

There is much truth in this, and the awakening of a sense of need has been identified by most writers on adult learning as a precondition of effective learning. But we have to tread carefully here. Not all purposeful learning comes from a sense of need; some for example comes from an increased interest.

'Needs', then, is a dangerous concept in adult education. It often leads to an assumption that 'I know what you need to learn even though you don't know what you need.' 'Needs' are externally identified; 'wants' are internally identified. Purposeful adult learning, the kind of voluntary learning episodes we have been talking about above, come from identified wants rather than externally set needs. It is a search for satisfaction in some sense or other.

Motivation and learning

Much has been written about motivation in relation to the education and training of adults. In many forms of adult education and extension in developing countries, it forms the keystone of the training programme. But in the West, rather less consideration has been given to it in practice. In most forms of adult education (except perhaps those industrial and professional development programmes where some of the participants may be seen to be reluctant participants), we tend to rely on the fact that adult student learners come to us of their own free will, that they are already interested in the subject, that they are already motivated to learn. We forget that initial motivation to learn may be weak and can die; alternatively that it can be strengthened and directed into new channels. This is the task of the teacher of adults – and as such we need to understand motivation.

Motivation is usually defined as those factors that energise and direct behavioural patterns organised around a goal. It is frequently seen as a force within the individual that moves him or her to act in a certain way. Motivation in learning is that compulsion which keeps a person within the learning situation and encourages him or her to learn.

Motivation is seen as being dependent on either *intrinsic* or *extrinsic* factors. Extrinsic factors consist of those external incentives or pressures such as attendance requirements, external punishments or examinations to which many learners in formal settings are subjected. These, if internalised, create an intention to engage in the learning programme. Intrinsic factors consist of that series of inner pressures and/or rational decisions which create a desire for learning changes.

Most adult learning episodes are already dependent on intrinsic motivational factors; but not all of them are. It has been argued that intrinsic factors are stronger and more enduring than extrinsic factors. But even within intrinsic motivation, there is a hierarchy of factors. For example, a desire to please some other person or loyalty to a group which may keep a person within a learning programme even when bored with the subject are seen as intrinsic motives of a lower order than a desire to complete a particular task in itself.

There are three main groups of ideas behind the development of a theory of motivation. The first says that motivation is an inner drive to fulfil various needs. The second says that motivation can be learned. And the third claims that motivation relates to goals set or accepted by oneself.

Needs-related motivation

Many people see motivation as internal urges and drives based on needs. All individuals vary in the composition of these needs and their intensity. At their simplest instinctual level, they may be the avoidance of pain and the search for pleasure, or the Freudian drives related to life, death, sex and aggression; but all such instincts can be modified by learning.

Most theorists see a motive as a learned drive directed towards a goal, often regarded as a search for the reduction of tension or conflict. Boshier (1989) and others see this as having two main dimensions: the reduction in inner conflicts between different parts of the self and different experiences (intra-resolution); and the reduction of conflicts and tensions between the self and the external social and physical environment (extra-resolution). The individual is seeking for harmony, for peace. Such directed drives may be aroused and sustained, as we have seen, by incentives (external factors) and by goals set or accepted by the individual (internal factors).

Some writers have distinguished between needs (seen to be physical) and drives (psychological). More often however the distinction is drawn between primary needs (viscerogenic, related to bodily functions) and secondary needs (psychogenic). The latter come into play only when primary needs are to a large extent met.

Two major writers, Carl Rogers (1974) and Abraham Maslow (1968), have helped us to see learning as the main process of meeting the compulsions of inner urges and drives rather than responding to stimuli or meeting the demands of new knowledge. Whether viewed as goal-seeking (based on limited and specific goals set by themselves) or ideal-seeking (related to objectives set by the value system the learners have come to accept and hold), both argue that the learner is impelled to seek out learning changes from within rather than by outside imperatives. Rogers viewed this as a series of drives towards adulthood – autonomy, responsibility, self-direction – though it is now clear that the precise forms which such drives take are culturally bound, varying from society to society. Maslow concentrated on the urge to satisfy in part or in whole a hierarchy of needs.

Abraham Maslow is recognised as the apostle of the 'needs' school of thought. He distinguished basic drives from temporary needs, and established a hierarchy which is often quoted (Fig. 17); and he developed a theory of 'pre-potency' – that one need must be largely satisfied before the next need can come into full play.

Maslow argued that all people are driven through the first four stages of basic needs. As each lower need is in part met, the next higher level of need is triggered. Several levels of need can be in operation at the same time. The

Figure 17 Maslow's hierarchy of needs

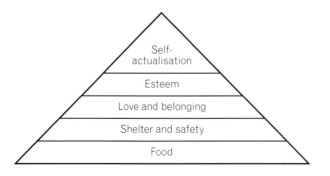

highest level of need, self-actualisation, may not be reached by some individuals on more than an occasional basis. This level consists of a need to create, to appreciate, to know and to understand. (Maslow indicated in his teaching a further level of need above self-actualisation: self-transcendence, a need to express tangibly concern for others, but this hardly appears in his writings.)

Maslow's concern for self-actualisation accounts for the increasing popularity of the many adult education programmes of today designed to enhance the students' understanding of the 'self' – programmes like learner-generated 'life histories' or autobiographies, and the programmes of creative writing aimed at increasing self-confidence and self-expression.

From the point of view of the teacher of adults, Maslow's work will be a reminder that within any group of adult learners there will be a wide variety of needs, and within each individual student participant there will be a different mixture of needs. This mixture will be constantly changing as the learning proceeds and as the individual's life situation changes. This is why predetermined and uniform learning outcomes can never be achieved in adult learning programmes, why each adult learner will take away from any learning situation what he or she will require, why adult learning is unique to each learner and uncertain.

But Maslow's hierarchy of needs fails us as adult educators precisely at the point we need it most. It offers us an analysis of the *preconditions* to the type of learning we are most interested in: the self-evident truth that the prior personal and social needs (food, security, personal relationships and a sense of esteem) must be satisfied, at least in part, before motivation for the more creative, evaluative and self-fulfilling kinds of learning will be aroused. But it also reminds us that when some of our student participants come to our programmes from a desire for social relationships or to gain some sense of esteem, as many do, they are being driven by needs that must be met at least partially before further learning can take place.

Maslow also suggests that if the lower levels of needs are satisfied in part, the motivation to self-actualisation will be automatically triggered because it is inherent within each person. If it is not so triggered, this is because one of the lower levels of need has been inadequately met. This is by no means certain: and in any case, it does not explain the motivation towards different forms of self-actualisation which occurs between individuals.

To explain this, we need to turn to other work on motivation. We have already noted Carl Rogers's view of the drive towards adulthood – towards maturity and autonomy. Houle (1961) sees motivation as more complex, as being related to the goal-orientation or process-orientation or subject-orientation that comprises the inherent learning drives of the individual. A different picture is that of a spectrum consisting at one end of those who are 'high-achievement oriented' (not just ambitious, though it includes them: this group embraces those who seek to play chess or do crosswords or make bread or breed pigeons better than their neighbours) and at the other end those who are anxious about failure. The former experience has been called an 'approach motivation', a drive towards engaging in some activity or other, while the latter experience an 'avoidance motivation'. Success encourages the former, and failure does not put them off easily, it can become a further challenge; whereas both success (generally regarded as a 'flash in a pan' that will not necessarily be repeated) and failure alike encourage the latter to withdraw.

The danger with this – as with so many such schemes of categorisation – is that of assigning individual student learners to particular categories; for such 'personality types' can themselves become a hindrance to learning, a demotivator. The very designation itself may prescribe the way in which people will behave and will certainly determine the way we view other people. There is some value in knowing that such factors are at work; but they are not determinants but explanations of what is happening.

Learned motivation

Such achievement orientation suggests that motivation can be learned. It is thus seen by some as the fruit of the reward-and-punishment systems that people have been exposed to during the course of their prior development. If this is true, then perhaps motivation may be altered by a new system of approvals and disapprovals, by specific training activities accompanied by a change of the learning environment to emphasise achievement rather than failure. Exactly what the factors are that lead to motivation being learned is not clear. Stimulus–response theories may help here; success and pleasure in early educational experiences seem to play a part. It is pointed out, for example, how many of those who liked their schooling and were a success in educational environments return to participate in adult education activities of both a formal and non-formal kind, while although others use the lack of education to rationalise their lack of success, relatively few are motivated by this lack to return to education. But the issues remain unclear.

Motivation and goals

The third group of ideas centre themselves round the concept that motivation is related to the goals set and accepted by the participants for themselves. It has been noted that motivation is highest among those who are most concerned with the process involved, who are satisfying their goals in each task, whereas those who have their sights set on goals which are further away (to pass an examination or to get a better job after the course is over) have a lower level of motivation. Motivation then seems to be related to the nearness of achieving the desired goal.

The importance of this to the teacher is that the student participants need to see clearly the immediate goals, to accept them for themselves, to believe them to be achievable and to be able to see some progress towards their attainment, if their motivation to learn is to be kept at the highest possible level. But there is a further factor here: confidence. Individuals will be more positively motivated if they are confident that they can not only cope with the learning situation but alter it to meet their own needs.

The learning situation

For it is important for us to realise that motivation relates as much to the situation in which the learning episode is taking place as to the individual. So far most of the theories of motivation have regarded the learner as a person divorced from any particular setting. But all learning is located within a particular time and place; and we know from the work of Herzberg (1972) and others that this setting influences motivation as much as the internal drives and avoidances.

Herzberg's work related to industrial activities; but it is of direct relevance to learning. He developed the concept of 'motivators' and what he called 'hygiene' factors (demotivators). He saw 'motivators' as those factors which make the participants 'feel good' about their work – a sense of achievement, recognition, responsibility, advancement and personal growth. Most of these are internal factors; and when they are present, the participants have a positive attitude towards their tasks. These feelings however are not on the whole long-lasting, they need to be continually reinforced. But they spring directly from the work in hand.

In contrast, the 'hygiene' factors that create a sense of dissatisfaction normally spring from external factors in the context of the activity – from inappropriate direction or methods, inadequate working conditions, unsatisfactory relationships within the group and so on. These tend to be longer-lasting in their nature.

These two sets of factors are not the plus and minus of the motivational situation. The presence of motivators and the reduction of hygiene factors are both necessary to achieve positive motivation. Removing the hygiene factors alone without increasing the presence of motivators will not help the task, and similarly strengthening the motivators without removing the de-motivators will not increase effectiveness.

It is thus clear that motivation factors in learning lie as much within the learning situation as within the individual student participants themselves. In this context, the teacher of adults plays a vital role. Motivation is as often in the eye of the beholder as is beauty. We need to be reminded of McGregor's Theory X and Theory Y: that the teacher may assume that all learners have an inherent dislike of work and will avoid it if they can (Theory X), that they wish to escape from responsibility, that they have a static range of abilities that nothing within the learning situation will improve, that it is the func-tion of the teacher to direct them to the work of learning (McGregor 1960).

Theory X	*Theory Y*
The average human being has an inherent dislike of work and will avoid it if he/she can.	The expenditure of physical and mental effort in work is as natural as play and rest.
Because of this, most people need to be coerced, controlled, directed and threatened with punishment to get them to put enough effort to contribute to organisational goals.	External control and threats of punishment are not the only means to encourage them to make an effort to contribute to organisational goals. People will engage in self-direction and self-control to achieve objectives to which they are committed through the rewards which the achievement itself brings.
The average person prefers to be directed, wishes to avoid any responsibility, has relatively little ambition, and wants security above all.	The average person, under the right conditions, learns not only to accept but to seek responsibility. The capacity to exercise a fairly high degree of imagination, ingenuity and creativity in the solution of organisational problems is widely, not narrowly, distributed. In most societies, the intellectual potential of the average person is not fully utilised.

In this case, in the way of all self-fulfilling prophecies, we as teachers become part of the extrinsic factors influencing motivation; we become a hygiene factor ourselves, a demotivator. Or (Theory Y) we can assume that learning changes are natural to all human beings and certainly are the expressed desire of our student-learners; that they are willing to accept responsibility for their own learning; that it is external factors such as the educational system itself and the existing patterns of work in society rather than internal factors that are inhibiting the student participants from exercising their imagination, creativity and ingenuity; that all students are capable of breaking out. In this case, the teacher will become a 'motivator' in the learning environment. Motivation then depends as much on the attitudes of the teacher as on the attitudes of the students.

The implication of all of this for the teacher of adults is varied. Although it is useful to look at needs and at other views of initial motivation, it is probably best for the teacher not to rely solely on this original impetus but to seek to build up new kinds of drive in relation to the subject-matter itself. An emphasis on the extrinsic factors of motivation rather than the intrinsic will not lead to a durable level of motivation towards achieving the learning task. Although many adults are motivated by such concerns, it would seem that, particularly for adults, a stress on attendance, examinations and discipline is not an appropriate way to heighten or build new forms of motivation, although other forms of incentive may be helpful in some circumstances.

Further reading

Belbin, E. and Belbin, R. M. (1972) *Problems in Adult Retraining*. London: Heinemann.

Bloom, B. S. (1965) *Taxonomy of Educational Objectives*. London: Longman.

Gagné, R. M. (1972) Domains of Learning, *Interchange* 3(1): 1–8.

Gagné, R. M. (1975) *The Conditions of Learning*. New York: Holt, Rinehart and Winston.

Habermas, J. (1978) *Knowledge and Human Interest*. London: Heinemann.

Lenz, E. (1982) *The Art of Teaching Adults*. New York: Holt, Rinehart and Winston.

Lovell, R. B. (1980) *Adult Learning*. Beckenham: Croom Helm.

Maslow, A. H. (1968) *Towards a Psychology of Being*. New York: Van Nostrand.

Rogers, A. (1992) *Adults Learning for Development*. London: Cassell, and Reading: Education for Development.

Rogers, A. (1993) Adult learning maps and the teaching process. *Studies in the Education of Adults*, 22(2): 199–220.

Schön, D. A. (1983) *The Reflective Practitioner: How Professionals Think in Action*. New York: Basic Books.

Smith, R. M. (1983) *Helping Adults Learn How to Learn*. San Francisco, CA: Jossey Bass.

Smith, R. M. (1984) *Learning How to Learn: Applied Theory For Adults*. Milton Keynes: Open University Press.

Squires, G. (1987) *The Curriculum Beyond School*. London: Hodder and Stoughton.

5
LEARNING AND ADULT EDUCATION

How can we promote it...?

How do we learn?

There is a distinction to be drawn between the *type* of learning change desired (the development of new skills or the acquisition of new knowledge, for example) and the *processes* by which those learning changes are brought about. It is here that the greatest differences of opinion have been expressed by educational theorists.

A few general points may be made first, however. The first of these is that learning is active, not passive. Once again this needs to be stressed because there are still many people who speak about learning as if it was something which the teacher does to the learner. They talk of the teacher 'imparting' knowledge or skills to the learners. They seem to assume that if a teacher teaches, the student learner will inevitably learn. Learning however is not filling up an empty pot with knowledge; it is not even watering a plant so that it grows naturally. Learning is a positive action on the part of the learner calling in almost all cases for an act of the will.

The second thing that needs to be said is that there are many different ways in which we learn. It is not possible to list all the strategies for learning but some of them can be identified. Weinrich, talking about the learning that is socialisation, lists four main processes: reward and punishment; imitation of role models; identification, 'a process which is more powerful than imitation, through which the [learner] incorporates and internalises the roles and values of the . . . significant adult'; and structuring, in which the learners 'actively seek to structure the world, to make sense and order of the environment' (quoted in Henriques 1984: 19).

Among the many ways in which we learn, we can identify the following:

- the acquisition of facts, information;
- the memorisation of data or processes;

- the changes inspired by watching others;
- the sudden and apparently unassisted insights which we all experience from time to time;
- the learning that comes from the successful (i.e. the rewarded) completion of some task;
- haphazard experimentation and exploration.

The choice which each of us exercises between these strategies would seem to be determined by our preferred learning style (see pages 109–11). Nevertheless, studies have suggested that a range of strategies are used more commonly by adults than by younger learners:

- *Analogical thinking* and *trial and error* are used frequently in the adult learning episode. Through calling upon the resources of our existing knowledge and experience and the accumulated experience of others in an attempt to see possible similarities that may indicate a solution, through matching bits and pieces and creating relationships between them to identify where analogies may lie, we explore different ways of dealing with the learning situation. The learning involved relies upon the adaptation of knowledge and experience gained in other spheres of activity to the current issue. It proceeds by being highly selective of the material felt to be relevant to the task in hand and trying out a number of possible solutions by relating different elements to each other. When learning to mend a lawnmower for example, we may call upon half-forgotten experiences of motorcycles in our youth; when learning to cope with an infant, we may make all kinds of experiments suggested by our own or other people's previous experiences.
- Adults often tend to rely on the creation of *meaningful wholes* to master new material. They create patterns focused on key issues. These structured shapes and relationships summoned up by cues are employed to make the newly learned patterns of responses more permanent and enable the adult to incorporate the newly learned material into existing patterns of knowing and behaving.
- Parallel with this, adults rely *less on memory and rote learning* to retain what has been learned. Along with some of the sensory-motor skills, the process of ageing is often accompanied by a decline in both the ability to remember and the ability to concentrate – a frequent cause of much concern, as with other signs of physical change such as declining eyesight.
- Adults share with younger people the ability and need to learn by *imitation*. They will often quickly grasp something demonstrated to them, but in general they will not retain it without constant use as easily as their younger counterparts. Some adults will however seek to move quickly from such imitation (conformism) to independence, though others will be content to remain conformist in their learning.

Learning theories

It is important to stress the fact that there are many strategies for learning, because some recent writers have suggested that there is only one way in which all learning is done (we shall talk about one or two of these strategies later in this section). We need to be wary of adopting any all-embracing theory of learning which implies exclusivity.

It will be useful to summarise the many different learning theories briefly. They may be divided for simplicity's sake into three main groups. There are the *behaviourist* theories, mostly of the stimulus–response variety of differing degrees of complexity. There are the *cognitive* theories, based on a different view of the nature of knowledge. And there are those theories that have been called *humanist*; these rely on various analyses of personality and of society.

Before looking at these in more detail, one or two comments need to be made. First, it is tempting to identify the stimulus–response learning theories with the 'conformist' view of education which we noted above (pages 47–9) and the humanist with the 'liberation' view. There is some truth in this in that the humanists often talk in terms of liberation. But this is too simplistic: the divide between these two approaches runs right through all three sets of theories. The behavioural theories range from a simple reinforcement of the desired responses through to an exploration of the many different possible responses; the cognitive theories can talk at one extreme of the discipline of the subject and at the other end of the continuum of open discovery learning; and the humanist theories can describe the importance of role imitation in attitudinal development on the one hand and the freedom of the learning group on the other.

Secondly, however, there does seem to be a correlation between each of these groups of learning theories and the three main elements in the teaching–learning encounter. Education consists of a dynamic interaction

Figure 18

Learning theories	Conformist-oriented	(continuum)	Liberation-oriented
Behavioural; teacher-centred	Reinforcement of desired responses		Exploration of different responses
Cognitive; subject-centred	Discipline of subject		Discovery learning
Humanist; learner-centred	Imitation of norms		Group learning

involving three parties – the teacher-planner, the student participant(s), and the subject-matter. Each of the three groups of learning theories tends to exalt the primacy of one of these three elements. Behavioural theories stress the role of the teacher-agent in providing the stimulus and selecting and re-inforcing the approved responses; cognitive theories emphasise the content of the material; while the humanist theories (the most complex group) direct attention to the active involvement of the student participant.

It will not be possible to do more than outline the different groups of theories here. Those who feel they need more should refer to some of the more recent general books on the psychology of education.

Behaviourist theories

This group of theories suggests that we learn by receiving stimuli from our environment that provoke a response. The teacher can direct this process by selecting the stimuli and by reinforcing the approved responses while dis-couraging the 'wrong' responses. Learning is thus brought about by an association between the desired responses and the reinforcement (rewards and punishments through a complicated system of success and failure indi-cators).

These theories stress the active role of the teacher-agent. The student-learner is often seen as more passive. Although the learner offers a variety of responses, it is only the teacher who can determine the 'right' response and who can reward it appropriately, discouraging the other responses. Feed-back, the return from the learner to the teacher, thus stands on its own, sep-arate from and following after the learning process.

The behaviourist theories are based on a view of knowledge which distin-guishes sharply between right and wrong. They assume that knowledge is truth and can be known; it is independent of both teacher and learner; it is the same for all learners.

Stimulus–response theories are not seen by their proponents as just applic-able to low-level learning. They also apply at more advanced levels. Nor are they confined to skill learning; they form the basis for cognitive and atti-tudinal learning as well – to the understanding of historical processes and the appreciation of music. Indeed, the general validity of the theory is that it is often seen to underlie most of the other theories of learning. Cognitive theories stress the inherent demands of the subject-matter but they still rely on an assumption that responses are called out by different stimuli. And humanist theories urge that the stimuli arise from our social and life context, that the variety of our responses is dependent on our individual experiences and personalities, and that at an early stage of life we all learn by a system of approvals and disapprovals which indicate whether our social patterns of behaviour are acceptable or not. Stimulus and response form part of almost all theories of learning in some form or other.

Cognitive theories

Since the 1960s, a number of theories have emerged that direct attention to the activity of the learner in processing the response and to the nature of knowledge itself. These form a distinct group.

These theories point to the active engagement of the mind in learning. They stress the processes involved in creating responses, the organisation of perceptions, the development of insights. In order to learn, understanding is necessary. The material must be marshalled step by step and then mastered. The setting of goals is related to each part of the material encountered. Feedback is an essential part of the process of learning, not separate from it.

Although the learner is seen to be active rather than passive, the activity itself is controlled by the inherent structure of knowledge itself. The material which the teacher-agent orders and which the learner seeks to master dominates the process. The words 'must' and 'necessary' and 'discipline' which occur frequently in connection with this view of learning reveal that teacher and learner are faced by something which is bigger than both of them, something to which they must adapt themselves. The world of knowledge lies outside of themselves.

This group of views is not confined to the acquisition of new knowledge or the development of new understandings. It applies to learning new skills and new attitudes as well.

Both kinds of learning theories, behavioural and cognitive, posit hierarchies of learning: that there are strategies for low-level learning and strategies for higher-level learning. Learning advances as more and more learning takes place; there are higher levels of learning which not all learners attain to.

Bloom, who drew a distinction between learning in the cognitive domain and learning in the affective domain, may be taken as an example of this. He suggests (1965) that the steps to learning in each domain parallel each other. Thus the process of cognitive learning consists of the recall and recognition of *knowledge*; *comprehension*, understanding the material, exploring it more actively; the *application* of the comprehended knowledge, using it in concrete situations; then exploring each new situation by breaking it down into its constituted parts (*analysis*) and building it up into new concepts (*synthesis*); and finally *evaluation* in which the learners come to assess the new knowledge, to judge its value in relation to the realisation of their goals. On the affective side, there is a similar progression: *receiving* stimuli, paying attention, developing awareness, being willing to receive and eventually using selective attention; then *responding* willingly, the emergence of a sense of satisfaction with the response; thirdly, *valuing* the concepts and the process they are engaged in, making an assessment that the activity is worth doing, so that the learners come to express their preferences and eventually their commitment; then *conceptualising*, making judgements, attaching concepts to each of the values they have identified; and finally *organising*

Figure 19 Bloom and Gagné: hierarchies of learning

Bloom		Gagné
Cognitive	*Affective*	Signal
		Stimulus–response
Knowledge	Receiving	Chaining
Comprehension	Responding	Verbal association
Application	Valuing	Multiple discrimination
Analysis–synthesis	Conceptualising	Concept learning
Evaluation	Organising	Principle learning
		Problem-solving

these values into a system that in the end comes to characterise each individual. He suggests that the steps to learning are the same in all learners. Gagné (1972) too drew up a progression of learning from the simple 'signal' learning through stimulus–response to the very complex 'problem-solving' learning.

Humanist theories

Such hierarchies however do not seem to characterise many forms of humanist learning theories. These are more recent in origin and are not so coherent as those in the other two groups.

Humanist learning theories spring from an understanding of the major contemporary changes in culture – away from the certainties of empirical science, the relatively simple and universally valid conclusions of objective research, the stability and general applicability of scientific laws, the generally accepted values, the positivism of August Comte and others – into the modern world of living complexity, uncertainty, instability, the uniqueness of individual response and the conflicts of values (Schein 1972). Humanist learning theories stress once more the active nature of the learner. Indeed, the learner's actions largely create the learning situation. They emphasise the urges and drives of the personality, movements towards (for example) increased autonomy and competence, the compulsion towards growth and development, the active search for meaning, the fulfilment of goals which individuals set for themselves. They stress the particular social settings within which learning operates. Learning and setting goals for oneself are seen to be natural processes, calling into play the personal learning abilities that the learners have already developed and which they seek to enhance. Learning comes largely from drawing upon all the experience that goes to make up the self and upon the resources of the wider community. Motivation for learning comes from within; and the material on which the learning drive fastens is the whole of life, the cultural and interpersonal relationships that form the social context.

These views also stress the autonomy of the learners and emphasise that all the other theories talk about 'controls', about the learner being controlled by the stimuli, by the teacher, by the subject-matter. The humanist views on the other hand see learning as part of a process of conflict in which the learners are seeking to take control of their own life processes. It is the engagement of the learners with the world around them and with themselves that creates the learning milieu. The material on which they exercise their learning skills is less important than the goals they have set themselves. The role of the teacher is to increase the range of experiences so that the student participants can use these in any way they please to achieve their own desired learning changes.

It will be necessary for us to spend a little more time looking at these newer views, for they will influence the way in which adult education will develop over the coming years, before we can draw some general conclusions from them. It will be convenient to divide them into two main groups: those which focus on the *personality* factors and those which focus on the social or *environmental* context with which the learner is in dialogue.

Personality theories

Most personality learning theories depend on prior concepts relating to the distribution of personality types along a spectrum of one kind or another – between the extrovert and the introvert, for instance, or between those who see the 'locus of control' as within themselves and those who see it as outside of themselves ('I was ill because I ate bad meat' as against 'the food in that restaurant made me ill'), or between the fatalist and the self-confident (Rotter 1982).

Those who locate people on such external–internal scales tend to suggest that people placed at the external end of the continuum have a general expectancy that positive reinforcements are not under their control; that they may tend to lack self-confidence, to possess feelings of inferiority, even to expect failure and to rely more on luck, fate, chance or God. They suggest that in terms of learning, these people often feel that what they don't know is so vast and what they do know is so small that they may be discouraged from attempting to master new fields. At the opposite extreme, it is suggested, are those who believe that reinforcement is contingent on their own behaviour. These people are usually thought to be more independent, resisting manipulation; they will act, pay attention and (if they feel it necessary to the achievement of some goal they have set for themselves) remember. They are seen to draw upon the information and other resources provided by their environment, to select activities in which they have already been successful, and to feel confident that what they already know will help them to master further skills and knowledge. Most people however are thought to occupy mid-points between these two extremes or to display characteristics of both of these types at different times and in different circumstances.

Various learning theories have been built on these analyses of personality types. We have already noted the work of Carl Rogers, Abraham Maslow and Cy Houle. McClintock (1972) is a further example. He drew attention to the fact that in different learning situations, the relationship between knowledge (K), attitudes (A) and practice (P) will vary. He described four kinds of learning:

- behavioural modification
- functional learning (the satisfaction of basic needs)
- the development of consistency (the reduction of inner tensions)
- information processing.

In each of these, the way in which K, A and P relate to each other is different.

The importance of attitudes in the learning process and the relationship of attitudes to knowledge is the great contribution of these theories to our understanding of learning. Learning does not just affect the head (as so much in cognitive learning theories suggests). Berne (1970), for instance, built his view of learning to a large extent on the difference within each person of the 'parent' (P), the 'adult' (A) and the 'child' (C). He argued that communication between people may go seriously wrong if these attitudes become confused, if the lines get crossed, if for example one person speaking as 'adult' is responded to as 'child'.

Environmental learning theories

These writers emphasise that 'no man is an island'. The learning process, especially when self-impelled in the way the personality theorists suggest, calls upon the resources of the environment in which the learner is situated. But these writers go further than this: they suggest that learning is created by the active encounter between the person and the outside world more than by the inner drives and urges. Four main sets of social and environmental learning theories may be identified.

In brief, *human communications theory* indicates that communications link people together into an organisation to achieve a common purpose. Communication is not just a one-way tool; it is a system or network of events. Communication is a transaction, a series of two-way processes which involve a source (initiator), a transmission, a message and a receiver. There is inevitably interference and distortion in the transmission, and feedback is a necessary, though independent, part of the process in order to check whether what has been received is perceived as being equivalent to what has been sent. Interpretation is an essential element of the transaction, and in this the receiver is active, not passive. Learning is thus a process of change that comes about through reactions to the continuous reception of messages which is the inevitable consequence of each person being part of a human communications network or society.

Human communications theory tends towards the 'external' end of the scale; *social learning theory* on the other hand stresses the 'internal' factors. It is based on the study of the interaction of the individual and the social environment. The interaction starts with the members of the family and widens out from there, and much of the learning consists of imitation and the internalisation of value systems acquired from others. Recent studies, for instance, have stressed the need for direct human contact in attitudinal development; and the importance of peer group pressure has also become clear. Like the human communications theory, this is not just a stimulus–response theory. It emphasises the active engagement of the person with the environment, a dialectic with all the potential for conflict and the need for conflict resolution.

Some modern learning theories have seen the engagement of the individual with the environment in a holistic sense – the *total environment*, not just the social environment. The physical world in which we live, the built environment which we have made for ourselves, the mental world which we have created (what the French call *mentalités*) as well as the social environment are all elements with which we are bound in a perpetual engagement.

Some writers have seen this engagement in terms of a struggle, a desperate search for freedom. Habermas (1978), like Carl Rogers, views human life as a quest for self-emancipation, a search for autonomy through self-formative processes. Like others, he has drawn on the seminal work of Paulo Freire (1972) who identified three stages of learning: activities which are task-related; secondly, activities concerned with personal relationships; and thirdly, what he calls 'conscientization', a concept that implies the transformation of the awareness of surrounding reality, the development of a concern for change, and a realistic assessment of the resources of and hindrances to such a process and the conflicts it is bound to provoke. Learning is only learning when it leads to action for change.

Habermas similarly identifies three kinds of learning which form something of a hierarchy:

- *instrumental learning* – how to manipulate the environment; the acquisition of skills and understanding needed to control the world we live in (it is interesting that Habermas places scientific learning on the lowest rung of his scale);
- *communicative learning* – learning changes in the realm of interpersonal relations and concerned with increasing interpersonal understanding;
- *emancipatory learning* – self-understanding, awareness and transformation of cultural and personal presuppositions that are always with us and affect the way we act.

It is interesting that these three kinds of learning seem to approximate to the three dimensions of adulthood we identified earlier: maturity, the development of the individual's talents and potential, perspective and autonomy.

Habermas suggests that these different kinds of learning have different methods of investigation, of teaching and of evaluation. Any teaching–learning situation will call upon all three kinds of learning in different proportions. Because the teaching–learning encounter is part of the wider struggle of the individual and his/her total environment, it will involve a complete transformation of the relationship between learner, teacher (mediator of knowledge) and knowledge (sometimes seen as 'competencies').

A further group of humanist learning theories relate to what is called *paradigm transformation*. This view argues that the environment we live in is the result of our own creative processes; that we build, name and manipulate the environment for ourselves; and that learning is a process of rebuilding, renaming and remanipulating that environment. It calls for the modification and adaptation of those paradigms (i.e. accepted and usually unchallenged world-pictures on which we build our lives) that underlie our personality and all our actions.

One way of looking at this is to use the metaphor of 'learning maps' (Rogers 1993). People draw maps in their head: they place every experience, concept and activity on this map at some distance from themselves at the centre of these maps. Those who like cooking and feel themselves to be good at it, for example, will locate 'cooking' close to the self-centre, whereas they may well locate 'computers' closer to the periphery because they feel less at ease with this feature of modern society or because it seems to be distant from their main preoccupations. Learning, it has been suggested, is easiest among those subjects which are close to the centre; and this implies that learning includes a process of redrawing these maps so as to bring the desired learning subjects closer to the self-centre. So long as adults feel that any subject is 'not for me', they will experience great difficulties in learning.

Creating knowledge

Perhaps the most influential expressions of this group of theories is George Kelly's 'personal construct theory'. Kelly (1955) argues that learning is not something determined by external influences but that we create our own learning. By observing and reflecting on experience, we form our own personal constructs (units of meaning) from our ideas, feelings, memories and evaluations about events, places and people in our lives. In this way, we make sense of the world and manipulate it rather than respond to stimuli. The act of learning is then largely initiated by the learner, exploring and extending his or her own understanding, holding what has been called a 'learning conversation with him-/herself'.

This school of thought rejects the notion of knowledge existing outside of ourselves, an objective reality to be discovered by research. Rather all knowledge is contingent; it is 'contested and provisional'. What exist are the various 'acts of knowing' that we all engage in. Knowledge creation does not mean so much the uncovering of hidden truth as the construction of new perceptions. Those who search after truth are faced with choosing between all the various 'acts of knowing'. The focus thus switches from trying to establish the validity of the knowledge itself to the criteria by which we can judge the validity of the questions asked and the answers arrived at in each individual case; how can we determine which 'act of knowing' carries with it some experiential validity for ourselves?

Some have gone further. They have denied the existence of the mind as a finite, fixed entity in favour of 'a dynamic, ever-changing flux with unknown potential'. They claim that those psychologists who speak in terms of fixed measures like intelligence, aptitude and personality traits for what are seen by others to be 'temporary stabilised states' are to be regarded as perpetuating myths and creating blocks to a 'true' perception of the personality as fluid and active in its own quest.

We are thus back with the views that see learning as dependent on the innate drives of men and women towards autonomy and understanding in an attempt to control rather than be controlled, in a search for liberation. But it is a different form of theory. Learning is not seen by these writers as merely the satisfaction of a sense of urges, seeking a state of rest and harmony, the diminishing of a sense of anxiety, the relief of tension. Rather, learning through life is to be viewed as an active engagement with our environment and with ourselves, a struggle that may actually increase tension, a dialectic in which we seek to alter both our environment and ourselves in the constant search for something better, some ideal, a struggle that will never end. Learning is seen as the process by which our sense of discontent with the now and here and the search for transcendence expresses itself in a quest for perfectibility.

Some common elements

Through all the discussions about learning, especially in relation to adult education, some common elements now seem to be emerging.

Transfer of knowledge versus construction of knowledge

There is still a debate about the relationship between the transfer of information in learning and the construction of knowledge. Many modern writers are uncompromising about this: knowledge cannot be transferred from expert to ignorant. A recent issue of the journal *Lifelong Education in Finland* contained the following passage:

Current research has led to certain general conclusions which are of fundamental relevance for the organization and objectives of teaching. Although the modern approach is somewhat fragmented and contains several different theoretical elements, a number of widely accepted principles have emerged. The most general one, characterizing all the current trends, is a well-nigh total commitment to the constructivist notion of the origin of human knowledge.

This means that all knowledge which man [*sic*] has of the surrounding reality is the result of his own mental processes; in this sense, it is of his own construction. The constructivist view is a very different one from the traditional one which is often associated with teaching. Whether consciously or not, learning and teaching have traditionally been seen in terms of a direct transfer of information from the teacher to the learner. In denying the possibility of this kind of direct transfer, the constructivist theory opens up new challenges for teaching. If learning is an individual's active construction process in interaction with the physical and social environment, what kind of role can teaching play in such a process?

(LEIF 1990: 14)

This view has grown widely not just in adult education circles but outside it as well. For example, in management:

Learning is not finding out what other people already know but solving our own problems for our own purposes by questioning, thinking and testing until the solution is part of our life.

(Charles Handy, quoted in Ball 1991)

And in development:

Development . . . is not possible with somebody else's thinking and knowledge. . . . Knowledge cannot be transferred – it can be memorised for mechanical application, but learning is always an act of self-search and discovery. In this search and discovery, one may be stimulated and assisted but cannot be taught.

(Md Anisur Rahman 1993: 219, 222)

As Carl Rogers has put it,

The only learning which significantly influences behavior is self-discovered, self-appropriated learning . . . which has been personally appropriated and assimilated in experience.

(quoted in Christensen and Hansen 1987: 135)

There are, then, many writers who insist that knowledge cannot be transferred in learning. Yet that seems to contradict common sense; we seem to see the transfer of information at many different levels. There are others like Dudley (1993) who suggest that these two models are not opposed exclusives but that they complement each other. They argue that some learning changes are brought about by receiving uncritically information from someone else, what is sometimes called an 'information-assimilational' model of learning; but that other learning changes come from thinking, testing and experimenting for ourselves on the basis of our experience. They suggest that sometimes we can rely on transfer of knowledge, sometimes on discovering and creating knowledge for ourselves.

But there are some who suggest that a learning experience based on 'transfer of information' is unlikely to be very effective. For one thing, it creates dependency: it suggests that learning can only take place when a teaching source is present in some form or other. Secondly, it relies too heavily on memory and the uncritical acceptance of other people's knowledge.

Md Anisur Rahman (1993) tackles this question head-on and takes the argument further. He suggests that every individual possesses the capacity for discovery and constructive learning, and that the transfer of information will destroy this capacity: 'Those . . . who seek to transfer knowledge and skills serve mainly to disorient the capacity that is in every healthy individual to creatively search for and discover knowledge' (p. 22).

Those who build their education and training programmes on a 'tell and listen' basis (the teacher tells the learner what the ignorant learner needs to know) will actually weaken the ability which the learners have and which they often exercise in the process of their natural learning to 'work things out for themselves'. The distinction is between what may be called the 'input' model of learning, in which the learner is more or less passive, responding to learning inputs from outside, in which knowledge and skills and understanding are 'given' or 'imparted' to the learners, as in much formal education; and the 'action' model of learning in which the learners are searching out the material they need, trying to make sense of their experience (see above). It is not just a matter of choosing between two equally effective strategies of promoting learning; the one is seen to be the enemy of the other. Human beings are not like jugs to be filled with knowledge from their teachers; they are not like plants, dependent for growth on inputs which are controlled by outsiders. They can decide and take the initiative in their own learning.

Mechanical learning versus creative learning

Anisur Rahman is one of those who have also drawn a distinction between what is sometimes called 'mechanical learning' (which he links with training) and 'creative learning'. We have seen above (page 45) the distinction between education (which increases choices) and training (which limits choices by indicating the 'right' way to do something, the 'right' knowledge). Rahman goes further than this. He not only talks about 'memorising for mechanical application', but he analyses the impact of all forms of training: 'Nor can one be "trained" except to perform tasks which are mechanical, not creative' (p. 222). Training, memorising, the transfer of knowledge are contrasted starkly with creative or critical learning. Training will bring about 'mechanical' learning – which may be acceptable in some forms of child education; but what we seek above all in all forms of adult learning is to promote independence, self-reliance, creative and critical learning.

Learning programmes which are appropriate for adults will lay greater stress on developing creative learning rather than on mechanical learning. There is a growing consensus that 'transfer of knowledge' modes of adult learning are ineffective, dependency-making and inappropriate to the development of critical adults.

Experiential learning and the learning cycle

There is growing consensus too that experience forms the basis of all learning. Many modern writers suggest that at the heart of all learning is the search for meaning in experience. Mezirow (1981) has stressed this above all else. Learning is creating meanings, finding the keys, making sense of experience – a process which is as natural to all adults as breathing.

The process by which this search for meaning is conducted is, according to many contemporary writers, *critical reflection on experience*. Freire and others have suggested that learning is accomplished by critically analysing experience. They have spoken of a learning cycle starting with experience, proceeding through reflection on experience, and leading to action which in its turn becomes the concrete experience for further reflection and thus the next stage of the cycle (Fig. 20a). They argue that action is an essential part of the learning process, not a result of learning, not an add-on at the end. Without action, learning has not effectively taken place.

We need to modify this learning cycle in three ways if we are to understand it fully. First, the process of reflection is complex. It involves making a judgement on experience, assessing it in the light of some other standard which is drawn from other experience, either one's own or other people's experience. It means trying to determine how to explain the experience, to assess in what ways the experience could have been different. Farmers, faced with a new pest or disease, will ask their neighbours, 'What is it? We have never seen it before'; they thus reveal that they have first searched their own experience and are now actively seeking to access the experience of others.

In learning through critical reflection on experience there is the active

Figure 20a The learning cycle

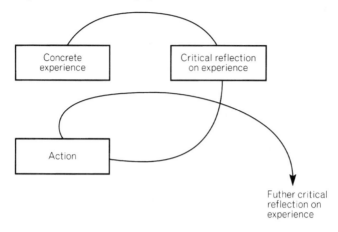

search for new material against which experience can be judged. The learning cycle needs then to be adapted as follows (Fig. 20b):

Figure 20b The learning cycle and the search for new knowledge

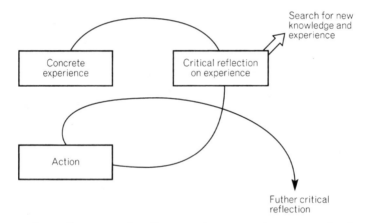

Secondly, as David Kolb (1984) has pointed out, critical reflection will lead in some cases to the drawing of conclusions, to developing generalisations, general principles ('abstract conceptualisation' as he puts it). Critical reflection can be seen as asking questions about experience in the light of other experience; abstract conceptualisation may be seen as identifying possible answers. Hypotheses are formed from the process of critical reflection on experience which can be tested in new situations (Fig. 20c).

Thirdly, however, learning includes goals, purposes, intentions, choice and decision-making, and it is not at all clear where these elements fit into the learning cycle. Decisions are needed to determine which other forms of

Figure 20c The learning cycle and conceptualisation

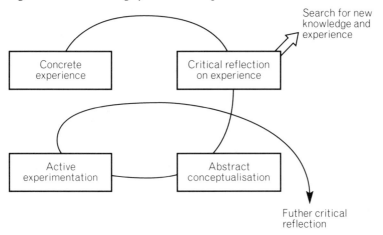

experience are used for critical reflection; decisions are certainly needed before translating abstract conceptualisation into active experimentation; and decisions and goals occur at other points in the cycle. These have tended to be omitted from discussions of the learning cycle (Fig. 20d).

There is then a widespread acceptance that critical reflection on experience leading to action forms a large part of the process of learning. But it is probably unacceptable to suggest (as some writers do) that this is *the* way in which we learn. As we have seen above, there are many different strategies of learning, and we clearly use them all at some time or other. Critical reflection on experience would seem to be the key strategy in the process of creating meaning out of experience; it is certainly the main way in which critical learning is developed. But there is more to learning than the search for meanings.

Figure 20d The learning cycle and decision-making

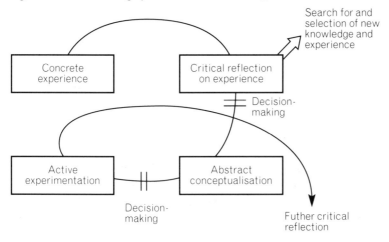

The importance of new knowledge cannot be exaggerated. It is against new knowledge, against our earlier experience or against the experience of others, however that is mediated to us (through teaching or speech or the written word or observation, etc.), that we measure the experience which forms the basis of learning, that we pass judgement on it, that we seek to make meaning; it is through such other knowledge that we reflect critically on experience. Without new knowledge there can be no critical reflection.

Learning styles

One common element in modern discussions of adult learning relates to what are called 'learning styles'. As mentioned above (page 80–2), we have all engaged for the whole of our lives in natural learning and from time to time in the more purposeful and structured 'learning episodes'. In the course of this, we have developed our own learning styles.

The subject of learning styles is too extensive to explore fully in these pages, but an outline of recent current thinking is necessary. The most relevant material is that based on the learning cycle which David Kolb elaborated and which is discussed above. The argument goes like this. Each of the stages of the learning cycle calls for different learning approaches and appeals to different kinds of persons (see Fig. 21).

Figure 21 Learning styles

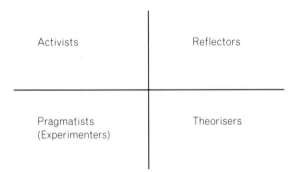

Every individual develops through experience one or more *preferred* learning styles. It is important to stress that we all tend to use all of these styles, we do not confine our learning efforts to one only. But we prefer to use one or perhaps two modes of learning above the others; we feel stronger at learning through one approach rather than through any of the others. What is clear is that we all learn actively and that we do it in different ways (see Fig. 22).

Two conclusions for the teacher of adults come from this view of learning styles. The first is that in any adult learning group there will always be people with a range of different learning styles. We can never assume that all our

Figure 22 Table of preferred learning styles

We all have certain preferences in the way we learn.

Active learners
Some of us prefer to learn by doing something immediately. We don't bother to wait to listen to all the instructions, to read the manual first but we get on with the job; we try to find out how it works. These people get impatient when someone tells them all about the task first. When they are asked a question, they give an immediate answer without waiting to work it out fully. They tend to be enthusiastic about new things; they like lots of new experiences ('I'll try anything once'). When they have finished one activity, they want to pass quickly to the next one. They want to see as many new things as possible; they like to meet lots of new people. They will often volunteer to take the lead in any activity. They like short-term goals and are usually bored by the slower work of implementing and consolidating a programme. They tend to believe what they are told. These people want to find out things for themselves.

Reflective learners
Some of us prefer to 'wait and see'. We sit back and watch others doing the task first, we listen to the talk of others. These people don't give the first answer that comes into their heads; when they are asked a question, they take time to think, they hesitate and are often uncertain. They want more information before they can give a real answer ('I want to sleep on it'). Before making a decision, they try to think through all the implications, both for themselves and for others. These people tend to like sharing their learning with others because this helps them to collect different opinions before they make up their minds.

Theorising learners
Some of us like to build systems, to get down to first principles. We don't want to deal with 'real cases' – they are thought to be too limited; rather we want to understand the whole, general principles first ('What does it really mean? How does this fit with that?'). They speak in general rather than in concrete terms. They question the basic assumptions. They make rules out of all cases. They usually think problems through step by step. They try to make coherent pictures out of complex material (they often represent ideas in diagrams showing relationships). They try to be objective, detached; they are less sympathetic to human feelings, to other people's subjective judgements. These people want the world to be logical; they do not like too many different opinions.

Experimental learners
Some of us like to experiment, to apply our new insights. We come back from training courses full of enthusiasm and full of new ideas which we want to try out. Having been told something, these people do not believe it until they see it for themselves ('It may work for you but I want to see if it will work for me'). They try to find new and more effective ways of doing things. They take short cuts or devise new modes of working. They tend to be confident, energetic, impatient of what they see as too much talk. They like solving problems and see new situations as a challenge from which they can learn a good deal. They like being shown how to do something but become frustrated if they are not allowed to do it for themselves very quickly.

(adapted from the works of Kolb 1976, 1984; Honey and Mumford 1986) student participants will prefer to learn only through one form of activity. This means that it is necessary for any teacher to adopt a wide range of teaching–learning activities in order to help those who prefer to learn through active engagement with experience, those who prefer to reflect critically, those who prefer to develop more generalised views, and those who prefer to experiment and test out other people's theories.

The second conclusion is that the development of understandings about learning styles was never intended to enable the teacher of adults to put people into a particular learning style category. It was developed to help explain what is going on. Some student participants will wish to strengthen those learning styles with which they feel less comfortable, which they feel are weaker. Some activists may thus wish to develop their skills of critical reflection or abstract conceptualisation, for example. But others will seek to use their strongest style to maximise their learning. It is never safe to rely upon any one conclusion in adult education.

There is still much that is not known about learning styles. We do not know for instance whether we use exactly the same learning styles for all learning situations. For example, if Habermas is right and there are three quite different kinds of learning, it is not clear if our learning styles will vary according to the kind of learning being engaged in. Emancipatory learning may call for more reflective styles than for activist styles. Again we do not know if these learning styles are common to all societies and all cultures or whether they are culture-bound (most of the research has been undertaken in Western rich societies). Equally we do not know if learning styles remain the same with ageing: do older learners continue to learn through the style they preferred when they were younger? While learning styles theories have been tested empirically with certain learning groups in a limited range of cultures (Honey and Mumford 1986), these aspects have not yet been properly studied.

Concerns of the teacher of adults

Some practical conclusions may be drawn from all of this for the teacher of adults.

The existence of natural 'learning episodes' suggests a series of principles for those whose function is to create purposeful, systematic and structured learning opportunities for adults. The task of the teacher is twofold – to build upon these processes but at the same time to seek to go beyond them in a number of ways:

- not just to use but also to build up and enhance the participants' existing learning techniques, to help to make them more efficient;
- to start with the specific issue but then to help the learner to move from the concrete to the more general, to draw out the principles underlying the particular instances;

- to help the learner make the learning more permanent, more available for later use, rather than being simply a one-off incident of learning;
- to urge that the process should not stop once the immediate task is completed but lead on to further purposeful learning.

These form part of the goals of the teacher, using as our base the natural learning processes of our adult student participants.

Some of the more important considerations to be drawn from the adult learning episodes and borne in mind during the planning and teaching process would thus seem to include (Fig. 23):

- If learning is episodic and not continuous, then perhaps we should rely on short bursts of learning activity. Material is more easily mastered if it is broken down into manageable units, provided that each such unit is linked to other items of learning, not left to stand on its own.
- If the natural learning process is focused on concrete and immediate issues, the material of our programmes needs to be made relevant to the present felt needs of the student participants. Their learning intentions should be used to encourage them to set goals for themselves. They must choose what they want to learn.
- If learning is focused on a specific issue, it will be necessary to start not with the logical introductory material appropriate to the academic study of any subject but with the area of greatest concern to the student participants. To start as it were in the middle of the manual or textbook and to move from there both backwards and forwards rather than to start at Chapter 1 and move inexorably to the last page is often more appropriate to adult learners.
- If learning is more naturally done actively than by passively receiving other people's wisdom, then it will be useful to engage directly with the activity under discussion rather than try to learn about it first and then to practise it subsequently. Learning by doing the task at once rather than preparing for doing it is more appropriate to adults. One learns cakemaking best by making cakes, not watching demonstrations; one learns history best by making one's own history rather than by listening to lectures or reading textbooks of other people's history.
- If each of the student participants who have joined us in the teaching–learning programme is already well experienced in undertaking learning tasks, and if they each have developed their own style of learning, their own preferred learning strategies, then it follows that the teacher needs to use of a wide range of different teaching–learning methodologies. The teacher of adults needs to discover what these learning styles are and to devise activities that allow the participants to use and develop them further. It is not of course always practicable for the teacher to explore with every member of the learning group their own way of working; it is certainly not possible to devise a common learning programme that will

incorporate all the different learning styles into one *omnium gatherum*. What needs to be developed is a range of activities that the student participants can try for themselves, using their own learning strategies to maximum advantage. And as much attention should be given to the skills of learning in any adult learning group as to the subject in hand – to learning how to learn about history and cakemaking and management – as it is to learn about these subjects. The imposition of the teacher's particular learning style on all the student-learners will often slow them down.

- If the learners in our programmes are accustomed to organising, planning, implementing and evaluating their own natural learning episodes, then the teachers should not seek to do everything *for* the participants. The participants need to be involved in every stage of the planning and implementing of the teaching–learning process.

- If adults tend to use analogical thinking as a strategy for learning, this suggests that the teacher should encourage rather than discourage the participants to relate the new material to their own experience, to assist them to bring that experience into play during the learning process and to make it available to the group as a whole. Students who discuss their own experience in class are rarely being irrelevant; they are almost always working on the new material, exploring it in relation to their existing knowledge.

- If adults employ trial and error as a mode of learning, the active exploration of alternatives from what the teacher is presenting should be encouraged by participatory and discovery learning methods. The learners need to be active, not passive recipients of instructions and information. There is a need for practice and for reinforcement. Constant feedback should be built into the programme so that both teacher and learners can assess regularly how the participants are progressing. This takes time: adults need time for learning.

- The decline in memory which many adults face as they grow older suggests that the teacher should rely more on understanding for retention, not memorising. Rote learning on its own is an inappropriate strategy for adults.

- The reliance on meaningful wholes for understanding and retention implies that the learners should be helped to build up units of new material so as to create wholes for themselves. Together teacher and learners should select out essential units from non-essential units.

- Since imitation is as important for adults as for younger learners, demonstration should form an essential part of all forms of helping adults to learn. Except in special circumstances (for example, when used as a deliberate technique of learning), the participants should not be asked to perform a task without the teacher having first worked through an example with the group.

- The lack of interest in general principles indicates that the teacher of adults should start with concrete issues and move to more general matters instead

Figure 23 The learning episode and the implications for the teacher of adults

Characteristic	Implications
1 Episodic, not continuous	• Rely on short bursts of learning activity. • Break material into manageable units; but hook each one on to other items of learning.
2 Problem-centred, not curriculum oriented; immediate goals based on needs and intentions; concrete situation; immediate, not future application; short term	• Make relevant to students' needs for motivation. • Be aware of students' intentions. • Students to set goals. • Start where they are, not necessarily at the beginning. • Do activity now, not prepare for it in the future.
3 Learning styles:	• Be aware of different learning styles; build up learning skills.
• analogical thinking; use of existing knowledge and experience	• Relate new material to existing experience and knowledge. • Be sensitive to range and use of experience.
• trial and error	• Discovery learning; students to be active, not passive recipients. • Need for reinforcement; build in feedback. • Need for practice.
• meaningful wholes	• Move from simplified wholes to more complex wholes. • Help students to build up units to create whole; select out essential units from non-essential.
• less memory; but imitation	• Rely on understanding for retention, not memory. • Use of demonstration.
4 Lack of interest in general principles	• Move from concrete to general, not from general to concrete; encourage questioning of general principles; build up relationships.
• stops when need is met	• Remotivate to further learning.

of the more academic process of stating general principles first and illus-
trating these with concrete examples. The use of particular instances and
their implications to arrive at general conclusions would seem to be a more
natural form of adult learning. With adults, theory tends to arise from
experience rather than theory leading to practice.

- If adults learn constantly throughout life, the participants should be
encouraged to link the teacher-led learning experience with further learning when the class finishes. Any dependency that the adults may develop,
by which they come to feel that the learning process must come to an end
when our class or group ceases, needs to be avoided. We should be seeking
to encourage the participants to learn without our help, to make ourselves
redundant as teachers. The teacher's main aim is to help the participants
to become more effective independent learners.

Conclusion

There are many different theories about learning. Most of them rely upon
some form of stimulus–response, but recent work suggests that the individual is engaged in learning through a process of active interrelating with
either new knowledge or with his/her social or total environment. Learning
takes place in a number of different domains, and different strategies are
called into play to cope with different types of learning. All these theories
have something to teach us about what we are doing, they each contribute
to the list of factors that will make for the effective teaching of adults.

Rather than suggest that any one of these groups of learning theories is
'right' and the others are 'wrong', I have directed attention to the 'natural
learning episode', those incidents in which adults throughout their lives
engage in purposeful and structured learning using their own preferred learning style in order to achieve a particular goal or solve a specific problem.
These episodes remind us that our student participants are already experienced learners; and they will help us to understand more clearly how to structure our own learning opportunities for adults. Our purpose as teachers of
adults is to go beyond this natural learning process – to help the learners to
make its results more permanent; to help them to draw out general principles;
to use the process to lead on to further purposeful learning; to encourage
them, in short, to become free in their own learning. We can use the characteristics of these learning episodes as a basis for creating adult learning
episodes for our student participants.

Note

The recommended titles for further reading relevant to Chapter 4 and given on page
93 are also appropriate to this chapter.

6

GOALS AND OBJECTIVES
What is it all for . . . ?

Aims, goals and objectives

Much unnecessary obscurity has been created by some writers about the subject of goals and objectives in education. The matter is relatively straightforward; goals are what we want to achieve, the reason why we engage in it at all.

Every teacher has goals. If education is the process of contriving purposeful learning opportunities, then the goals are those purposes that the learning is intended to bring about, the learning changes that will result from the activity. Both teachers and programme planners set out to construct situations in which the student participants undertake certain activities in order to accomplish something: mastering a skill, coming to understand something, behaving in a new way to meet new demands, growing in confidence and maturity. The goals are the *intended outcomes* of the teaching–learning activities.

Some people, especially some of those engaged in forms of community education, would argue that such a model of education is too directive (see pages 42–3), that we should not set goals for the learners, that we should seek only to fulfil the varied goals the student participants set for themselves, or that we should provide an open-ended learning situation so that the student participants can each achieve what they want in the programme without undue interference from the teacher. There is a good deal of truth in this. It provides a useful reminder of a number of points:

- Because a contract to learn is involved in the process of teaching adults, the student participants have come to the programme bringing with them their own expectations and intentions, their *desired outcomes*. The objectives of the learners are a real force in the dynamic interaction of adult learning.

- These student objectives will *vary widely* from each other. Each of the student participants will take from the learning situation what he or she wants. It is a salutory lesson for the teacher of adults, especially those of us who have a message to give, that our carefully planned objectives may be set on one side by our students and that they may well go off with some other truth than the one we have to 'sell'.
- Because the learning situation consists of a dynamic relationship and because three parties are involved in this encounter – teacher, learner and subject-matter – the *real outcomes* of the process may well be different from both the teacher's planned and the students' desired outcomes. The teacher and the student participants should be aware of the possibility of these unexpected outcomes, the unplanned results of the teaching–learning process.
- Sometimes the results of the learning activity are *long delayed* and do not appear during or immediately after the conclusion of the class or course.

Nevertheless these facts, that the goals of the learners may be different from those of the teacher and that the real outcomes (both immediate and long-term) may be different from both of these (see Fig. 24), do not mean that the teacher should not set goals at all. Indeed, in planning any programme of learning for the student participants, we cannot avoid having goals. They may be open goals, general in nature (personal growth, for

Figure 24

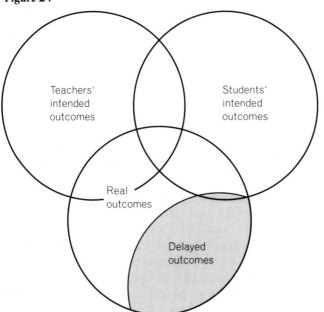

Teachers' intended outcomes

Students' intended outcomes

Real outcomes

Delayed outcomes

instance, or 'an opportunity for the participants to reassess their own priorities in life'); or they may be more limited goals (to learn to make Carrickmacross lace, say). But they will exist all the same.

The student participants will normally be recruited into the learning programme on the basis of goals set by the teacher:

Marshes and Moorlands
This class is intended for all those who wish to be able to identify the flora and fauna of these great tracts of the natural environment . . .

The intended outcome (goal) of this course is relatively clear. At the end of the course, the participants should be able to identify several species of animals, birds and plants that flourish in marshland and moorland habitats. Some of those who desire to attain such a goal will join this programme of learning (although others, less specifically motivated, may also join).

Despite this selection process on the basis of the goals set by the teacher, there will usually be occasions when the participants – because they are adults, each with their own range of different experience and each coming with their own intentions – challenge the teacher-set goals. In this lies part of the dynamism of the interaction between teacher and taught, so unlike the work done in most schools and colleges.

Even when accepted, such set goals leave room for a wide range of different options on the part of teacher and student alike. To take the example above, by the end of that course, the participants may be able to identify some of the most common forms of wildlife in these areas but may be in ignorance of others; or they may have begun to learn the processes of identification so that they can continue to explore and improve their skills when the course is over or during their own field-trips; or they may each have become expert in one particular field (orchids, say), the rest being irrelevant to their concerns. These are matters that require a process of negotiation between the teacher and each of the student participants.

Defining the goals

Too often, as we saw in Chapter 1, the goals are left undefined. It is assumed that the potential student participants will understand what is implied when they read the course blurb or programme. An adult class labelled 'Dressmaking' with no further indication of what is intended to be achieved during the course will recruit students with a wide range of expectations. Even when the programme of learning has been negotiated with the student participants, the goals frequently remain vague. But since goals play such a large part in the learning process and since they are one of the keys to learner motivation, it is important that they are not left unstated, assumed or uncertain.

- The more clearly goals are defined, the more effective the recruitment is. Those who join the learning programme on the basis of clearly defined goals are more willing to engage in the learning activities and contribute fully to the work of the group.
- The more clearly goals are defined, the greater the learning that takes place. The student participant needs clear guidance as to the direction in which the desired learning changes are to be made. If the goals are left vague, the learner is uncertain what responses are needed, what learning changes are intended.
- The more clearly goals are defined, the better the teacher can choose appropriate teaching–learning strategies, materials and methods. If the goals are left vague, the teacher too tends to flounder about.
- The more clearly goals are defined, the easier it is for the student participants and the teacher to evaluate progress, to assess how much and what kind of learning is going on. Such constant evaluation is necessary to build up and sustain motivation. If the goals are left vague, neither party is sure if they are achieving anything or not.

It is precisely here that the issue we raised earlier (page 83) on learning objectives as 'clearing up messes' will be most important. In association with the student-learners, the teacher will need to try to determine just how the participants are structuring the situation which has caused them to enter the adult educational programme, what sort of 'mess' they see and what kind of answer they will be seeking. Objectives may thus vary from one student-learner to another – which does not make for an easy life for the teacher. It is easier if we can help them to come to a clear-cut learning objective – but that will not always be possible.

Levels of goals

There are different kinds of goal. Some people have tried to describe these distinctions using different terms – *aims* being general, overall goals, frequently ultimate in nature; *goals* being the main purpose of the activity; and *objectives* being nearer still, those targets which, once achieved, lead on to further objectives and contribute towards the goals. This is perhaps an unnecessary sophistication; the words can be used more interchangeably.

Nevertheless, the distinction has some value; for while we may specify clearly our objectives at one level, we often leave the other levels unstated. Much of our work thus is based on unexplored goals that we have accepted for ourselves and we assume others have also accepted merely because they are present in our classes and groups.

The various levels of goals and objectives may be described as follows:

1 Overall goals (aims)

Behind every learning situation contrived by the teacher is a set of assumptions about the nature of personality and society. We are vaguely conscious of the range of desired changes we would wish to help bring about in order to make our lives in particular and the world in general better. This is our value system which informs much of what we do, the purpose for which most of us engage in adult education at all. A teacher of gardening, for instance, can hardly teach the subject without a belief that gardens are a 'good thing' and that gardening practice and appreciation should be improved and become more widely distributed throughout society. The same is true of most of the subjects we teach; we 'believe' in them in some sense or other.

Overall goals in this sense are usually those longer-term goals that inform as a whole the programme within which we teach. They consist of those ideals – a more just society or a richer quality of life, for example – to be aimed at even if never fully realised, which may be used to test our work by.

These goals are rarely made explicit; they are assumptions that we imagine others (especially our students) share. But such assumptions may be challenged by these student participants at any stage in the learning process, because their assumptions may be different from our own. We may believe that training for health and safety at work or a knowledge of some religious writing is in itself a desirable thing; and we may assume that our students share these judgements. But we may be wrong. Sometimes the challenge is open: 'Why do we have to do these tasks, learn all this stuff?' Usually it is more polite, a withdrawal with the comment: 'I couldn't see the point of it all.'

2 Specific goals

These are the shorter-term goals we set, sometimes fully consciously, for our courses. Teachers have, in most forms of teaching adults at least, a fairly clear idea in their own mind (though not perhaps on paper) of the kind of changes in skills, knowledge, understanding and attitudes they may wish to encourage the student participants to bring about for themselves. Thus they may plan to offer the student participants the opportunity to become something they are not yet: a better geologist or gardener, joiner or dressmaker, a 'fitter' person or a more active, thoughtful and understanding Christian, a more assertive person or more effective teacher of adults, a more efficient and happier worker, a more literate individual. The more clearly these specific goals are seen and accepted by the student-learners, the more effective will be the learning process. When the learners' expectations (goals) and those of the teacher are far apart is when a learning group is most ineffective.

This is the area where the tension that we have seen to exist within all education – between learning as discipline and learning as growth into freedom – is felt most keenly. Setting the goals out clearly will cause us some concern about being too directive in relation to our student participants. It is also in this area that the assumptions we ourselves make about the nature of knowledge and reality and the role of the teacher express themselves most fully. The process of making clear and precise our goals at this level will not only help us to construct a more effective learning experience for our students; it will also enable us as teachers to see how we work and what assumptions we make, and thus to test the validity of these assumptions for ourselves; and it will enable us more easily to renegotiate these goals with the student participants.

3 Immediate goals (objectives)

In order to achieve our specific goals it is necessary to break down the task in hand into manageable units – to learn how to handle wood or sewing machines, to learn how to relax or to read old documents, to use new machinery or processes, to read and discuss, to do all the multitude of things that go to make up the learning activity. These goals lie within each teaching session or each learning exercise. For the learning to be effective, it is necessary for the learners not only to see the desired learning change clearly but also to see the relevance of the present task to the specific goal.

A hierarchy of goals

Setting goals is a more complicated exercise than this threefold division might suggest. Whilst it is attractive to relate these three levels to the rather different objectives of the programme (aims), the course (goals) and the class session or individual teaching unit (objectives), it is important to remember that there are various levels of objective that come between each of these three main tiers. In any case, all will be operating all the time. Nevertheless, the distinction between overall, specific and immediate goals may be helpful as we plan our programme of adult learning.

There is a relationship between these three levels. The lower levels are usually built on the assumptions and contribute towards the attainment of the higher levels. On occasion, however, one level may contradict the assumptions held at other levels. It is possible for teachers of adults to engage in some forms of teaching adults because they believe (overall goal) that the participants should be encouraged to become more confident and self-reliant, and yet for the immediate goals they set in each teaching session to deny the learners the opportunity for self-expression and independence of thought and action.

Exercise

Most teachers of adults start setting their goals with the middle tier (specific goals). An exercise, based upon the course or class you listed above, may help you to see this more clearly. Across the *middle* of Fig 25a, page 124, put down in one sentence what you see as the *specific* goal of the course. It may well take the form of completing the sentence.

'The aim of this course is/was to . . .'

Once you have done this, draw a short arrow upwards and try to answer the question 'Why?' Then ask 'Why?' again, and then again, if possible, until you reach into the area of your *overall* goals (to make people happy, to build a more just and less unequal society, to help people become better workers, etc.) – up until the question 'Why?' no longer seems relevant, the answer is self-evident.

Then below the central statement, the specific goal, draw an arrow downwards and try to answer the question 'How?' This too can be done time and again until you have reached the smaller elements (*immediate* goals) of the learning activity.

It may be helpful to give you an example from my own experience (see Fig. 25b).

One of the problems of taking any particular example is that there will always be those teachers who say that such an example (in the case on page 125, local history teaching) is a special case, that the exercise doesn't work for their subject (music appreciation, for example, industrial training, adult literacy or flower arranging). But it is possible to ask three simple questions about any piece of teaching you may be thinking of undertaking:

1 What is the purpose of this piece of teaching? (*specific goal*)
2 Why do I want to do it? (*overall goal*)
3 How can I best help the students to achieve the purpose? (*immediate goals*)

We can also note from our case study two general points about objectives. First, there is no single 'right' answer to any of the questions; each of us might give a different response. For instance, in reply to the question, 'Why do I want to teach local history?' (or its alternative, 'Why do I want the student participants to learn about local history?'), some teachers will answer, 'Because the students have expressed a desire to learn about the history of their local community, and I see my role as helping them to do what they want to do, nothing more.' This is for them enough justification; whereas (as Fig. 25b shows) I see a social purpose in the task as well.

Figure 25a

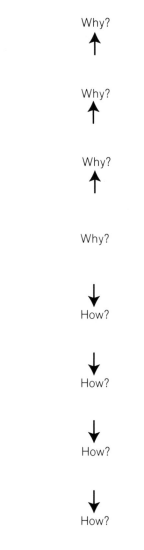

Secondly, most of the 'How?' questions lend themselves to a 'doing' response. This may be expressed as the teacher doing something (lecturing, talking, presenting, etc.) or as the student-learner doing something (reading, practising, discussing, writing, visiting, asking, etc.). It is worth repeating that adult learning is most effective when the student participants are active, not passive, when they are 'doing' the various activities that will lead to the attainment of the goals.

Figure 25b

Because I believe that strong local communities will benefit all their members

↑

Why?

To help build up stronger local communities as support groups for all of their members

↑

Why?

To help build up groups of people who are interested in and concerned for the amenities of their local communities

↑

Why?

| The aim of this course is to help people to understand and (if they so wish) to practise the tasks of the local historian |

How?

↓ ↓ ↓

| By asking intelligent questions about the past of their own community | By coming to know about the range of source material available and searching for it | By developing the skills of analysis and interpretation of the sources and of writing up the results of their studies |

How? How? How?

↓ ↓ ↓

By reading about the background to their history	By visiting record offices, libraries and museums	By discussing examples of local records in class
By reading other local histories	By visiting surviving monuments	By trying to read old handwriting under supervision (practice, exercises)
By looking around them and questioning what they see	By looking at other local histories to see the sources they have used	By practising writing up small parts of the work under supervision
By asking questions about the local community today		

Setting the goals

Lying behind every adult class and every adult course, in every context, is a set of objectives, an understanding of which can be arrived at by asking ourselves (as teacher-planners) what we are trying to do, why we want to do it and how we plan to go about it. Two questions arise in relation to these goals: how does the teacher set them, and how do they relate to the students' goals? This implies a further, preliminary question, whether the teacher has the 'right' to set the goals. For it can be argued that goals and purposes of this kind can be seen as an act of manipulation, of aggression against the minds and personalities of our students.

By what right?

The basis for the teacher's actions in this respect is expertise. We are teachers precisely because we have some form of expertise. It may be a *direct* expertise; we may be a qualified joiner, cook, athlete, archaeologist or engineer. Or it may be an *oblique* expertise; we may have experience of groups, tools or methods of study without being an expert in all aspects of the subject under discussion. But whether direct or oblique, a recognition of expertise is essential if we are to acquire that measure of respect needed for the voluntary learner participants to accord us the role of teacher or group leader, to accept our creation of the learning opportunity, our guidance, our conduct of the class.

There will be those who object to such a statement, to the teacher adopting such a role. They may assert that our task as 'teacher' is to lay our experience and expertise at the disposal of the group of adults who may wish to learn with us, reminding us that we are a resource for the student participants. This is true, but such a role is common to *all* members of the learning group. In adult education, each person brings his or her experience and knowledge and shares these with all the others. The teacher's role in the adult class goes further than this. We are not just a member of the group like all the others. We have been given the role of creator of the purposeful learning opportunity and director of the programme of work; we set out and generally oversee the activities (the *immediate* goals) through which the participants can move towards the more general (*specific*) goal, and to do this we have to determine the nature of this specific goal, the purpose of the programme of learning, first.

How do we set the goals?

As teachers we set not only the 'specific' goals for the course, the purpose of the activity, but also the 'immediate' goals, the programme (or schedule of learning) for the participants to follow. There are many different paths to tread, and from our experience and expertise we select those that seem most useful if the participants are to learn what they have demonstrated they want to learn.

The choice of these paths is indicated to us by the various answers we have given to the question 'How? in the exercise above; and they may be set out in some form for the participants to see – in a *syllabus* or programme incorporating the ground to be covered and the methods to be employed. It is not an unchanging syllabus, a permanent programme of immediate goals, to be ticked off automatically in sequence; for as the needs of the student participants become clearer or change during the learning process, so the programme will change. As the field is explored, as the subject is learned, so the range of enquiries and the activities to be pursued will develop. As time passes, so the world (even of dressmaking or Christian understanding) will change.

The immediate goals are expressed in the 'methods/content' part of the learning situation. Adult education is a process, a 'doing', rather than a system or a set of structures. So the teacher (in negotiation with the student participants wherever possible) has to decide what the learners need to *do* in order to achieve the specific goal. Do they need to watch? To practise? To listen? To read? To write? What they need to do will determine both the methods and the content of the programme of learning. If, for example, the goal is the performance of a skill – to learn how to use a sewing machine, for instance – then they need to watch a demonstration, to handle, practise and in the end use it meaningfully. If the goal is to understand, then they need to grapple with the various concepts that form part of the subject-matter, play with them, rearrange and use them in writing and/or discussion. If the goal is the production of a community magazine, then they need to debate (the contents), to select, to explore, to collect material, to write, to discover information. If the goal is to pass an examination, then they need to understand, to memorise, to practise writing under restricted conditions. The construction of the sequence of immediate objectives, from simple concrete tasks to more elaborate ones, is part of the role of the teacher. It is our job to devise, modify and reconstruct the series of steps (the learning schedule) by which new skills, knowledge and understanding are acquired and developed. This is as true of literature and music, of computers and labour studies, of health studies and craft training, of bridge and fencing and flower arranging, as it is of advanced engineering and accountancy updating courses.

Types of objective

This emphasis on activities, on 'doing', as part of the adult learning process leads us to ask whether all goals and objectives can be expressed in behavioural terms or whether there are other kinds of objective. E. W. Eisner (1985) suggested that there are two types of objective: behavioural and expressive.

Behavioural objectives are the 'doing' objectives that can be precisely stated: an ability to swim or to draw or to write a report. They are used particularly in learning skills (technical training, for example) and are of especial value in helping the teacher and learners to assess the course arrangements and design and in measuring progress, the effectiveness of the curriculum in achieving these objectives. It is however sometimes urged that behavioural goals cannot apply in large areas of adult learning – understanding poetry, for instance, or appreciating art – and that in any case most adult student participants need, value and demand a coherent body of knowledge rather than just a set of competencies.

The other kind of goals are *expressive objectives*. Whereas behavioural goals are usually set by the teacher as 'predictive' objectives and can be precisely stated, expressive objectives are usually set by the learners and are unpredictable in their results. The learners seek to expand on, elaborate and make unique to themselves the skills, knowledge and understanding they acquire through the learning opportunity. They do not know in which direction they will 'take off', and each of them will 'take off' in this sense in different directions.

Expressive objectives are complex. Behavioural objectives tend to be simple and linear in nature; once the learners can complete one task, they can move to the next. Such objectives can be tested by a series of increasingly advanced tests. But for adults particularly many activities are not only unique to the learner concerned; they are unique to the occasions they are engaged in. Reading a text, for example, or sewing a piece of fabric is not just a simple skill; on each occasion the actions engaged in operate on several different levels at once. They may be done hesitantly or confidently: they may be done at an elementary level or at a more advanced level; they will be done for a particular purpose, unique to that occasion; and they may or may not achieve the desired result (see Fig. 26). These dimensions lie behind each learning activity, form the expressive objectives of the adult student participant and accompany all behavioural objectives.

This division of objectives into behavioural and expressive corresponds with the distinction that can be drawn between the *public* effects of our

Figure 26

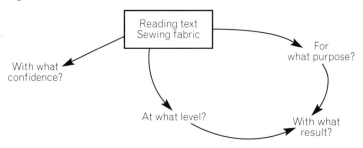

teaching (the way the learning will display itself in public) and the *private* effects (those internal changes in understanding, attitudes or skills of learning that contribute towards the overall development of the individual). This distinction is useful.

The value of behavioural objectives

Behavioural objectives cannot encompass the whole of the learning process; there is much going on behind the behavioural changes we wish our student participants to learn. Nevertheless, we cannot see *any* part of the learning process unless it results in changed patterns of behaviour. 'Inner' learning will reveal itself through actions or expressed preferences. Learning to appreciate literature, music or art will reveal itself in a number of different ways, not least in a desire to make contact with more of the subject. Learning to understand the historical process will express itself in the range of concepts used in discussion and possibly in other activities such as visits to historic places; learning new attitudes towards other people or coming to understand some scientific process will equally reveal itself in changed practices and behaviour.

While remembering that such objectives cannot describe all that is going on, all learning goals can be expressed in terms of some behavioural changes. Such observable changes will however vary for each individual learner. The activities that will reveal the deeper levels of learning will take a variety of forms. One person may express their new understanding of local history and the new attitudes this understanding has brought with it by joining a local history society; another may become an ardent conservationist, while still others may prefer to work on their own, reading more, writing or collecting artefacts. All will display in their lives the learning changes that have sprung from the common achieved objectives, the acquiring of more knowledge of and insight into the history of their local community. One of the tasks of the teacher is to try to determine in association with the student participants some of the particular ways in which the inner (private) learning changes may express themselves in (public) actions. These then will become the behavioural objectives for the course.

To help the student participants to achieve such behavioural objectives, the student participants need to be given opportunities to engage in such activities under supervision *during* the course. They should not have to wait until the course is over before they begin to practise their new competencies or to express their new learning. And the tasks involved need to be seen to be realistic, useful, purposeful, not meaningless exercises. They should not, except in some few circumstances, be artificial – activities that will never be tried again outside the class. To develop the ability to write an essay is perhaps rarely an appropriate objective, for writing essays is not for most people an activity engaged in real life (some people however may like to do it; a number may wish to contribute to some publication, while a few may earn extra money writing for local newspapers or magazines). If such an artificial objective is set before the learners, then they must be able to see how the task contributes to the whole programme of learning, to the general goal. They should not be asked to accept it as a 'given' part of the programme.

Many behavioural objectives have been determined by the teacher stating what the student-learners are expected to *be able to do* at the end of the course. Brochures continue to proliferate with statements such as 'At the end of this course, you will be able to . . .' and there follows a list of activities which the participants will be able to undertake, the new skills/knowledge/understanding and/or attitudes which will be expressed in action when the programme has ended.

But such a process is not really adequate. For the aim of any adult learning programme is to affect actual behaviour, not potential behaviour. It is not important what the student-learners *can* do after the end of the course; what is important is what they *do* do. When, in an adult literacy programme, the participants at the end of the class show that they can read but after a short time it is clear that they are not actually reading, that programme will inevitably be regarded as a failure, not a success.

Conditions

Objectives, at all levels, should be expressed in terms of accompanying behavioural changes. But not just in simple words of action. We need to set out not only *what* we hope the learners will be able to do but also the contextual *conditions* under which the behaviour will need to be practised (how fast or slow, perhaps, or with or without help, and so on) and the *standards*, the level, of the activity – not just that they should be able to do something but as far as they can to do it to a certain level of competence. This is relatively easier for those programmes designed to achieve a particular skill, to perform a task – courses such as woodwork or crafts, art or languages; but even in these cases we will need to spell out the conditions under which we anticipate that the task can be performed. Not only shorthand and typing set levels of speed and accuracy as part of the learning goals; in adult literacy, for instance, we set as our goal not that the learners should be able to 'read' in a vacuum but that they should be able to read something specific, read it fluently and read it with understanding. In the case of music appreciation, the goal is not just going to more concerts or buying more records but listening with discrimination, and this will express itself in decisions about the kinds of music preferred and in other ways.

The teacher needs to set the objectives of the programme of learning not just in terms of intended observable behavioural changes but also in terms of inner (private or expressive) learning. Both sets of objectives will be needed. We cannot afford to concentrate on just the one or the other, on the competencies arising from the learning without any concern for changes in understanding and attitudes, or on the internal personal changes in appreciation without any concern whether these express themselves in changed patterns of behaviour or not. Of the two, the inner learning changes are the more important. It is not just a matter of what we as teachers expect the learners to be able to *do* after the course is over; rather it is what we hope they will *be* and how that will express itself in action. Our aim is not just a trained person but someone whose understanding and attitudes have been enhanced. Equally, we want someone who reflects the enhancement in practice. And above all, we want to help them to continue to learn purposefully after the end of the course. As we have seen above, long-term continued learning will depend on developing further the ability and the confidence to engage in critical reflection on their experience and to act upon that critical reflection. Developing learning skills further needs to form part of every course for adults.

Exercise

Is it possible to express the goals of your course in terms of

- expressive objectives (private effects)?

- behavioural learning objectives (public effects), stating the conditions under which such achievements should be performed?

How do the goals relate to the learners' expectations?

The teacher needs to give attention to the relationship between his or her goals and the student participants' goals. Adult students come to learn to achieve particular purposes, and they usually express their goals in behavioural rather than expressive terms; their objectives are frequently concrete and immediate. This is not always true, and the teacher will need to explore just what the students have in mind when they come to the course; but in most cases they will be thinking in terms of some learning change that they can recognise and use at once. They will want to be able to do something new or better at the end of the learning programme, something that they and others can see.

Further, they have usually selected themselves for the course according to the expressed goals of the teacher – the middle-level, specific goals rather than either the immediate or the overall goals. They will tend to leave the setting of the immediate goals, the various stages of the learning process, to the expertise of the teacher, while the overall goals are, as we have seen, largely determined by the institution providing the programme or the setting in which it is placed – the church, local authority adult education agency, voluntary society, development organisation, community association, university or training agency, for instance, and the public image it presents. The student participants themselves have come in order to join in the stated activity of the group, to produce a particular product (a pot or a report) or to learn something – how to make a table or a dress, how to keep fit, how to market a new product.

Exercise
Set out in writing what specific goals you think your student participants will have come to your group for.

Two caveats must be entered here:

First, the *wide range of student expectations*. In many forms of adult education a number of student participants will say that they have joined a group in order to achieve the same goals as the teacher-planner has set out, but in reality they are there for some other reason. Student participants come to adult classes from all sorts of motives and for all sorts of purposes, often unstated.

Thus adult student groups contain a wide spectrum of differing expectations, related directly to their individual needs and intentions (Fig. 27a). At one end of the spectrum is the person who has come in out of the cold or whose regular night out is to attend some form (it does not much matter what) of adult class. At the other end is the person who wants to do just one part of the whole exercise. In a local history or commercial subjects class, for example, we may have at one extreme the attender who seeks companionship and comfort without disturbance, who has no real goals of learning, and at the other extreme the participant who wants to trace their own genealogy or to learn how to type, nothing more.

If the aim of education is to meet needs alone, the task of the teacher in these circumstances would be impossible. But we have seen that education is not just meeting needs, it is purposeful learning. So the teacher has a purpose, a goal. Those of the learners whose goals are closest to the teacher's goals will learn most quickly, most efficiently and most permanently (Fig. 27a); those who are further away will have greater difficulty in learning and may even prevent the other participants from learning. We will see later how a learning group can help to deal with this situation.

The range of student expectations is not evenly distributed throughout the spectrum; they will tend to come in clusters. Nor will the teacher's goal necessarily be at the centre, it may well be to one side. This can be explored

Figure 27a

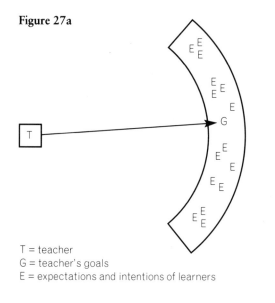

T = teacher
G = teacher's goals
E = expectations and intentions of learners

only once the teacher has met with the learning group. If the preponderance of student expectations lies away from the teacher's goal, then it would make for more effective learning if we were to move our goal nearer to those of the majority of our student participants. If in a woodworking class we intended to focus on making tables, and the majority of the participants wanted to make garden furniture instead, it would be in the interest of all parties including our own to change our goal rather than expect the learners to change theirs.

But we need not change the *specific* goals, for these lie behind the immediate goals. It may be that the main purpose of the class is not just to make one type of furniture but for the student participants to learn general approaches to woodworking. In this case, the teacher can accept and go through the widely varying goals of all (or at least most) of the student-learners and still direct them to the goal of the course as a whole (Fig. 27b). It will however be difficult to do this for those at the very edge of the spectrum, who frequently do not want to learn much or who are willing to learn only over a very narrow territory.

> *Exercise*
> Write down some of the expectations and hopes of the student participants in your class; try to grade them on a scale of closeness to or distance from your own goal.

Figure 27b

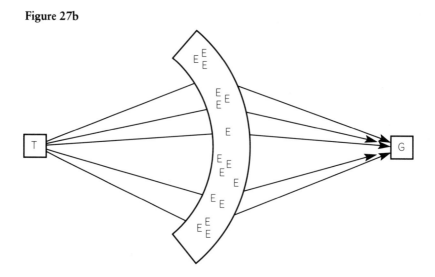

A second problem may arise in that some of the student participants, even when they come to accept the teacher's goal, may see *a different picture* from the teacher. The dress, the table, the fitness exercises, the type of local history arrived at may all be very different in the minds of the learners and of the teacher. How many clergy have failed to realise that the lay view of a practising Christian is so different from that of the parsonage? It is a valuable exercise for us to spend some time exploring the minds of our student participants to discover their understanding of the task in hand.

Nor should we assume that, once we have done this, the picture we possess will remain static or that the goals will remain unchanged. One of the main characteristics of goals is that, the nearer one comes to achieving them, not only does the picture of them change but they exert less and less pull on the learners who begin to look beyond that goal to the next one. We should listen and explore with our student participants what goals they have and how these are expressed; and we should continue to discuss this as time goes on. We will learn much of misapprehension in our students and in ourselves.

Exercise
Try to write down some of the different pictures of the 'end product' of the course that you think your student participants may hold. How can you test if you are right?

To summarise: in order to create purposeful learning, the teacher will set a series of goals for the learners and from them construct a programme (curriculum) for the student participants to arrive at the goal of the course. But the participants may have their own goal or, even when they indicate that their goal is the same as the teacher's, the picture they may hold of that goal may be different. Only as the teacher and the student participants interact can these hindrances to learning become clear and be removed.

The relationship of the various parties to the different level of goals may be set out as in Fig. 28.

Widening the goals

So far we have concentrated on the 'How?' side in our discussion of setting the goals. A consideration of the 'Why?' will also help us to be more effective in the programme we draw up for our student-learners.

There is space for only one example, which is taken from woodworking, though it could just as easily be drawn from dressmaking, local history, geology, health and nutrition, music, computer studies or industrial training programmes. For here we consider the long-term purposes of teaching adults. The purposeful learning opportunities that we plan for adults will, we hope, lead not just to temporary but to permanent learning changes. In the end these will lead to changes in the way of life of the individual and thus contribute towards change in society at large.

Our goals may be narrow, specific and limited, or they may be wider, designed to extend and maximise the changes in the individual. We can express this in a series of scenarios.

Scenario 1

A class comes together to learn to make a table. The *goal* is limited: to make a table (specific goal). The *programme* thus is limited: to learn how to handle the wood, the tools and to make the joints needed to make a table (immediate goals). The *achievement* too is limited to the skill of making tables (overall goal). We can express it as in Fig. 29a.

Scenario 2

We may widen the *goal*: to make a range of furniture *through* making a table. the *programme* then is wider: to learn a wider use of wood, tools and joints, going beyond the point of making a table. The *achievement* too is wider; the learner is freed to innovate with new tools and new joints, to make new furniture (Fig. 29b).

Figure 28 Levels of goals: teacher–learner interaction

	Teacher-agent	Student participant	How set out
1 Overall ultimate goals (aims)	Usually set by the *programme organiser*, but the teacher will possess own version of these goals	*Students* rarely directly interested in this level	Rarely spelled out, usually assumed; implicit in whole programme
2 Specific goals	Usually devised by the *teacher* in association with or independent of the *organiser*; the main purpose of the teaching–learning situation as the teacher sees it	*Students* will have an unformulated version of this goal, but this will usually become clearer as the course progresses; it will not (at first, at least) be their main interest	Usually set out briefly in the course blurb
3 Immediate goals (objectives)	The narrower goals of each learning task; often clear in the mind of the *teacher*	Usually what the *learners* will hold as their goals, the reason for attending the course; what they are most interested in	Sometimes set out in the syllabus or schedule of work, but usually discussed class by class, task by task

Figure 29a

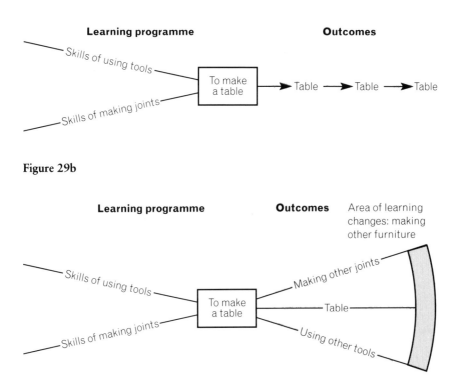

Figure 29b

Scenario 3

We can widen the *goals* still further, though still using the table. The goals then will be to understand and appreciate furniture through making a table. The *programme* will be much wider: to learn how to design a table and make comparison with other tables; to study and analyse wood and develop a feeling for it; to acquire a wide range of skills of using wood, tools and joints. And the area of *achievement*, of learning changes, has also been widened so that the student participant has developed critical attitudes as well as technical skills (Fig. 29c).

Goals, then, may be set by the teacher on a narrow or a wider basis, and as a result of these goals, learning will tend to be either narrow in confine or wider. We must allow for the active involvement of the adult student participants. Some will be able to use even the narrow-goal-based teaching to learn over a wide front, but their task will not be easy. In any case, it is the intention of the teacher-planner that concerns us most at this point: whether we plan that our student participants should learn over a wide field or over a narrow field. This is our choice.

Figure 29c

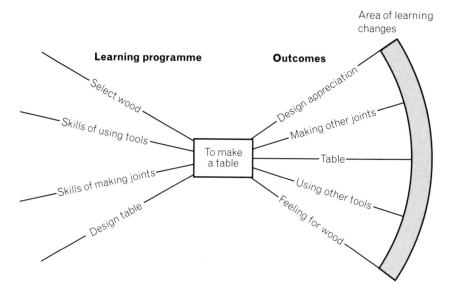

The value of training

We saw (pages 44–6) the distinction to be drawn between training, education and indoctrination. I suggested that the main purpose of education is to confirm and increase the adulthood of the participants, to help them to become free to innovate, to develop critical reflection, to increase the range of choices before them. The increase of the ability to achieve in one field will contribute towards achievement in general. In this respect, training – the acquisition of a particular skill, the growth of knowing how to do something, the practice of the ability – has greater long-term benefits for the learner than has a process of 'informing' that will lead to a sense of dependency of the learner on the teacher.

In this we can see one of the distinctions between training and indoctrination. Training, that development of knowledge, understanding and skills leading to mastery over some narrowly defined area of activity or study, is one of the essential steps towards education as freedom and may be used as a basis for a widening approach to learning. Indoctrination, in contrast, a confinement of ways of thinking and behaving, can never lead to freedom.

Elements of training will inform a good deal of what we do in teaching adults. Some recent writers have claimed that *all* teaching–learning tasks can be expressed in terms of *competencies*, so that all learning can be precisely evaluated. But this is hotly disputed by other educationalists. A more balanced view would suggest that some of the goals of the teacher will be narrow (the acquisition of particular skills or data), and some will be wider (building awareness, developing understanding of relationships and the like); and it will help the learning task greatly if both the teacher and the student participants are able to distinguish the wider from the narrower goals. Both will be involved in our teaching. Training lies at the basis of education; the use of training objectives, the development of specific skills, will contribute to widening the perspectives and increasing the confidence of the learners. But it is not education in itself; more than this is needed. In the pursuit of greater adulthood, teachers of adults should not confine their goals to specific narrow training goals; part of their aim is to widen the horizons before the individual participants. We do not want to encourage mechanical but creative and critical learning.

Should the teacher attempt to lead the student-learners from the narrower to the wider goals in this way? Is not such an approach in itself indoctrination? This question has received a good deal of attention. We need to remind ourselves

1 that teachers inevitably possess goals as they pursue with the student participants that purposeful learning which is education – such goals are inescapable;
2 that in treating the student participants as adults, the teacher will seek to make sure that they are aware of what these goals are, so that they may (a) opt in or out of the learning situation and (b) contribute to their formulation and reformulation.

Without this, such teachers will be denying the adulthood of the learners. The continual modification of the teacher's set goals in the light of the changing goals, intentions and aspirations of the student participants is part of the dialectic of teaching adults. Setting and modifying goals is paradoxically a process by which the teacher may contribute towards the students' growth towards greater adulthood and freedom; but equally the surrender of autonomy by the teacher in this area is part of the process of building up the autonomy of the learner.

Further reading

Davies, I. K. (1976) *Objectives in Curriculum Design*. London: McGraw-Hill.
Knowles, M. S. (1980) *The Modern Practice of Adult Education: From Pedagogy to Andragogy*. New York: Association Press.
Mager, R. (1991) *Preparing Instructional Objectives*. London: Kogan Page.

PAUSE FOR THOUGHT

So far we have seen that teaching adults in any sphere is a process of providing an opportunity for others to engage for themselves in a more or less intensive bout of individual creative learning, and of encouraging and helping them to bring about within themselves changes in skills, knowledge and understanding, changes that will be reflected in altered attitudes and patterns of behaviour. Such learning depends on the motivations and intentions of the learners and on the range of knowledge and experience they already possess and which they bring to the learning task, as much as (or even more than) it does on their learning abilities. We have to take these factors into account when planning our teaching.

However, the range of these three elements in the teaching–learning situation – the intentions, experience, and learning abilities of the student participants – is in all groups of adults (even those most carefully selected and graded) enormously varied. It is invariably impracticable to assess adequately the needs, existing knowledge and abilities of each and every one of the student participants.

In these circumstances, to ensure that all of the student participants can directly relate the new material being learned to their own expectations and experience, we can

- turn the class into a 'learning group' in which all members can engage with the subject in their own way and at their own level;
- and, secondly, devise active learning strategies for the student participants to engage in.

It is not always easy to do both of these at the same time, but the possibility of pursuing both lies before us as teachers. The next part of this book seeks to explore these two avenues.

7

ADULT LEARNING GROUPS

How does it work . . . ?

Learning is individual. Each person comes to claim for themselves something new and in the process changes their thought patterns, their competencies and their behaviour to a smaller or greater extent. Such learning changes come from direct interaction between the individual learner on the one hand and their environment, including the subject-matter, on the other.

Most of us however have to teach, and learn, in groups. There are one-to-one teaching–learning situations – in adult literacy programmes, for instance, or with community and social workers, health visitors and the like who engage in systematic and structured programmes of learning in the home. But the large majority of the teaching of adults is done in a class or other form of group.

There are a number of reasons for this:

1 Schooling has habitually structured itself in this way. We ourselves learned in groups (classes) and on the whole we expect and even prefer to teach in groups.
2 The use of a class seems to be the most efficient way to use the resource of a single teacher.
3 Most adult students seem to prefer groups as a context for learning. Although opportunities for individualised learning are increasing (correspondence courses, the Open University and the increasing use of libraries and manuals by home students are some of the signs of this trend), a reaction against these forms of 'lone-ranger' education can often be seen in the demands for more face-to-face contact between teacher and taught and between the learners themselves.
4 There are sound educational advantages in group learning. The learning group can often achieve more for its members than a one-to-one situation can do.

But whether the existence of learning–teaching groups is more a question of habit or economics or gregariousness or educational effectiveness, the fact remains that learning is individual while teaching in practice is usually a group matter. Here lies tension. The group may be a great help towards achieving learning; but equally it may inhibit the sort of individually determined learning change we hope will be achieved. The teacher of adults needs to balance the usefulness of the group against the growth of individualism, discrimination and self-reliance which constitute the goals of so much of what we set out to do. It is another form of that tension between education as conformity and education as liberation.

Exercise
Before we go on to explore the nature of learning groups, you may find it helpful to write down in your own words and from your own experience some of the practical *values* of a group for your student participants and some of the *hindrances* that the learner might find in a group.

Values

e.g. viewpoints of more than one person (teacher) are available

Hindrances

e.g. learners might be put off from trying by the presence in the group of others 'better' than themselves

---

What is a group?

A group is more than a collection of individuals. It is an entity, something whole in itself. There is a continuum of groups: at one end, the tightly knit team, the integrated group where all the members have submerged their individuality; at the other, the loose-knit bundle. There are elements beyond each end of this continuum – the *folie à deux* at the integrated end and the collection of isolates (such as a cinema audience) at the other – but these lie outside any definition of 'group'. Most of the classes or other types of groups we teach will be at some point along this spectrum (see Fig. 30).

For a group to exist, there must be some form of common identity, but of itself this is not enough. The group has to be distinguished from the collection

Figure 30

or 'set' (all redheads, for instance) which although possessing a common characteristic cannot be classified as a group because it has no interaction. So two features are essential to a group: common identity (usually a common purpose), even if it is unspoken, for all of its members, and secondly interaction between the members allowing for the development of shared attitudes and feelings, some emotional involvement, a minimum set of agreed values or standards. For many groups, there is a third factor. Groups are not static but dynamic. They grow, they develop. Successful groups are those which feel that they are moving forward in one way or another.

The term 'group' covers a wide array of social units. Even in the field of formal education, groups are not all the same. A lecture audience is frequently large and loose-knit; a class is usually rather smaller but at times it is equally loose-knit, closer to the 'collection of individuals' end of the spectrum as each of the learners works on their own (the 'no-talking-in-class' syndrome). A discussion group is often smaller still and closer; a task-oriented group, set on problem-solving or producing a cooperative piece of work (as in group project work), may be even smaller and may generate a good deal of warmth, if not heat; while a 'buzz-group' is sometimes smaller still, but it is unlikely to be able to maintain the strength of interaction for any length of time.

Exercise

You may find it helpful before we go further to jot down one or two groups (not necessarily educational: it could be a committee, for example, or a band) with which you are associated, so that you can test the characteristics to be discussed against your own experience. (Fill in only the first two columns at this stage.)

Name of group	Size (approx.)	(a)	(b)	(c)	Comments

Moreover, groups do not stay still. One group may well pass through a number of stages at different times, changing its nature according to its function. Groups may move up and down the continuum continuously, and it is useful for the teacher to ask at each stage, 'What is this group doing now?'

Types of group

There are different types of group, each with their own characteristics.

1 Formal groups

In these groups the structure is set before any member joins, and the new recruit does not contribute materially (the army, for example). Sanctions may be brought to bear on the members, and the group is not altered in any way by its changing membership, only by outside orders. Such groups do not in general concern adult education – though it has been suggested that some schools and classes on occasion display characteristics of formal groups. Most forms of adult education groups, being voluntary and participatory, are informal.

2 Informal groups

These are usually divided into primary and secondary groups. *Primary* groups are normally small face-to-face groups, a close-knit team based on mutual acceptance of roles. A family, a committee, a house church are usually primary groups. Each member is influenced by the others and a sense of loyalty exists, founded on regular contact. In this group, a member may have a strong sense of affiliation, but at the same time the individual will be very exposed to the group.

Secondary groups are usually too large to have regular face-to-face relationships. It is even possible for them never to meet, despite the fact that the ties are clearly felt. The extended family network, for example, or the members of an order of monks form secondary groups. More often, however, the secondary group will meet in some way or maintain some other means of contact (newsletter, etc.). This group will affect the behaviour, attitudes and outlook of each of its members; and although the individual will not be so exposed as in the primary group, the influence of the group will still be strong.

Primary and secondary groups are not two clearly distinguished forms; rather, once again there is a continuous spectrum, with many shades of grey between black and white. As we have seen, any one group may be mobile, moving backwards and forwards along this spectrum. A group may display at different times some of the characteristics of a primary group and some of a secondary group. Groups have a life of their own, largely independent of the wills of the individual members. Also, primary and secondary groups overlap; they are not mutually exclusive. A Methodist will belong to his or her chapel and even to the choir within that chapel – two different primary groups – and also to the Methodist circuit, district and communion (secondary groups). All those who come to learn in adult education, teacher and student participant alike, bring with them many different and overlapping primary and secondary groups.

A general point concerning the members of groups may be helpful. Those who seek to use the group to defend themselves from the outside world can do so only by exposing themselves more and more completely within the group; those who reject the openness demanded by the group will find themselves unable to use membership of the group as a defence against the outside. It is not possible to belong fully to a group without being willing to expose oneself in some measure to its influence. This is an important point in connection with motivation.

3 Reference groups

The reference group is hardly a group at all, but it concerns us for the influence it exerts on us and our student participants. The reference group covers the people from whom we draw values, standards, aims and goals by our own sense of affiliation. The group itself doesn't know we belong to it (we may not even be official members of the group) but *we* know. The reference group of our Methodist friend is the Christian church (or more likely the Protestant branch of the Christian church). Other such reference groups might be socialists, cricketers, farmers, teachers, clergymen – a sense of identity towards whom will help to determine the range of attitudes we possess.

Adult learning groups

Our adult learning group, to begin with, may not be much of a group at all. Rather it may consist of a collection of individual hopeful typists or French-language speakers. Normally, however, it will quickly become a primary group with secondary and reference attachments. One secondary group to which the members may belong may consist of all the other adult students in the centre where they are learning; another may include those elsewhere who are engaged in the same sort of activity as that of the class. Participants in a local history group, for example, will relate to other adult students nearby, if there are any, and/or to other people interested in local history in the region. Managers taking an advanced course will each bring with them to the primary learning group the secondary groups of their own businesses as well as the institution within which the course is being held. Beyond these there is the reference group: all adult education students (the 1980s Save Adult Education campaign in the United Kingdom for a short time brought a sense of coherence to this reference group and Adult Learners' Week is currently doing much the same), for instance, or the world of local history or all managers.

Exercise

It will now be useful for you to determine for each of the groups you have listed (page 143) what are its primary – column (a) – and secondary – (b) – forms. Do not worry if you have difficulty in determining between them, but have a try.

Most adult learning groups seem to work most effectively as small primary groups (say between ten members as a minimum and 25 as a maximum) that meet regularly (say, once or twice a week or for short intensive periods of a few days) and share common tasks between each meeting. A larger group than this may prevent effective interaction between all its members; a smaller group is often too vulnerable to sickness and other causes of absence to ensure continuity of learning, and this inhibits the growth of group coherence and performance.

Group structures

The primary group will structure itself in a number of different ways. The first is the *task group* – that is, the way the group members relate to each other in order to achieve the common aim. A cricket team illustrates this; it has its own structure, and the members play mutually recognised roles to fulfil the task. Task groups are usually primary groups, only rarely secondary groups, and they are distinguished by two features, a defined goal and a recognised leadership structure.

Groups are made up of individuals who may be willing for a time to submerge their own preferences in order to achieve the task but who remain individuals and relate to each other independently of the task. Some of them may dislike particular members with whom they work closely while they may interact with others at deeper levels. At some distance from the task, then, the primary group may adopt another structure; its members may fill roles other than those they occupy in the task group. Such a group is called a *socio-emotional group*, and it has its own rewards as well as its own structures. It is, for example, not always the case that the cricket captain is the team's best after-dinner speaker; that leadership role off the field may belong to another member of the group.

An amateur dramatic society, to take another example, has a particular structure during rehearsals. The producer or director is the recognised leader, often a tyrannical leader at that. But after rehearsal in a more convivial atmosphere, he or she may as likely as not sink back exhausted and remain silent for long periods; the leadership role comes to be adopted by another member of the group. Many new roles emerge in the social environment that are not displayed in the rehearsal hall.

The task group and the socio-emotional group are the same group acting in different ways. The former stresses the function of the group, the latter its social relationships. Some groups have no task orientation or structure. My drinking partners who meet most evenings in the corner of the bar that I frequent are there only to enjoy themselves and to exchange useful and useless pieces of information; it is clearly a socio-emotional group but hardly a task group. On the other hand, few if any task groups will fail to have socio-emotional aspects.

A primary group devoted to a task at times swings in its activities and in its structures from one aspect to the other. It can rarely remain all the time in the task aspect alone. Such a switch is healthy; it helps to facilitate the task and to increase the strength of the bonds in the group by relaxing the tensions created by the task orientation.

Such changes are most easily made when the task structure and the socio-emotional structure are not too far apart. If however the structure of the task group and the socio-emotional group become too distant, or if the socio-emotional structure becomes too strong – if for instance the leader of the socio-emotional group is expected to play a clearly subordinated role in the task group with no recognition of the position the rest of the group accords to him or her – then the performance of the task group can be damaged. If, in our example above, the producer or director of the play and the leader of the socio-emotional group clash over the task and their respective roles in the task (if, say, the leader of the socio-emotional group objects to some of the casting), then the whole production suffers. The group works best when the two structures are different but not too different, and when the socio-emotional structure is subordinate, with everyone's consent, to the task.

The second structure, then, serves as a *maintenance group*. It exists to help the task group to attain its goals. But a maintenance group and a socio-emotional group can be distinguished, for the maintenance group has the task before it and ceases to exist once the task has been completed, whereas the socio-emotional group seeks to keep itself in existence, perhaps by choosing another task. In this case, the task comes to serve the ends of the socio-emotional group rather than the other way round.

Exercise
We can now ask of each of the groups we listed (page 143) whether they are predominantly task groups or socio-emotional groups, which of these two structures predominates – column (c). In some cases, it will be half and half, but in others one type of group structure will stand out clearly.

Groups in adult education

How can we adapt all of this to our adult courses and programmes? Apart from the important but often overlooked point that all of our student participants will bring with them a number of overlapping primary, secondary and reference groups of which they are members, what is the relevance of all this to our teaching? Do we need to convert a 'class' of individual learners, which most of us teach, into a primary group with both task and socio-emotional orientations; and if so, how do we go about it? What are the advantages of adults coming together into groups to learn? How can the presence of other learners help, and hinder, our student participants?

Advantages and disadvantages of groups to adult learning

Views differ about the advantages and disadvantages of groups in adult learning. What will seem to some to be a help will be a cause of concern for others. Nevertheless, four main values appear to flow from the use of groups in teaching adults:

- they provide a *supportive* environment for learning;
- they provide a constant *challenge* to the learner;
- they provide resources to build richer and *more complex* structures for learning;
- they have a *life* of their own, which can assist the learning.

Each of these needs elaboration.

Advantages of groups for learning

1 *Supportive environment.* There is a sense of solidarity in the group in which the student participants can undertake learning changes more easily. The social context is one where all the members of the group are engaged in the same task. The individual will be supported by the group. For example:

- The group calls for conformity to its norms. In this way the group provides a measure of *suggestibility* and reinforces patterns of change.
- The group establishes the *status* of the learner and thus provides encouragement. Endorsement of one's worth, acknowledgement of one's potential, recognition of the role one is capable of playing within the group (especially a task group) and which the group is willing to accept – all of these can enhance the learners' self-image and encourage them to greater effort.
- The group *rewards* success. The warmth of fellowship and other emotional interchanges help to overcome the anxiety over changes that many learners experience. The group gives confidence. The shared

empathies that spring from the awareness of others in the same situation encourage the student participant to launch out and experiment. In this inner circle, ideas can be tested out first before their assertion in the outside world, skills can be practised prior to their demonstration before all and sundry. With many adult students, it is their vulnerability that is most touched upon in learning; and the group can provide that security needed for personal development. It is even possible for fellow participants to criticise another student at times when it is not possible for the teacher to do so; the group can provide the evaluation and reinforcement needed for learning.

All this depends on the members accepting and internalising the group goals and norms.

2 *Challenge*. The group provides an additional challenge to the learner. It creates a new setting calling for novelty in interrelationships. 'Newness' is in the air from the start. Most of us are accustomed to changing groups and joining new ones – from our family to school to work and leisure groups, new family groups and so on. We accept all of these, usually willingly, and build up new norms. An adult teaching–learning group is another such group. We meet new ranges of views, prejudices and experiences, all of them calling for learning changes and widening horizons. This is particularly true for changed attitudes; the existence of the group often provides the stimulus for change. Some adults come to educational programmes more for the experience of newness than for anything else.

3 *Building complex structures*. The group, drawing upon the increased variety of experience possessed by its members, can build larger and more complex cognitive structures, can create more satisfying products, can present a wider range of possible solutions to problems, can bring into play more evaluative judgements than can any learning environment consisting of teacher and student only. Because all the participants have their own well-trusted learning styles, the methods available in the teaching–learning process are greatly multiplied; it has not been unknown for a student participant to teach another member of the group a particular skill or concept when the teacher's methods have failed. The resources that both student participant and teacher can call upon are greatly increased by the existence of the group.

4 *Dynamic*. The group has a life of its own, a momentum that carries the participant along, helps to create and maintain motivation, and sets a pace of learning that is satisfying to most of its members. The teacher's task in these areas is greatly eased.

Disadvantages of groups for learning

Each of these same characteristics of learning groups however may also act as a hindrance to learning in certain cases.

1 *Learning environment*. The pressure to conformity, the *suggestibility* that the group exerts on the individual member, can promote imitation, not the free exercise of experiment. The group may smother the individual. At times (this often happens in an adult class) pre-existing prejudices and expectations are confirmed and strengthened by the presence of other participants who share them. Thus conflict between some or all of the student participants on the one hand and the newer ideas and ways of other student participants and of the teacher on the other may be generated and made more bitter. Trying to convince one or two students out of ten that their way of holding a chisel is inefficient and dangerous is relatively easy – until they are strengthened by the presence of even a few other people who share their idiosyncrasy. The group, in whole or in part, can thus become a new form of authority to which the individual is expected to conform.

The *status* offered by the group may become restrictive; the individual may become typecast by the group into a set role and may thus find it hard to break out and adopt another role (see Chapter 7).

What is more, the success of the group in providing *reinforcement* for its members can lead to some of the participants experiencing anxiety and fear of isolation, of being an outcast from the group if any of them experiments with a new way of doing something or expresses a divergent point of view. The participant can so easily become dependent upon the group, and even come to fear the rivalry of other groups. Such dependency can lead to learning ceasing rather than continuing when the group disperses.

2 *Challenge*. The closeness of the group, as each member engages in the similar 'new' activity, can become a threat to some of the more individualistic learners. At times the challenge may be so strong as to deter experimentation by those who are less confident.

3 *Building complex structures*. Some learners may find it difficult to cope with the variety of experience and views that others see as the richness of the adult learning group. The more elaborate structures that the group builds may in their case lack the necessary foundations for comprehension.

4 *Dynamic*. The pace set by the group may not be that needed by the individual member, and thus additional pressures can be created by the group. Some learning groups can be very intolerant of those who are felt to move unusually fast or slowly. Again, the relationships within the group may be inimicable to the personality traits of the learner.

Forming the group

Economics, educational considerations, student expectations and existing traditions of schooling all help to create a situation in which most of us find ourselves teaching a number of student participants at the same time. Each of us will have to weigh up how far in our particular circumstances a coherent learning group is necessary or whether we will teach our students without encouraging them to form themselves into a group, a cooperative for learning. But if we do decide to follow this second path, what steps do we need to take to help turn these separate individuals into a group? Will it happen by itself?

There are several different models of how groups coalesce and develop. The one that has most currency would appear to be as follows. The first stage is when a collection of socialised individuals, seeing a common goal, come together and express their need and willingness to interact. There is a common bond. Then comes an exploration stage, during which the individual members set and explore goals, when their inner inclinations become aligned on to the agreed goal. During this stage, members interact because they see that others are looking towards the same (or similar) goals as their own. They express their mutual dependence and begin to explore other bonds they may share, such as common interests, concerns or acquaintances. Thirdly, the group begins to structure itself; its members start to adopt roles, and these – after a period of experimentation, jostling and even conflict – stabilise into the formation of agreed role identities and the acceptance of common rules for all members of the group. Finally, the organisation completes itself into a

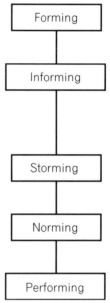

working group, dynamic, not static, with interlocking roles, specialisations and division of functions. In other words, the group has become something of a team, dedicated to the achievement of commonly agreed goals.

Not all groups, nor even all adult classes, pass through all of these stages, though many will. Perhaps the first lesson for us as teacher or leader of a group of adult learners is to watch what is going on in the group, not to be worried when conflicts arise, and to do all in our power to help the group achieve a measure of self-consciousness in identifying and achieving its goals. Nor must we assume that, once the group has begun to perform in relation to the common task, its structure will remain stable; as we shall see (pages 158–61), roles will constantly be changing in the group, and this will make some of the members feel uncomfortable. It does not harm most groups to get them to discuss from time to time the nature of the interrelations within the group.

This becomes particularly true of the group that takes off on its own, that begins to move towards the formal end of the spectrum. The mutual identification – in which the group meets the socio-emotional needs of the members as well as the task needs – leads the members to join with each other against outsiders. Praise, good luck, blame and even persecution of individual members are shared, and the concept of 'we' becomes exclusive. Loyalty and solidarity are expressed in a group symbol (a name, headed notepaper, etc.), then a badge, insignia, tie, dress or uniform. It is not long before ranks and titles emerge; taboo behaviour is laid down and jargon encouraged. The group is still a group; standards, values, attitudes and customs are shared, and norms are learned. But it has become more formal.

This is a very powerful tool of conformist learning but it scarcely leads to self-development, to increasing choices before the members. Formal groups of this kind have their uses and are especially effective in achieving some goals (political change, for example), but they are hardly education making for adulthood. Nevertheless, some long-running adult education groups seem to have gone a good way down this road.

The teacher and the group

What can the teacher of adults do positively to encourage effective learning in the group? First, we need to help the group to emerge from the collection of individual learners who have joined the class by encouraging the members to coalesce. Frequent face-to-face exchanges, together with some emotional involvement (for instance, cooperation on a common short-term or immediate task) will help in this. People who have nothing to share will never become a group. Students who come to classes and sit saying nothing, waiting for the teacher to begin to teach, with a coldness that suggests a lack of emotional commitment to the exercise, will remain a collection of individual learners, not introducing each other to the combined riches of the group. Equally dominance of the group by the teacher will not help at all; without a shared ownership of the task and a sense of achievement arising from its completion ('*We* did it'), the learners will remain in loose affiliation.

Figure 31a
Seats in rows prevent members in the front from talking to those behind them, while the only face that all the learners can see is that of the teacher.

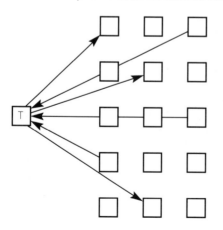

Figure 31b
Circular seating helps all members to talk freely with each other as well as with the teacher. Even when engaged on individual tasks, such an arrangement allows for interaction (sewing machines and typewriters can with advantage be set out in this rather than the more usual formal format).

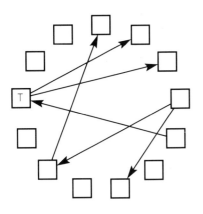

Figure 31c
Even a large table doesn't always help. The members at the far end have formed their own group; watch out if the same people sit there every time.

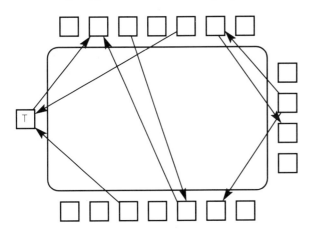

Seating patterns can help. Figure 31 suggests that such arrangements can contribute to the interrelations between group members; but we must be careful not to be too deterministic in this.

Secondly, we need to watch the balance between the personal self-development of each learner and the supportive/challenging role of the group. Both are desirable, but the needs of the learner should always take precedence. Each participant ought to be given opportunities to exercise their skills and express their views without fear of criticism, contradiction or exclusion by the group. As teachers, we should constantly try to be aware of the pressures the participants in our groups are under. All of them should be able to experiment and practise, play their own games, explore their own concepts. Each must add his or her particular contribution to the common pool. We should remember especially that the capacity of each individual for affiliation varies, and no one ought to be pressed too hard.

Thirdly, we must pay attention to the task structure of the group and to its socio-emotional structure. We should not perhaps try to discourage the emergence of informal, non-task-related interactions (a short break from the task, such as for refreshments, is a great opportunity for this, as well as the periods at the start and end of each meeting), but we need to ensure that the socio-emotional structure is subordinate and contributory to the task group, that it helps on the work of the group as a maintenance group. The task is, after all, learning, in whatever field of activity the class is concerned with. If both structures are contributing towards the task, the teacher will not be unduly worried when the group continually moves in and out of its distinct aspects, not even when the socio-emotional structure seems to predominate for a time ('What about our party this year?'). But it is not always easy to keep a balance, to keep the common goal before the group when so many of its members seem to wish to engage in anything except the learning task.

Sometimes it may be desirable to break up the group, to form new sub-groups, new roles and new structures, in order to encourage the learning task. But this can lead to the formation of cliques; and when the participants are reluctant to come back from their sub-groups into the full group, it may well be that the sub-groups are satisfying some need that the full group isn't meeting. If such a sub-group becomes permanent, especially if it gets between the group and the goal, conflicts will arise. In these cases, setting a closer subordinate goal, a short-term task with its own sense of achievement, will sometimes help to re-create the whole group.

On occasion, however, it can be the teacher who wittingly or unwittingly encourages such a division in the group. An in-group centred on the teacher (especially one who adjourns to a nearby bar with some of the members after each group meeting) and a consequent out-group frequently occur in adult education. The out-groupers may be willing to accept the role assigned to them, but they will not be as keen on the learning task as they were when the group was whole. The in-groupers for their part will often assert their role, either displaying a proprietary interest in the teacher (asking specialised questions, for instance) or preserving an attitude of aloofness during the class as if to keep their contributions until later when the out-groupers are excluded and they can have the teacher on their own.

Throughout this minefield, we will need to tread carefully. The most important attribute for any teacher to develop is *sensitivity*: awareness for example of the group members' non-verbal as well as verbal interactions;

awareness of group tension and its release symptoms (jokes, laughter, etc.); awareness of its signs of satisfaction. The way a group member sits on the edge of (or even outside) the group, the way they lean forward or draw a breath preparatory to taking the plunge into the common activity, anxious to make a point as soon as there is a reasonable break – these and many other signals will be absorbed, often half-consciously, by the teacher. Some teachers are born; they seem to take to this naturally. But all of us can increase our awareness, by understanding the ways groups operate and by learning to watch.

Note: Killing the group

The sensitivity of group dynamics has been expressed with sardonic humour in Clyde Reid's book, *Groups Alive – Church Alive: The Effective Use of Small Groups in the Local Church* (1969). Although intended for church discussion groups, it can be applied to many other situations. I have used the following extract from the book with several groups of teachers of adults; it is naturally not to be taken too seriously.

The Fine Art of Squelching Small Groups

The ability to squelch the life out of a small group may be thought of as an art. Because of the strong interest in this new art, the following ground rules are offered to give direction and purpose to would-be squelchers who wish to develop their talents in this direction.

1 Keep the small group too large for the members to really get to know each other. By all means have at least twenty or twenty-five members in order to do this.
2 Complain at every meeting about how few people have turned out. This will give group members a size-consciousness and sense of guilt. They will either quit coming or they will invite their friends and the small group will soon grow into oblivion; it will become a large group.
3 Arrange the seats in formal rows like a classroom. Don't permit informality to sneak in by sitting in a friendly circle. In that situation group members might feel encouraged to express themselves and not want to give up the group.
4 Include a long business meeting with each group session and bore everyone to tears. The group will rapidly wither.
5 Dominate the group from the beginning. Establish yourself as the authority on all matters that may come before the group. Make all the basic decisions yourself, while giving the impression of a democratic spirit to the group members.

6 If possible, establish yourself as the teacher of the group and deliver a learned lecture at each meeting. (Our rock-bound guarantee: the group won't last more than three months this way or your money back.)

7 Pay no attention to the needs and interests of the group members. Most people don't know what is best for them anyhow.

8 Answer all questions yourself. Don't let group members speak to each other or answer each other's questions. What do they know that you can't say better?

9 Don't permit the fiction to arise that group members should take turns leading the discussion. They're liable to get too deeply involved and interested and keep the group alive in spite of your efforts.

10 Never allow group members to share anything personal. Change the subject to a nice safe intellectual discussion when this happens. That way they won't get too involved with each other at a depth level. Groups in which this happens become devilishly hard to squelch.

11 By all means, don't encourage members of the group to express themselves. Limit the participation to the more vocal, intellectual members to keep the conversation on a high plane of sophistication. They will bore each other to sleep.

12 Keep the discussion on a theoretical plane, preferably in the realm of theology and philosophy. Mention names like Kant, Schleiermacher, and Tillich occasionally to make the others feel inferior.

13 Allow one or two persons to dominate the discussion. That way the others will become quietly angry and the group will fold up in no time. By all means, don't point out to the dominators what they are doing. This might lead to some hurt feelings and personal growth – things to be avoided at all costs in squelching a group.

14 Don't urge the silent members of the group to speak up. They might get the idea that you really care about them and that their ideas count after all. They will be more difficult to discourage as a result.

15 By all means don't let the group members express any hostility towards each other. You may find them understanding each other too well as a result and the group will become tenacious of continuing.

Note. It is recommended that every group leader express his own unique personality in using the above rules. There is a squelching method that is uniquely yours. You may have found ways to squelch a group that haven't even been thought of yet. But follow any one of these rules with dogged persistence and you need not fear. You will have expressed yourself. The group will certainly collapse, for you will have violated a principle of human nature.

Further reading

Banbury, J. and Carter, G. (1982) *Teaching Groups: a Basic Education Handbook*. London: Adult Literacy and Basic Skills Unit.

Blumberg, A. and Gloembiewski, R. T. (1976) *Learning and Change in Groups*. Harmondsworth: Penguin.

Douglas, T. (1983) *Groups: Understanding People Gathered Together*. London: Tavistock.

Egan, G. (1973) *Face to Face: the Small Group Experience and Interpersonal Growth*. Montercy, CA: Brooks/Cole.

Jacques, D. (1984) *Learning in Groups*. Beckenham: Croom Helm.

Knowles, M. and Knowles, H. (1972) *Introduction to Group Dynamics*. New York: Association Press.

Sork, T. J. (ed.) (1984) *Designing and Implementing Effective Workshops*. San Francisco, CA: Jossey Bass.

Zander, A. (1982) *Making Groups Effective*. San Francisco, CA: Jossey Bass.

8
ROLES AND THE TEACHER
What part shall we play . . . ?

Roles and changing roles

Groups rely on roles, mutually recognised and accepted, both to achieve a task and also to work effectively in their socio-emotional and maintenance aspects. The fact that a group has a structure implies roles; in the learning group, all of the members (including the teacher) will play some part towards its functioning. Such roles are fulfilled in meeting different situations, performing various activities and engaging in patterns of behaviour.

The way each of the members of the group views his or her role may differ from how others in the group see the same role. To ensure group coherence and performance, there needs to be a measure of agreement about and acceptance of roles through the pressures of suggestibility, through conformity to and internalisation of the assigned place in the group – although, as we have seen, the capacity for affiliation that each member possesses will vary.

Equally, engagement with the new material on which the learning changes will be based will call for each group member to adopt new roles – at first in relation to the new material and subsequently (and consequently) in relation to the other group members. Part of the learning process for each of the group members (including the teacher) is to change roles; and part of the teaching process is to encourage and help all members of the group to enter new roles and to interpret old roles in new ways.

Group roles

There is a wide variety of roles that will exist in any one group. In the exercise on the next page is a list collected from a number of teachers of adults of some of the titles they have used to describe particular members of their learning groups. There is no particular significance in the order in which they are given, and in most cases the meaning of the epithet is clear.

A few comments on the list below will be useful. First, such a list can never be complete; the roles are too diverse, and in any case we will each see them in different terms. Secondly, titles like these describe a series of activities

---

Exercise

This list contains 'titles' given to particular roles which some adult student participants have adopted. You can do two things with this list: use each title to describe how you think such a student participant will behave, both in and out of the group; and secondly, add to this list other titles from your own experience, if possible.

Title	*Description*
Student leader	Speaks for the group
Questioner	More interested in asking than in listening to answers
Queen	
Jester	
Professional simpleton	
Leader of the opposition	
Expert	
Prefect/monitor	
Cynic	
Know-all	
Last-worder	
Eavesdropper	
Ignoramus	
Special disciple	
Deviator	
Arguer	

Now add your own list.

undertaken by the group members and depend on judgements of motives made by other members of the group. Thirdly, since these roles depend on reactions to different situations, all members of the group in their time will play several parts – roles in relation to the teacher (or group leader), to the subject-matter and to the other members of the group. A given title must not imply that any person will adopt that role to the exclusion of all others. Fourthly, there are dangers in giving such labels (which some people will in any case see as patronising); it can so easily lead to stereotyping and even to self-fulfilling prophecies. But such titles can help to point out the wide range of reactions within any one group of adults engaged in learning under our supervision. Finally, the *teacher* will be called upon to adopt some of these roles during the course (you may find it useful to mark these items on your list).

Breaking roles

Each member of the adult learning group, be it class, lecture course, training group or voluntary body, will play a role in the group. All these roles must be accepted by the group in some way if the person is to feel fully a member of the group. Rejection of the role is interpreted as rejection of the individual. However, the role may be tolerated only in so far as it helps in the achievement of the goal; and this fact can create tensions between those members who have set themselves roles that do not in themselves contribute to the task and those members who are committed to the group objective. It will be the teacher's task to minimise these tensions. Part of our work, then, is to watch for the signs of these roles: to be sensitive to the cues that indicate the nature and strength of the role being played.

Perhaps the greatest problem with these roles, and with giving titles to them, is that they may quickly become fossilised. The 'talker' at the first meeting may remain for ever the 'talker' and thus stop the 'listener' from becoming for a time a talker; the 'show-off' will continue to demonstrate their skills to all and sundry, in the process not only limiting their own learning changes but undermining the confidence of other group members not so proficient. There is often considerable group pressure on members to keep to their roles, although equally it is sometimes surprising how much effort a group as a whole will expend in its attempts to limit troublesome roles (to quieten down the 'joker', for instance) and to encourage the 'quitter' (the 'I-know-I-can't-do-it-so-I'm-not-going-to-try' type) or the 'quiet one' to join in.

These actions of the group, when they occur, are valuable and show the contribution of the whole group towards the learning task. They will complement the efforts of the teacher to encourage changing roles in the course of learning. The teacher's main aim is to help the student participants to learn, first through the group and later independently of the group. Learning must not become dependent on the group or on the role played within the group. Role changes will be necessary if learning is to take place. So the teacher needs to resist any tendency to fossilise roles, joining with the group when it seeks to urge some of its members to break roles, and even if necessary to break up the group structure if it will help members to change their roles.

Although some of the student participants will change their roles willingly, in a spirit of exploration and experimentation, others will be more hesitant. Their sense of identity in the group, their security, depends on the role they have acquired, which has been accepted by the other members. One useful way around this problem is the use of smaller sub-groups, dedicated to achieving a significant part of the task yet providing opportunities (even perhaps the necessity) for members to adopt roles different from those they possess in the full group. It is also possible to use the group itself, its loyalty and sympathy, to encourage such changes in individual members.

The roles of the teacher of adults

Just as each of the student participants brings with them a package of experience and expectations and concerns, so too the teacher brings his or her own package – and this fact needs to be recognised and acknowledged. The teacher is at one and the same time an adult learner, engaging in learning episodes with their own preferred learning style. All that is stated above about the adult learner applies to the teacher as a learner in his or her own life.

It has often been suggested that the teacher is the most important single element in setting the whole tone of the learning group. But if there is a tension inside the group between its coherence and the call for individual learning, so too there are a number of tensions within the role of the teacher in relation to the group. We will have at least four main parts to play:

1 as *leader of the group*, whose purpose is to keep the group together, to keep things going;
2 as *teacher*, an agent of change;
3 as *member of the group*, subject to the pressures it exerts;
4 as *audience*, outside of the group, the person before whom the group members will perform their newly acquired learning in search of evaluation and reinforcement.

It is a daunting role, but the rewards more than compensate for the difficulties.

1 ... as group leader

The teacher is the group leader; our role in this respect is clearly recognised and accepted by the group. We cease to be a teacher when we abandon this role. There have been many, and increasingly complicated, attempts to describe the role of the group leader. One way to discuss this subject is under the three subheadings of task, interaction and maintenance, as suggested by Ivor Davies (1976).

Task

The group leader identifies and clarifies the task ahead, whether it be improving skills, learning a subject or solving a problem. The leader sets and offers to the participants a goal and – with the participants – clarifies the goals that they set for themselves; he or she keeps the worthwhileness of the whole enterprise constantly before the group; and evaluates with the group, as the learning process goes on, what progress towards achieving these goals has been made and is being made.

Interaction

Although part of the group, nevertheless the teacher is the one person who is outside the group and who can therefore watch what is happening from a position of committed detachment, involved and yet an observer. The teacher monitors the interactions within the group and the structure it builds for itself; sees the roles each of the group members adopts, and seeks to assert that all the individual members of the group count; acts as arbiter if necessary so as to ensure that monopolies or persecutions do not arise; watches out for special relationships that occur and seeks to use them creatively, so that in the end every member will contribute positively and meaningfully towards the achievement of the common task, the learning. The teacher as group leader can, and often should, help the group to see for itself what is happening.

Maintenance

The teacher is the person who helps the group to identify the resources available to them and the constraints under which they operate; the one to mobilise the necessary resources and materials – the equipment, the books, the speakers, the exercises needed for learning. This may often consist of persuading individual group members to utilise the resources that are at their own disposal.

Most of these roles can and often should be shared with the participants rather than kept to one person. But the person who is ultimately responsible for seeing that these tasks, necessary for the performance of the group, are carried out is the teacher acting as group leader.

Problems sometimes spring from the creation of dependency syndromes. The group as a whole will tend to come to rely on us in direct proportion as we act effectively as its leader; and individuals in the group, especially those given special attention in the course of the group's activities, frequently develop such an attitude towards 'their' teacher. Some measure of dependency may be desirable, even necessary, in the production of a play, but in an adult learning class or group it will inhibit real education. This danger exists even where the teacher is attempting to develop the self-sufficiency of the learner, for group members will often try to keep us in the role of group leader even against our wishes. We must seek, as time goes on, to play a less dominant role as leader of the learning group, whatever pressures the group members may bring to bear on us.

2 . . . as teacher

The teacher is the promoter of learning changes, the encourager of the learners. The term 'change-agent' which has been used for the teacher in some circles is a good one. We aim to use the group to help bring about changes in knowledge, understanding, skills, attitudes and ultimately in behaviour. Teachers thus have to be 'stirrers', to achieve change without breaking up the group entirely.

The teacher operates in two ways in relation to the learning group, as manager of the learning process and as instructor.

Manager of learning

In this role, the teacher engages in four main types of activity: as planner, as organiser, as leader and as controller of the learning process for each of the members of the learning group.

- *Planner* – the teacher analyses the programme of learning, identifies the skills, knowledge and attitudes required, sets out the learning objectives and the individual learning tasks that need to be completed in order to achieve these goals, determines what resources will be necessary and constructs the learning sequences (the curriculum).
- *Organiser* – the teacher organises the learning tasks, the context within which the learning takes place, the environment of the class or group, the conditions in which the student participants engage in their work. The end purpose is to make it easier for the participants to work and learn together, and it is thus important that such organising should be done to meet the requirements of the learners. It is all done for their sakes rather than for administrative convenience or for an easy life for the teacher.
- *Leader* – the teacher encourages and motivates the student participants, selects and uses appropriate teaching–learning methods. For this part of our work, we need the most effective social tools we can find.
- *Controller* – the teacher determines the relevance of the activities and the

material to the task in hand and to the ultimate objectives of the course, revises the programme and changes direction when necessary. He or she rules out irrelevancies and maintains the momentum of the class group.

Instructor

Secondly, there is the teacher's other role, instructor.

Several attempts have been made to categorise the different styles teachers adopt in relation to their learners, ranging from what has been called the 'sheepdogging' approach to teaching (herding the flock by constantly snapping at them), to the opposite extreme, allowing the student-learners to 'free-range'. Some writers have divided teachers in their personal approach to the student-learners into different types such as 'lion-tamer', 'entertainer' or 'cultivator'; it is not difficult to see the force of these terms as they apply to teaching patterns. Others have reflected on the contrast in modes of relating to the group: the autocratic, the *laissez-faire* and the democratic, for example. Others again have spoken of those teachers who 'tell', those who 'sell', those who 'consult' and those who 'join' the group of learners. Such descriptions attempt to depict the spectrum of approaches to teaching (Fig. 32); they are not distinct categories.

Exercise

It may be helpful for you to describe briefly the sort of activity each of these teachers engages in; you could perhaps mark those you feel you most nearly approximate to.

Lion-tamer:	Autocratic:	Tells:	*Your own list*
Entertainer:	*Laissez-faire:*	Sells:	
Cultivator:	Democratic:	Consults:	
		Joins:	

Others have spoken of the teacher's manner: of those who on the one hand are aloof and egocentric as opposed to those who are friendly and understanding; of those who are dull and routine as against those who are stimulating and imaginative; of those who are evasive and whose work is

Figure 32 The continuum of approaches to teaching

unplanned as against those who are responsible and business-like. Such characteristics are major factors in creating the atmosphere within which we all have to work in a learning group.

Class climate

Teaching styles help to create a 'climate' for the adult class or learning group. The atmosphere of the learning group may be relaxed, warm and friendly, or it may be tense, cold and hostile. The responses of the student participants could be on the one hand apathetic, obstructive, uncertain and dependent, or on the other alert, responsible, confident and initiating. An attempt to assess the different elements to this climate has been made on the basis of four main characteristics:

- *Warmth* – the strength of emotions and identification between the teacher and the student participants; is the group welcoming, affirming, encouraging to the learner, not dismissive or exclusive?
- *Directness* – whether the interactions between the teacher and the student participants are direct or indirect, whether the teacher does all the work or whether the class stimulates the learners to do their own work.
- *Enthusiasm* – the way the teacher feels about the subject being taught, about the students and their learning; the commitment of both teacher and student participants to the learning task.
- *Organisation* – how far the teacher demonstrates competence in organising; the strength and efficiency of the process of managing the learning situation, devising carefully planned and purposeful exercises so that all involved feel they are not wasting time.

It is the teachers who to a large extent control all these elements and who largely create the climate of the classes or learning groups by their own styles. Their concern is both for promoting the emotional well-being of the student participants and for ensuring learning.

The climate of the class or learning group may be stable, with a consistent teaching style used throughout; or it may fluctuate as the teacher swings from one style to another. Sudden and unexpected changes of climate may leave many of the participants uncertain of their roles and less able to cope with the learning tasks; but some modifications of climate are probably desirable for learning changes to take place. A static climate may not encourage the experimentation that must accompany learning.

Implications for the teacher

The fact that there are different ways of describing the relationship between the teacher and the student participants prompts a number of thoughts. The first is that there can be no universally applicable way of depicting the very complex series of relations that go on within a learning group. Each of us can define these interactions in different ways. Further, it is easier for us to describe and classify the relationship of other teachers to their students than it is to do so for ourselves; we are aware how far such categories fall short of the complexity of reality in our own case.

Figure 33 indicates the two main sets of factors controlled by the teacher and the sort of activity that may result from the varied teaching styles and class/learning group climates. You might consider where you prefer to operate on this matrix.

Figure 33 Matrix of class/learning group climate

Strong organisation, structure, management, administration

e.g. formal presentations

e.g. group work, simulation exercises

Subject-centred objectives

Personal growth objectives

e.g. project work, discovery learning

e.g. individual projects, self-exploration

Concentration on personal relations, loose structure

Secondly, most of us as teachers do not adopt any one approach consistently. We move about throughout these styles as the need presents itself. The effective teacher will probably use many of these different ways of relating to the learners in the group during the course of teaching.

Thirdly, we will sometimes find ourselves torn between the style adopted in relation to the whole group and the style needed for certain individual learners. How for instance shall we handle the situation of the slow learner who holds up the group? Or the very able who speed ahead and thus begin to distance themselves from the group? Which comes first, the welfare of the individual student participant or of the whole group?

And finally there may be – and often is – a tension between the role which the teacher wishes to adopt in relation to the adult learning group and the role which the student participants wish him or her to adopt. Many students want the teacher to teach formally, to present information; they sometimes regard discussions as a waste of time. And some teachers find this a role which they cannot easily adopt. A real tension can arise from dissatisfied teachers of adults who are unable to reconcile themselves to the desired approaches of the student participants.

It is impossible to answer such questions with universal rules. Each teacher must think about them and answer them for him/herself in the context of their own style of teaching. If each of the learners in our classes and other learning groups has their own learning style, which they have come to use effectively, it is also true that each of us as teachers has our own particular teaching style that we are happiest with, and this will to a large extent determine how we react in our learning groups. We need to recognise our own particular style for what it is; to improve it with practice; and to try to make sure that it accomplishes what it is intended to accomplish: student learning.

The course material

This will involve introducing the learner to the material comprising the learning task. The duty of the teacher is to persuade the student participants to engage directly with the subject-matter for themselves. Here the triangle of learner, teacher and subject-matter occurs again. Normally the subject-matter is at first mediated through the teacher; then the teacher gradually withdraws, urging the learners to encounter the material face to face, until we have rendered ourselves to a large extent (ultimately completely) redundant to the learning process (see Fig. 34). Unless we withdraw from this process of interaction between student participant and subject-matter, learning will tend to cease when the class comes to an end or the group disperses.

Figure 34

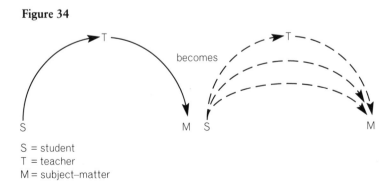

S = student
T = teacher
M = subject–matter

3. . . . as group member

As teachers of adults, we are concerned with the learning needs of our student participants. Their learning styles need to be practised, their learning skills strengthened and enriched. In this process the teacher's third role, as member of the group, becomes of importance. Not only will it enable us to experience something of what the other group members will be experiencing; it will directly assist us in helping the various members to learn. The teacher can become a model of learning for the student participants. It has been said that 'the most important attribute of the teacher [is that] he must be a learner himself. If he has lost his capacity for learning, he is not good enough to be in the company of those who have preserved theirs' (quoted in Kidd, 1973: 303). The way we ourselves learn and engage with the subject-matter can be used as an illustration of the way other learners in the group can relate to the subject-matter. All of us in the group, including the teacher, are learners; and we can all learn from each other how to learn.

The teacher and the class session

If we approach our learning group in this way, the class meetings assume a different perspective. Instead of seeing our students as 'attending classes', we, and they, will see ourselves as engaged in a course of study, a programme of work that will occupy a good deal of our time as long as we remain committed to it. As we ourselves learn between class/group meetings – as we engage with the subject-matter, prepare the material for the next learning step and evaluate progress made – so we can encourage the other members of the learning group to learn in similar ways. It is odd that so many teachers of adults expect their students to learn in class only, while they themselves learn on their own. Those teachers who aim to make their students independent learners will seek ways to enable them to learn as much *between* class meetings as in the group sessions.

There are two possible different models of the teaching session in relation to learning. Teachers may adopt either model to suit different sets of circumstances.

In the first, most of the learning activity is done during the class meeting: demonstration of a new method of working, for instance; reading and discussing a text; listening to a lecture; engaging in practical group exercises, etc. The period between each class/meeting is then spent by the learner reinforcing (by practice, reading, writing, etc.) the learning done in class (Fig. 35a). Part of each class session will be spent in feedback, an assessment of how much and what sort of learning has gone on since the last meeting. This is not a waste of time. Indeed, to expect all learning to be confined to those times when we are face to face will not only create dependency; it will waste all the time between each meeting available for reinforcement and run the risk of learning changes being lost.

Figure 35a

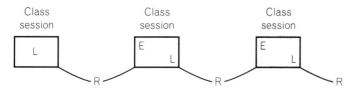

L = doing the learning exercise
R = exercises reinforcing the learning done in class
E = evaluating the reinforcement exercises

The alternative model moves the main learning process out of the class session to the period between each meeting. A task is thus set during the class, to be completed in the time before the next session. In this case, the next meeting will be spent partly assessing and evaluating how well the task has been performed and the material learned, and partly setting another task (or an adaptation of the same task if it has been inadequately or incorrectly learned). Most of the new learning will take place outside the class/group meeting (Fig. 35b).

Figure 35b

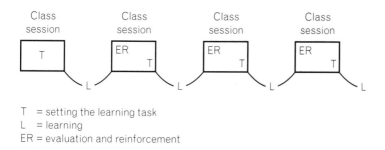

T = setting the learning task
L = learning
ER = evaluation and reinforcement

Using the space between meetings for learning will not occur automatically. As long as we concentrate on the teacher teaching, we shall think of the class session in isolation from the rest of the student-learners' lives; we shall believe that all learning goes on during the face-to-face encounter. Even when we reorientate ourselves and think more in terms of the students' learning as an ongoing process, continuing even when we are not present, there will be obstacles in the way of using to the best effect the time between each session. Most of the student participants will tend to see the encounter between teacher and learner as necessary for learning. We need therefore to take conscious steps to ensure that continued learning occurs outside of the group meetings and to evaluate what learning is taking place.

4. . . . as 'audience'

The fourth main aspect of our task as teacher is that of evaluator. By setting the learning tasks and calling for them to be performed before us for our comments and evaluation, we remove ourselves to some extent from the group. We become the criteria by which our student participants' learning efforts are judged; we are the expert, not just the instructor but the assessor.

The learners and the teacher

At this point the greatest change of role comes about in both teacher and learner. For in order to learn, the student participant needs to become for a time a teacher; the learner presents the newly acquired skill or newly learned material to the teacher, who in turn adopts the role of learner. Adult education has been described as an activity in which all the participants 'alternate between the roles of student, teacher and person' (Thompson 1980: 67). In using the material, the learners demonstrate (a teaching function) their mastery, while the teacher evaluates (a learning function). Every adult learner needs to come to teach. The teachers watch, listen, read and evaluate as they assess the student participants' work, just as the learner demonstrates, talks, writes and displays the new learning in other ways. The teacher–learner exchange of roles is the single most effective method of learning. (Formal institutions have long recognised this when they prescribe the writing of essays as a main tool of learning, though there are many better ways of the student undertaking teaching functions than writing essays, and essays are not of course appropriate for skill-based learning programmes.)

The teacher comes to make critical judgements about the work of the student participants. So it is essential that we come to know ourselves, become aware of those biases that influence the judgements we make. Such preferences include those between male and female, between white and black, between old and young, between professional and working class, between the law-abiding and the law-breaking, between the known and the unknown. We all possess them, and they affect all we do and think. We should try to be open with ourselves about such preferences.

The teacher makes demands on the student participants as learners. We set them tasks and call for them to be performed under our critical eye, until the stage has been reached when the subject-matter makes its own demands on learners. In many cases we are faced, on the part of some of the student participants, with a measure of resistance for several reasons:

- Some of the participants do not in fact want to change. They come to our classes and learning groups for many reasons (sometimes even believing that they want to learn), among which socio-emotional needs may be strongest – and these reasons often militate against change. Others may be there for career-related reasons rather than out of a desire for learning;

they want to get through the course and acquire the accolades that go with the completion of the programme of study but they do not want to learn, to change. Most groups of adult learners contain some members like this.

- Sometimes the roles played by the student participants establish their status in the group. Any abandonment of those roles may be seen as damaging to their status in the group. Several adults find engaging in group learning exercises embarrassing; they see such activities as damaging the picture they believe others have of them.
- Learning changes can be, as we have suggested, uncomfortable and even painful to make, the more so as the adult grows into a concept of self-maturity. To admit to learning needs is in itself challenging to some adults, while others resist the effort needed to change their views and attitudes.
- Perhaps most frequently many student-learners will object to the teacher who abandons the traditional role of instructor and expert, especially the teacher who occasionally admits ignorance. Some students may become anxious when a teacher engages in participatory activities; for a number of student participants want to be taught; they want authoritative guidance or reassurance and even discipline from a 'superior' person. Many groups will go to considerable lengths to keep the teacher as teacher and the learners as learners.

Fight or flight

When faced with a request to engage in learning activity, group resistance takes one of two main forms of reaction: fight or flight. In 'fight', open resistance ('We don't want to') is on the whole less common than the question, 'Why should we?' This is more often not so much a genuine enquiry, an expression indicating that the participants are unconvinced of the necessity of the particular learning task, as a statement meaning, 'We won't' (although many adult students are too polite to say so).

On the other hand, the alternative is just as effective. 'Flight' may be expressed in the form: 'We will, but later'; 'It's a good idea but we can't do it because/until . . .'; 'We must find the proper material first (or do this or that) before we can begin.' An alternative form of flight is compensation, the substitution of some other task for that set.

We should recognise these tactics for what they are. One effective way of dealing with them is to help the group themselves to become aware of them as avoidance techniques, as resistance to engaging in learning activities.

Expectations of the teacher

Most members of adult learning groups of all kinds expect the teacher to occupy the teaching role and the student participants to occupy the learning roles all the time. They see the teacher as both *an* authority (a specialist in the subject) and *in* authority (in command of the class/group). Many teachers see themselves in this way too; they collaborate with the pressures of the student participants. They feel safer being in charge of the whole process. They are often anxious about letting the student participants loose to experiment and learn by doing on their own – fearful that the learners will 'get it wrong'. They feel that they are not fulfilling their responsibilities as teachers, not fulfilling their students' expectations of them, even not 'earning their money'.

Just as the student roles are expressed non-verbally as well as verbally, so too are those of the anxious teacher. How often do we stand up before the class unnecessarily, especially when pressed with a question to which we are unsure of the answer? Standing above our students reasserts our authority both to them and to ourselves, like preaching from a pulpit, 'six feet above contradiction'. We convince ourselves that it is necessary to rise to point out something to the rest of the group or to use the blackboard, when it may not be necessary for us to stand at all. In non-verbal ways like this, we buttress our position when we feel challenged. We should try to become aware not just of how the roles of the learners are expressed but also of how we express the position we wish to occupy in the group.

This position is compounded of many different roles. The students call upon us to express many of these in the course of our encounter with them. Particularly, many group members expect the teacher to be a performer, what Richard Hoggart (in Jennifer Rogers's book, *Teaching on Equal Terms*, 1969) has called 'a Pied Piper of Hamelin', leading our flock by our playing to a dreamland of success. Some students consciously exert pressure to keep a teacher in this performing role: 'I could listen to you all day'; and some teachers respond to this demand willingly, adding one more role to the many they are already playing. 'Even more than most teaching, adult education invites its tutors to a range of attractive . . . forms of role-playing.'

Some of these roles contradict each other. The list in the following exercise, selected from the descriptions compiled by different groups of teachers over the years, indicates some of these roles; you may wish to add to it from your own experience.

It is no wonder that at the end of a discussion of these roles one teacher in the group exclaimed; 'We have just described God!'

Exercise

List some of the roles that teachers adopt in relation to their student participants. You may find it helpful to write notes against each of them to say how you expect the teacher to behave in these circumstances.

Expert: a resource, a source of knowledge	Expected to provide instant answers to all queries
Provider: gives access to resources	
Explainer: demonstrator	
Discipliner:	Especially against a disruptive or nonconformist group member
Organiser:	
Instructor:	
Motivator:	
Protector:	
Chairman: arbiter	
Examiner: evaluator	Assessor of the work done, the one who maintains standards, checks work, etc.
Counsellor:	The one who will help, advise, guide, reassure, support, encourage, etc. the individual learner
Others:	

Conclusion

This last remark provokes a few final comments about the role of the teacher.

Expect a life of isolation. As teacher, it will rarely be possible for you to join the group fully. You will always have one foot outside the group, however much you join in. You will nearly always be the 'audience' before whom the participants will practise their newly acquired learning and who will be expected to evaluate and judge their performance. The teacher is 'in' but not always 'of' the group.

Clearly a thorough knowledge of one's subject is essential for teaching adults. This is not low-level work, as many in other areas of education have suggested, for the learners frequently push the teacher by their questions to the very limits of the subject. The teacher of adults needs to be fully acquainted with all aspects of the subject, for unlike the university lecturer we cannot always choose what we teach about; the learners often determine that.

Equally, the teacher of adults must be prepared on occasion to say, 'I don't know.' We will have some idea of how to find out, and it is very rare that an adult group will respect any teacher the less for admitting gaps in his or her knowledge. They are themselves aware that the amount that is not known is far greater than what is known, and they will rarely expect the teacher to be an expert across the whole of any field.

Many teachers of adults feel threatened by their students. Some of these know more about the subject-matter or parts of the subject-matter than their teacher. Some possess many of the social skills which the teacher may wish he or she possessed. In such circumstances, there is a danger of the teacher falling back on to authority – the claim to leadership which the role of teaching endows. The teacher of adults needs to allow and indeed encourage the group to be student-led without feeling that their role has been usurped.

This suggests that social skills may be more important in selecting teachers of adults than subject specialism. It is not always the best policy to get the most up-to-date expert or series of experts to talk to a group of adult learners. Continuity of contact may be more important to allow for growth over a period of time rather than a series of individual teaching sessions by specialists.

If our task as teachers of adults is so demanding, it follows that we should seek out all the help we can get. Most teachers of adults work in isolation from each other, and we rarely spend enough time searching for the resources available in the community to assist us in the task. We need support, and it is up to us to find it. Our employing agency, if we have one, should help; but if not, there *are* other teachers of adults in our neighbourhood.

We must not become too self-conscious about our roles, our methods and our relationships. It is useful now and again to check how we and the group are performing; and every so often something will pull us up and make us realise the nature of the group reactions. But provided we are sensitive to what is happening, we can let things flow naturally, helping just a little here and there to direct the current towards the goals.

In view of the superhuman range of expectations that both we and the group hold of the teacher's role, we must not expect one hundred per cent success. Most of our classes will have at least one blatant error, sometimes many more. The task of being a teacher needs to be learned, and that takes time.

Further reading

Belbin, R. M. (1980) *The Discovery Method in Training*. Sheffield: Manpower Services Commission.

Davies, I. K. (1971) *The Management of Learning*. London: McGraw-Hill.

Hostler, J. (1982) The art of teaching adults, *Studies in Adult Education*, 14: 42–9.

Lenz, E. (1980) *The Art of Teaching Adults*. New York: Holt, Rinehart and Winston.

Rogers, A. (1991a) *Teaching Adults in Extension*. Reading: Education for Development.

Rogers, J. (1984) *Adults in Education*. London: BBC Publications.

Schön, D. A. (1995) *Educating the Reflective Practitioner*. San Francisco, CA: Jossey Bass.

Stephens, M. D. and Roderick, G. N. (1971) *Teaching Techniques in Adult Education*. Newton Abbot: David and Charles.

Verduin, J. R. (1983) *Adults Teaching Adults: Principles and Strategies*. Mansfield: University Associates.

9

TEACHING: CONTENT AND METHODS

How shall we do it . . . ?

We have seen that, in order to ensure that each of the student participants in our groups can learn in their own way, using their own learning techniques and styles and at their own pace, we can utilise the learning group and the various roles within it. But we can also use a varied range of teaching methods that will involve the student participants in their own programme of work. It is the purpose of this chapter to explore this second avenue.

Curriculum

Methods and content together make up the curriculum, and a word on curriculum is thus necessary. There is very little material related to curriculum in adult education; most of the work on curriculum has been done in relation to schools (Colin Griffin's pioneering study (1983) concentrates on philosophical concepts and tends to neglect more practical aspects of the curriculum). It is therefore necessary to adapt what is known about curriculum in schools to adult education.

Curriculum is often seen as a body of knowledge, the content of education to which the students need to be exposed. But curriculum is much wider than a list of subjects to be studied; it is not only what you say but how you say it! Curriculum is all the planned experiences to which the learner may be exposed in order to achieve the learning goals. R. M. W. Travers speaks of 'all the planned conditions and events to which the pupil is exposed for the purpose of promoting learning plus the framework of theory which gives these conditions and events a certain coherence' (Travers 1964).

Five elements have been seen as making up the curriculum:

1 *Philosophical framework* – part of the curriculum which the learners learn consists of those attitudes which underlie all of our teaching. Local

history may be taught as a leisure pursuit or as part of community development, and this difference will show in the way it is taught. Woodwork may be seen as a series of techniques or as part of a concern for good design and good living; family planning may be taught on its own, in isolation from all other subjects, or as part of a holistic approach to personal growth and family development and human sexuality. The philosophical framework relates to those overall goals discussed above (page 121). In particular, it will reflect our assumptions as to whether the education we are engaged in is designed to reproduce or transform existing social systems, whether it is aimed to lead to conformity or to liberation (pages 47–50).

2 *Context* – the learners will also learn much from the way in which the course is organised. There are two main aspects to this:

- The setting – the room, the furniture, the lighting and heating, the levels of noise and other distractions in the immediate learning environment. The amount of attention the teacher gives to these forms part of the curriculum experiences. But it goes further: the building itself, whether formal or non-formal, the location of the course, the social and academic environment in which it is set, whether it is close to or distant from the learner's base, whether the student participant can reach the centre easily or only with difficulty – all of these are part of the learning experiences and will teach the learners much.
- The climate – the atmosphere created in the class session by two sets of relationships, those between teacher and learners and those between learner and learner. The climate, as we have seen, may be warm, informal and open or it may be cold, formal and closed (page 165). In adult education particularly, the climate will reflect how seriously the organisers and teachers take the intentions of the learners, what importance they attach to the expectations and hopes of the student participants.

The most important factor in creating the climate in any programme of adult and continuing education is the staffing of the course. A series of lectures given by different experts may tend not only to create problems for the students in relating both to the teachers and also to the subject-matter (problems of overlap or gaps or contradictions between the material of different lectures, or establishing the relationships between the different material in each lecture); but it will also arouse a number of questions about the nature of knowledge itself and the relationship of the learners to knowledge. Are they expected, for example, to know everything that each of their different lecturers know? If not, which parts are important and which not? Who does knowledge belong to – the expert or the learner? Can the learner ever become an expert, and how? A course with more continuity of teacher–learner contact will reveal a care to help the learner to learn. It will indicate that learning is a continuous process, to be pursued consecutively, not a spasmodic series of events; that learning goes on all the time, not just in the lectures.

Again, frequent and arbitrary changes of timetable to suit the demands of the organisers and/or teacher will teach the learners the level of importance which the agent attaches to the programme – and the learners may begin not to take the course seriously themselves. A commitment to honour the contract to learn, clear indicators that the learners come first in every case, will form part of the learning experiences of the course. These will teach the learners much that is not discussed formally as part of the course.

3 *Content* – the material to be covered clearly forms part of the curriculum. But in addition, there is the *sequence* in which it is handled, and the *conditions* attached to the learning. The sequence is planned to facilitate learning; if a change is introduced because a particular teacher or resource is not available, the participants may learn that the order in which the material is pursued does not much matter. And the level of performance, the speed at which the task should be completed and so on, all form part of the curriculum. What is required of the learner is as much part of the learning experience as the subject-matter itself.

The content of a course is often set out in a syllabus. But syllabuses frequently include elements of methods as well as subject-matter. A management course syllabus may include not just topics such as 'personnel recruitment; selection procedures; career development; staff training; promotion criteria', etc., but also activities such as 'workshops; syndicate work; group discussion with report back to plenary session' and the like.

4 *Events* – the activities which the teacher plans and the learners experience, and the sequence in which they occur are all part of the curriculum. Some events of course occur which are not planned: the interruption of a course because of the weather or the interruption of a class by an organiser or supervisor to collect fees, mark a register or make an announcement, all form part of the learning experiences of the student participants. Such unplanned events will either contribute to or distract from the learning; and one of the traits of an effective teacher is the ability to innovate, to use such happenings as they occur to help forward the learning process, to direct even distractions towards the learners' goals.

5 *Processes of evaluation* – among the experiences of the learners are those planned processes of evaluation – examinations and tests, if they are used; activities for feedback; criticism and assessment; ways in which the learners can express their satisfactions and so on (see pages 221–32). These too form part of the total planned curriculum.

All these five elements go to make up the curriculum. We do not of course spend an equal amount of time on planning each of these but they all contribute to that sequence of experiences and the philosophy which embraces them which together go to make up the learning. It is the curriculum that brings the content and methods of our courses close together.

Approaches to learning

But the link between teaching methods and the contents of the teaching–learning encounter also depends upon the approach which we as teachers adopt towards our courses. An emphasis on content, a set amount of matter that must be covered, to a large extent prescribes the methods to be used in the class/group; while a concentration on methods, the processes of learning, means that relatively less of the content will be dealt with but it will be used as an example of how the rest of the material may be handled by the learners on their own.

The emphasis between these two elements varies according to whether the approach to learning is teacher-centred or learner-centred. This distinction corresponds to what Bruner (1974) describes as the *expository* approach to teaching–learning, in which 'the decisions concerning the mode and pace and style of exposition are principally determined by the teacher as expositor, the student as the listener', and the *hypothetical* approach, in which 'the teacher and the student are in a more co-operative position. . . . The student is not a bench listener but is taking part in the formulation and at times may play the principal role . . . [through] acts of discovery.'

There is on the whole a close correlation between these two sets of approaches. A content-/subject-based approach tends to be teacher-centred, to emphasise the teacher's presentation methods, the sort of activity the teacher engages in in the group; whereas a process-/methods-based approach will be more learner-oriented, more concerned with what the student participants do than with what the teacher does. But this is not necessarily the case, and a matrix (Fig. 36) would seem to be a better model. (It may be helpful to locate your own course on this matrix.)

In the course of our teaching most of us need to adopt varied approaches. Sometimes our work will be teacher-centred, sometimes learner-centred; sometimes it will be concerned with subject-matter, sometimes with process.

Figure 36 Matrix of methods/content in the adult learning process

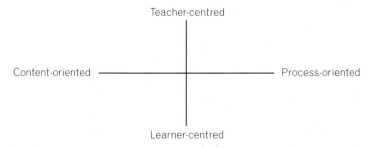

Both Bruner's 'expository' and 'hypothetical' approaches will be called upon at different times. Exposition is a valid tool of the teaching–learning situation, a necessary part of the process; it is one of the basic skills the teacher needs. Despite the protests of some adult educators, especially those in the field of community education, much learning by adults consists of the acquisition of new knowledge. The student participants do need to inform themselves, to learn new processes, to obtain new information and understanding from outside of themselves. They do not possess all the knowledge they need. They can of course do this in a variety of ways; and although presentation is a valid and widely used method of teaching, in order to promote independence of learning, the student participants will need at times to engage in 'acts of discovery' for themselves. The decision as to which approach to adopt will to a large extent be determined by our attitudes towards the balance between content and methods in our courses.

Content

There are two parts to our discussion of the acquisition of new knowledge: the amount of new knowledge needed to complete the learning task, and secondly the ways the students can acquire this new knowledge.

Amount

The amount of knowledge required for any specified learning task is almost always decided by the teacher. The evidence suggests that teachers in adult education regularly overestimate the amount of such 'input'. Many teachers try to insist on what they see as a 'complete' coverage of a topic. There are, it is true, some leisure and recreational courses where the amount of new knowledge is *under*estimated: 'Learn this skill and don't bother with the theory' is sometimes the approach. But there are signs that many adults wish to learn something of the background to the particular process they are engaged in learning, some framework of understanding within which to locate the newly acquired skill meaningfully. On the whole, however, most courses are over- rather than underloaded. Perhaps the reason for this is that teachers tend to take themselves and their own range of knowledge as the norm for their students. They often determine the amount of knowledge needed for the completion of the task by what they themselves know rather than by what the learners need to know. They judge the speed at which the student participants will be able to move by how quickly they themselves can learn. They assess the learners' ability to cope with new knowledge by their own abilities, and they tend to choose the processes of learning by taking the way they learned in the past as the norm. None of this may be correct.

The result is often undue pressure on the student-learner. The teachers set the pace of learning by judging the amount of material they have chosen against the time they have at their disposal, not by the abilities and commitments of the student-learners. The time allowed for the course is often limited; teachers of adults often think that ten meetings of one and a half or two hours each amount to more learning time than is in fact the case. But this is not a long time when seen as an isolated class, outside of any context of learning and against competing pressures on the learners. Also, some of the participants may not be able to go very fast. Acquiring skills and understanding takes time; and adults need to relate their new knowledge and understanding (present experience) to past experience, which also takes time. We may underestimate this and press on, bound by our material and the length of the course.

On the other hand, as teachers we need to recognise that we ourselves experience internal pressures. We have been asked to teach some subject or other, a subject for which we may possess considerable enthusiasm. We have in our minds the amount of material we think the learners *ought* to cover. There is a compulsion on us to round off our subject-matter, to bring the episode of learning to a satisfying conclusion; we will feel unresolved, incomplete, if only part of this matter is dealt with, if the material is 'broken off' before its 'natural end', if the syllabus is not finished.

This compulsion may encourage us to employ formal modes of presentation (lectures and the like). It is not inevitable that a concern for the comprehensive nature of the content of the course and the expository methods should go together. It is possible to choose an excess of material to be covered while trying to use participatory methods, just as one can combine a more realistic assessment of the amount of new knowledge needed with formal methods of instruction. But on the whole the pressure of trying to cover a good deal of subject-matter in a limited time leads to a concentration by teachers on their own presentation of the material to more or less passive students, and teachers tend to resist efforts to pursue anything other than the main line of the learning process. How many adult classes have sat there and heard a teacher say, 'I can't deal with that point now; I must get on'?

Yet there is no reason why the teacher 'must get on'; it is the learners who must get on. Relatively few adult classes still have externally set syllabuses to be covered and examinations to be passed, though the number of these is increasing. Even when these exist, it is more important that our student participants learn than that we complete for our own satisfaction the whole course. Many of the student participants will expect us to cover the ground, to deal with most of the important topics of the subject-matter, whether it be skills-related or knowledge-based. But if covering the whole of the material means going so fast that the learner cannot learn deeply enough and with understanding, then the class is not effective. What is the point in completing the syllabus if the learner does not really learn?

In most cases, such pressure is not only harmful; it is unnecessary. For the main aim of our work as teachers is to create more effective learners, people who will carry on their own learning when our course is over. They do not need to learn 'everything' from us. A view claiming that complete coverage of the subject-matter is desirable in an adult learning group is based on the assumption that the learners cannot be trusted with their own learning, that they can learn only when a teacher is present.

It is far better to help the students learn how to learn more effectively by concentrating on part of the syllabus and to let them do the rest for themselves than to try to teach them everything. A course on 'keep fit' does not need to cover all aspects of the subject; as new fashions of exercise and new equipment continue to become available, the range of learning is constantly widening, and the learners will need to cope with these for themselves. Similarly, a Church history course that sets out to cover the entire range from the Early Church through the Reformation to the modern Church will make unrealistic demands on both teacher and student participants. To concentrate instead on part of this field, however much it may offend the susceptibilities of academic or ecclesiastical authorities, may well provide the students with both a greater sense of satisfaction (intrinsic motivation) which will lead to a desire to pursue the learning further, and at the same time an acquaintance with the methods of continued learning to enable them to do so. By examining one or two shorter periods in depth, the learners will learn more of how to study history than a teacher-presented overview will teach them. The purpose of teaching adults is to help them to continue learning, not to teach them all they know and thus stop them from carrying on learning.

Methods of acquiring new knowledge

The adult learner needs to acquire new knowledge: practical knowledge of processes (how to do something), factual knowledge (data), and theoretical knowledge (concepts). The teacher is there not to *impart* anything – skills, knowledge or information – to the student participants but to help the learners to acquire these for themselves. We cannot impart literacy or the skills to run a cooperative, a knowledge of politics or an understanding of healing; the learners develop these for themselves. Our task is to help and encourage them to learn.

Research and experience suggest that the more active the student-learners are, the more effective is the learning process; the more passive they are, the less deep will be the learning. Figure 37 indicates those processes that are seen to be most potent in achieving learning, ranked on a scale from 1 to 6. As may be seen, a high emphasis is placed on student-centred activities, especially those in which the student participant engages with the teacher and/or with the material directly.

Substantial amounts of teacher-centred activity may not advance the cause of greater student learning. The straight lecture is one of the most inefficient methods of teaching. It calls for very advanced learning skills on the part of the listener (concentration over a long time, adaptation of the mental images and the use of trial-and-error learning *at the same time* as listening to yet further material, etc.), and the rate of forgetting the subject-matter is high

Figure 37 The figures indicate the relative effectiveness of these methods – 6 being high, 2 being low

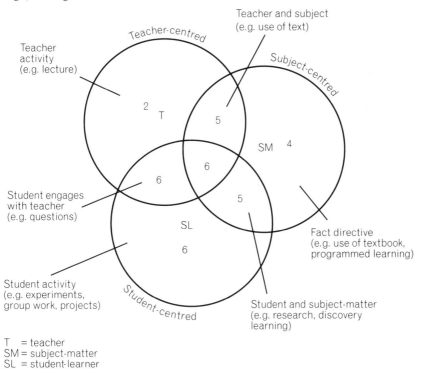

T   = teacher
SM = subject-matter
SL = student-learner

('What I hear, I forget; what I see, I remember; what I do, I learn'). Too often the lecturers choose their own ground to discuss rather than the concerns of the students, and there is little opportunity for feedback or further exploration, except perhaps at the end. So the listeners have to retain in their minds the points they wish to make or questions to ask while still paying attention to the next points the lecturer is making.

On some occasions a lecture has value – when summing up a previous complicated discussion, for instance, or when introducing an overview of a new area of study, or when as a part of the learning process one might say to the other participants, 'Allow me for a time without interruption to explore the implications of a particular argument to see where it leads us.' But these will all call for special learning skills on the part of the student participants, and they will thus be most appropriate to limited numbers of adult students. In every case the teacher could well ask whether there are other, more active, more effective ways in which the student-learners could acquire the new knowledge: by reading a text, by discussion, by discovery methods, and so on. There nearly always are better methods than direct exposition by the teacher.

Authoritarianism and unlearning

A combination of teacher-chosen subject-matter, teacher-determined amount of knowledge and teacher-presented material can create one of the greatest obstacles to effective adult learning: authoritarianism. Authoritarianism is not confined to the teacher; it can also attach itself to other statements such as a textbook or hand-out. There are several reasons for avoiding excessive reliance on such statements: the adulthood of the student-learners, the fact that their well-established learning patterns are usually based on testing the validity of all statements against their experience, the fact that such statements normally lay new patterns of knowledge (authority) on top of older patterns without disturbing them. A different approach, which disturbs the existing pattern of understandings, is needed. This calls for a range of social skills and attitudes towards the learner that the teacher of adults will come to only gradually (see pages 170–3).

There is a device used by social workers in group work that can be employed usefully by teachers seeking to avoid too great a reliance upon authoritative pronouncements. Instead of speaking to the student partici- pants in confrontation terms ('Do this . . .' or some other form of instruc- tion), we might (for a short time only – it would become too artificial otherwise) use the phrase 'I think that . . .' before each such communication ('I think that you might do this', etc.).

Once more a balance is necessary. At times the dynamics of the situation will call for the teacher to be assertive, for instance when constructing a learn- ing exercise or perhaps in relation to a participant who persistently slows down the group (see pages 195–202). The teacher will then want to be con- scious of the reactions of the other participants if the work of the class is being held up by one person. The sensitivity of the teacher to the needs and inten- tions of the individual learners and to the needs and intentions of the whole group will dictate the approach (i.e. methods and content) to be used.

The teachable moment

Teaching is not just a mechanical process; and teachers are not made to a set recipe, a packet of this, a pinch of that. Each teaching–learning situation (especially with adults) is unique, calling for innovation on the part of the teacher, untried and individual responses to new circumstances, the courage and willingness to venture into new methods, to experiment, to dare. All the skills, knowledge, experience, attitudes, understanding and emotions of the teacher come to be focused on to the one moment in which the learning may be successful. Once past, the opportunity may be lost. That moment should be flexible, not set by any textbook or manual of teaching; it should be inspired. Teaching is an event, a fusion of enthusiasm, of adaptability, of reacting on the spur of the moment.

Learning too consists of the same sort of inspiration, the catching of enthusiasm. It comes from encounter, interaction – either person-to-person interaction or learner-and-material interaction. Some people have seen this engagement in terms of struggle; a learner struggles to 'master' a new skill, subject, a tool or concept, and to use the new material. But it is perhaps better to see this interaction as a 'spark' between two poles, which fires the imagination, illuminates new fields, motivates the learner, gives power and throws light on new ways of looking at reality.

Such interactive learning requires three contributions from the learners: the use of their experience (it is increasingly appreciated that all forms of learning, even of young children, are dependent on what is already possessed by the learner and the way the new material engages with what is there); the exercise of their learning abilities (intelligence and learning skills); and effort (practice of the technique, reflection on the new material, collection of data, discrimination between the various elements of the learned matter). In determining the methods to be used in teaching, we should bear in mind these requirements on the part of the learners and provide them with opportunities

- to use their experience;
- to exercise their learning abilities;
- and to practise.

Teacher activity

Does this emphasis on the practical and direct involvement of the learner with the subject-matter mean that the teacher has nothing to do other than to set the tasks and watch the learners do them? Real learning can be going on in a group when everyone (especially the teacher) is silent, and perhaps we should try this more often. The existentialists have shown us that it is in the silence that those moments of crisis lie – moments of decision, of rearrangement, of change; and it is noteworthy that in some adult groups the student participants, rather than the teacher, try to avoid silence by any means.

But the role of the teacher is more than that of overseer and taskmaster. There are four main areas of activity:

1 Determining *the general approach* of the class – the goals of the learning, whether the programme will be curriculum- or process-oriented; whether the student participants are intended to learn something or to learn how to learn something (some may wish to do both at the same time). Our concern in this part of the task is with the end product: what the student-learners will have achieved by the end of the course. We cannot avoid taking up some sort of attitude towards this; it underlies everything that we and our student participants do together. We make a decision on this even when we are not conscious of doing so.

2 Selecting *what* will be learned, choosing the material and the way it is marshalled in order for learning. The overall subject of the programme will have been agreed by all members, but in general the detailed content of a learning opportunity on computers, keep fit, art, management or nutrition will be the concern of the teacher.

3 Deciding *how much* of this material can be covered in the time available – what will most help the learning process and what can be left to a later stage. As we have seen, most of us tend to overestimate the amount that adult learners can cover; it would be better to underestimate and surprise ourselves and perhaps the learners.

4 Determining *how* the student participants will engage with the material – whether they will watch and practise for themselves, whether they will listen, read, discuss, write, practise and so on. We will determine the steps the learners will need to take in order to complete the task, to learn the process or the subject-matter.

The learning steps

Such learning steps will be cumulative and sequential; they combine to make a course. Each of the learners will engage in them for themselves. Some writers have analysed the stages by which a new skill or concept is learned. One such list is as follows:

- *Stage 1* – 'Play': this is the encounter stage, when the learners meet the new elements, gain familiarity with them, lose their fears and begin to experiment – perhaps playing it backwards or asking 'Does it *always* work?', etc. A good deal of time is often needed for this stage.
- *Stage 2* – 'Structured play': trial-and-error exercises are planned. The material and situations are so arranged to lead in a certain direction, i.e. to stage 3. This stage too must not be rushed, it takes time.
- *Stage 3* – 'Grasping': the material 'falls into place'; it is related to other material, mostly by insightful learning – it 'clicks', makes sense, becomes 'real' or 'true'.
- *Stage 4* – 'Mastery': practice, not just learning but using, exploring the material or process further, discovering more relationships and properties, obtaining mastery over it. This in turn leads to further learning needs and intentions, new skills or concepts. The process is a dynamic ongoing one.

Such steps call upon us to set for ourselves and for the participants clear signposts throughout the programme of learning, indicating the point reached and the relationship of what is being done to what has gone before and what will follow. This is an important task for the teacher, often overlooked. Some student-learners may not be able to see the overall structure that we have in our minds unless we make special efforts to clarify it as we go along. Some sense of this structure of the learning process is required for effective learning to take place.

In this way the teacher sets the curriculum, the syllabus and the schedule of work for the group. This should as often as possible be done in discussion with the group, but in the end it is the teacher's responsibility. This task calls for a series of skills that are part of the essential equipment the teacher needs and which can be practised and learned:

- The skill of determining what is needed to achieve the goal – what basic concepts, facts and techniques are required to perform the task and how they relate to each other.
- The skill of selecting the tasks most suitable and of grading them in sequence. Again these will be related to each other, not isolated or compartmentalised. The relationship may be *vertical* (one task can be attempted only after another has been successfully mastered) or *horizontal* (a parallel task at the same level of complexity) or *oblique* (a mixture of both of these). Several of these tasks will overlap with others.
- The skill of breaking down the subject-matter and processes into steps for learning. For this activity we need to learn something of what goes on in the process of learning, based partly on theory and partly on experience of what works in practice.
- The skill of identifying and selecting the resources to be used – the equipment, materials, objects and texts, sequence of demonstrations, words of the teacher, discussions. We will devise some of this material for ourselves, other parts we will take from elsewhere. It is our task to choose, arrange and often present it; this is what the students will expect of us.

Methods

We have begun to see how the teacher selects the methods of the learning group. We need now to look at this in more detail.

Most teachers underestimate the number of different teaching–learning techniques available to choose from. We often tend to be unimaginative in this part of our work. In one group of teachers, we listed 49 different teaching–learning techniques by using a brainstorming session, and that did not exhaust the possibilities (see Fig. 38). Recent research suggests that when teachers feel unsure of themselves, threatened by inexperience, by new material, by lack of time or self-doubt, they frequently revert to those teaching methods by which they were themselves taught; perhaps we should all watch for this and see it for what it is. We need to think about and identify different methods, to experiment with them and select those that seem to suit us and our student participants for each particular purpose. We should test whether this or that method does in fact fit the students' learning practices and, if not, choose another one. We need to practise too, until we can use them effectively. A new method may not always go well for the first few occasions it is employed. We should also try out other methods with which we are less familiar. We can learn much about teaching while we are teaching.

The basic range

Methods may be divided into four main categories:

- *presentation* methods (teacher activities such as demonstration, exposition, use of blackboard, text or audio-visual media);
- *participatory* methods (interaction between teacher and learner, or learner and learner, such as questions, discussion, buzz-groups);
- *discovery* methods (in which the learners on their own or in groups work on tasks, exploring and discovering knowledge for themselves through practice, experiments, reading, writing).

In addition, the techniques we may adopt to *evaluate* the learning already done (tests, quizzes, role play) will in themselves become the means for further learning (Rogers 1992).

Figure 38
In the space below:
- List any teaching methods you can think of; you can add to it as time goes on and as new ideas or experiences present themselves.
- Indicate against each item whether it is *primarily* a teacher activity (T), a learner activity (L) or group activity (G).
- Mark those that are more content-oriented (C) and those that are more process-oriented (P).

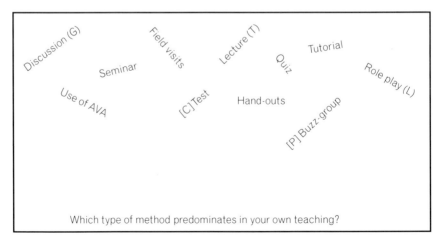

Which type of method predominates in your own teaching?

These vary from each other in the nature of the transactions involved. The first set are largely one-way, the others are two-way or more. They are normally closely related to each other, being built up into a complex range of activities. Thus exploratory methods may be followed by interaction methods as the learners present the results of their activities to the teacher for evaluation. And not all of these take place in the classroom; field visits and excursions frequently partake of all four kinds of method during the course of the activity.

The different methods can be divided in other ways. There are those, such as demonstrations, the use of texts, lectures, hand-outs, that are more concerned with the subject-matter of the course. Others, like simulation exercises and projects, are more concerned with the process of learning. Equally they may be divided into those that are primarily teacher activity, student activity or group activity (see Fig. 38).

Exercise

Looking again at the adult educational programme which you have chosen, which group of teaching–learning methods predominate in your course planning?

Presentation?

Participatory?

Discovery?

Evaluatory?

The basis of the selection

The determination of the approach most appropriate to the particular teaching–learning situation depends on a number of factors, of which the following are examples:

- the area(s) of learning involved: whether it is *primarily* skills, knowledge, understanding or attitudes;
- the need to get the learner actively engaged in the process of learning;
- the learning styles of the student participants, what they prefer and what they are able to do;
- the demands of the subject itself;
- the availability of resources.

Decisions on all these matters can often be taken jointly by teacher and learners, not by the teacher alone.

If, then, our classes and groups are really to promote learning, four things seem to be necessary, as Dewey pointed out (*How We Think*, 1933):

- An *experience* on the part of the learner. The learning group is an experience that ought to be maximised. 'All genuine education comes about through experience.'
- A *climate* in which the learners play their part in structuring the learning process, where there is 'a concern for the development of persons . . . [where] the growth of people has precedence over the accomplishment of things'.
- *Continuity* of encounter. The process of learning builds on what is already there. The present experience of the learning group must be related in the learner's mind to past experience; the latter must be used by the teacher, not left passive. 'Continuity of experience means that every experience both takes up something from those which have gone before and modifies in some way the quality of those which come after.'
- *Interaction* between the learner and the new material, either through the teacher, or directly, by practice; interaction between what is outside and what is inside the learner.

Student engagement

Many adult students seem to expect and even prefer teacher-centred and content-oriented methods. Some recent studies have suggested that in clearly goal-oriented classes (directed towards an examination, for example), where the learners themselves feel the speed of learning is more important than depth of learning and thus a leisurely pace cannot be afforded, the students achieved more of their intentions in a teacher-centred environment. Even outside these contexts, it is often urged that active learning methods are slow, that the material can be dealt with more quickly if the teacher instructs and expounds and the learners watch or listen. This is true. Much more ground can be 'covered' by expository methods than by participatory methods. But 'covering the ground' is not the purpose of the exercise; the goal is learning. The learners may listen but in listening they may not learn what the teacher intends.

Further, it is sometimes argued that such varied methods are not appropriate to some subjects or in some contexts. How can they be applied, for instance, to music appreciation, which will tend to involve listening to records often over long periods? A little imagination on the part of the teacher will quickly suggest a variety of methods, all appropriate to the subject-matter, apart from the ubiquitous discussion that dominates so many adult classes or learning groups. Why should not the student participants write their own programme notes or record-sleeve introductions or reviews of particular recordings? Why should not some of them present to other group members in a structured way a complete concert programme – why one piece of music 'goes' or does not 'go' with another? Why, in fact, should not the student participants do most if not all of the tasks that we as teachers reserve for ourselves?

It is not however just a case of the teacher devising situations in which the learners can use their new learning; it is a question of approaching the learners in a new way. Too often we treat the student participants as if they are totally incompetent or ignorant and have to be taught everything. But instead of seeing them as a long way from a finishing post, a long way from being able to make a table or to discriminate in music, for instance, we can begin to treat them in the learning group as if they have (at least in part) already arrived. Training courses in management have for a long time realised this truth; they do not treat the learners as trainees but as managers who are working under supervision and evaluation. Equally a local history teacher can treat the members as active local historians rather than simply listeners or readers who benefit from the work and knowledge of others but who are excluded from finding out new knowledge by and for themselves. A woodworking teacher can treat the participants as if they were to a large extent already capable of making what they want to make rather than entirely unskilful. A music appreciation group can view the student-learners as being knowledgeable, discriminating and appreciative listeners to music rather than completely ignorant and with no ear for music at all. Many of the students who come to adult education classes will cast themselves in the role of ignoramuses – 'you must teach us everything' (see page 65). It will be hard for the teacher to encourage these persons to learn by doing, by reflecting critically on what they already know and what they can already do, when they wish to learn by preparing for doing, when they seek to learn what they think they do not know or cannot do.

Such student engagement in learning activities cannot be restricted to those periods *between* each group meeting or class session while treating the learners as passive listeners *during* the class meeting. The way we treat the student participants *in* class and the methods of learning we select for them to use at other times should be consistent in approach. Further, even for adults it is not usually adequate for us to *tell* a group of learners what to do but rather to demonstrate it, to do it with them as a first run-through, whether it is woodwork or music appreciation. Student activity begins in class.

The teaching steps

The teacher's concern for the student participants' learning through active learning, the promotion of critical reflection on experience followed by action (CRE + A), thus comes to focus on four main points, each associated with a range of teaching–learning activities.

The learners need to encounter the material directly for themselves. The material can be embodied in the teacher – but this may make for dependency. The materials then should be separated from *the means of conveyance*, be

Figure 39 Applying the learning cycle to teaching adults

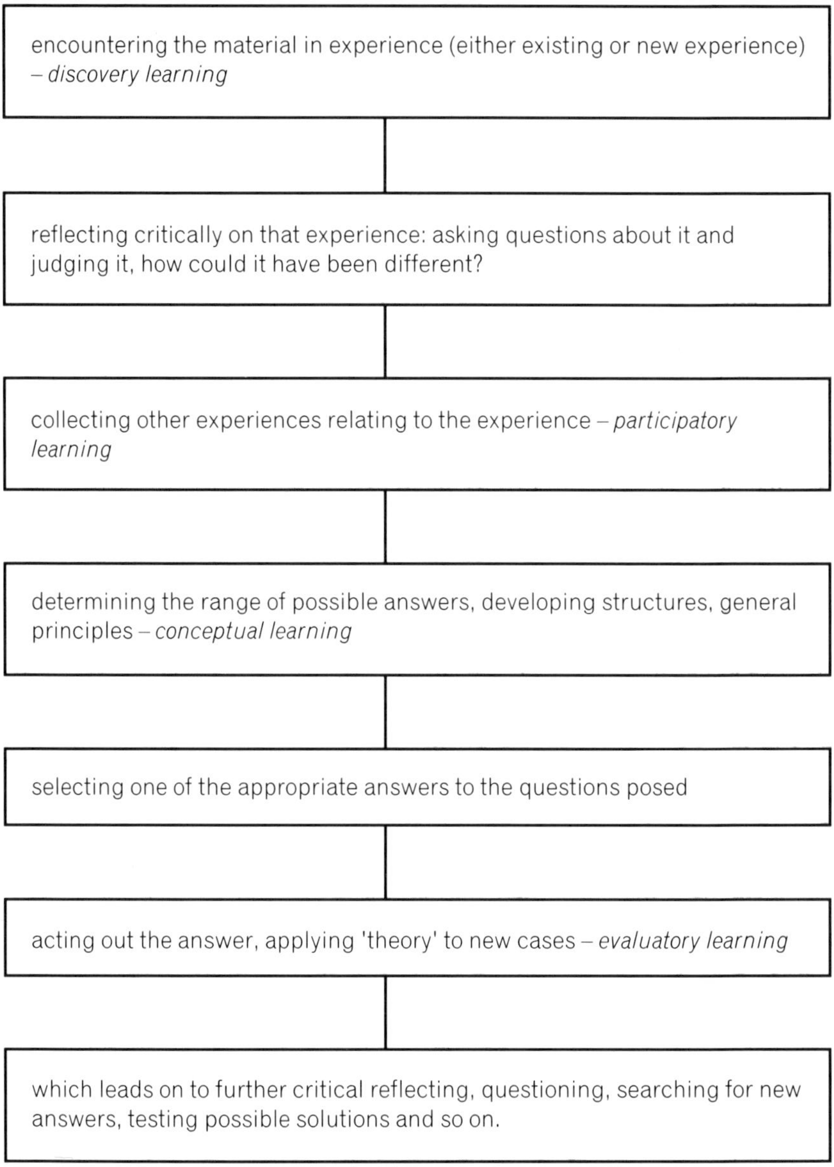

encountering the material in experience (either existing or new experience) – *discovery learning*

reflecting critically on that experience: asking questions about it and judging it, how could it have been different?

collecting other experiences relating to the experience – *participatory learning*

determining the range of possible answers, developing structures, general principles – *conceptual learning*

selecting one of the appropriate answers to the questions posed

acting out the answer, applying 'theory' to new cases – *evaluatory learning*

which leads on to further critical reflecting, questioning, searching for new answers, testing possible solutions and so on.

that teacher, film or book. This can be done by using more than one con- veyance for the same material (which incidentally reinforces the teaching– learning material) or by helping the student-learners to draw on their own experience or by creating opportunities for the participants to have a new direct experience of the subject-matter.

The student learners' activities should be *productive* – mastering processes, answering questions as actively as possible; not just watching or listening but doing, reading, writing, talking, etc. Only if the learners are engaged in meaningful, relevant activities will they learn and change. New skills will thus be grasped, new knowledge be acquired permanently, new understandings and concepts be formed.

The student participants need to understand that *learning is the task* they are engaged in. They need to continue to learn how to learn, with encouragement. They should spend the maximum amount of time on this process.

The student participants need to realise that learning is *not a matter of rote memorising* of processes and facts but a complicated matter of asking and answering questions, finding solutions, practising skills, spotting relationships and linkages, constructing explanations, making 'maps' in the mind. They need also to come to realise that this is done by producing fabricated work or written or spoken words, both for an immediate check by themselves and for a more considered check by others.

Such considerations as these help us to choose the most appropriate methods of learning – not just a demonstration (of flower arranging, say) by an expert but a fumbling practice by the learner, followed by an evaluation by the learner, by the teacher and even on occasion by other student participants as well; not just a lecture (on psychology, say) but a series of carefully constructed observational analyses and role plays; not just a slide show (on historical architecture) but the development of a new sense of awareness by looking at buildings in the neighbourhood; not just reading a text but the construction of an argument on the basis of the material contained in it.

Teaching

The role of the teacher of adults is thus wider than just that of a demonstrator, lecturer, presenter of information. Rather, the teacher constructs a sequence of learning activities for the student participants to engage in. But this does not mean that the traditional instructional activities are inappropriate to a teacher; we need both types of skill.

What, then, makes a good teacher of adults? At least four sets of things appear to be necessary:

First, a series of *attitudes towards the student-learners* – concern, sensitivity and support; attitudes of flexibility and innovativeness; a willingness to experiment, to adapt the material to meet the specific needs of the learning group, not just be stuck with one set of teaching–learning methods and content; and *attitudes towards the subject-matter*, an enthusiasm for the material and its philosophy.

Secondly, a *clear understanding of the philosophy of adult teaching*; for the effectiveness of what we do depends to a very large extent on the clarity with which we hold the logic frame of our activity. We need to know and understand the concepts of adult learning and adult teaching.

Thirdly, we need to develop *the skills of teaching* – of planning, of communication, of counselling, of evaluating – as well as the competencies which our subject-matter itself will demand:

- *Planning skills* – selection of teaching–learning strategies and the effective use of learning resources.
- *Communication skills* – the development of means of communication and a sensitivity as to how effective these are, an awareness of when (for example) the wrong message may have been received from the presentation. It is surprising how few teachers can place themselves in the position of the receiver of their messages, how often they use vocabulary, concepts and sentence construction way beyond some of the participants, how often they present written forms of language rather than spoken when expounding to the student-learners.
- *Caring-guidance skills* – counselling the participants, adjusting the learning tasks to the needs, intentions and capabilities of the individual learner.
- *Evaluation skills* – identifying the goals, monitoring progress and evaluating the usefulness of the learning process; presenting such evaluations to the participants.
- *Subject skills* – competencies in the subject-matter of the course; continued learning in this area.

But above all, we need to possess a measure of *self-confidence and self-respect* based on a belief in one's own competence, a feeling that will quickly communicate itself to the student-learners. Adult participants need to respect us as teachers in order to accept willingly the learning tasks we set for them, to adapt themselves to the methods we adopt for the class. This respect comes about only when we respect ourselves.

Working at teaching

We must not become too confident, however; and not confident without the skills and attitudes to go with it. It has been said that in adult education, as elsewhere in the educational world, there are no bad students; that if there is a failure to learn, or if attendance falls off, this is because the teacher has not prepared an adequate programme of learning or adopted appropriate teaching–learning methods. This may not always be true; but we must not expect our task to be an easy one. It is difficult, lengthy and at times tedious. We may have to prepare our own teaching material, adapted to the needs and intentions of the particular group of adult learners we are helping, which may be equivalent to writing and experimenting with a good-sized textbook with exercises. Even when we are able to use material prepared by others, we still need to fit it in with each situation, with each student group, and this too can be a time-consuming process. The teacher of adults cannot rush into teaching without preparation, relying on our experience and expertise to help us flannel our way through – though some adult teachers do this. Preparation and choice between alternatives lie at the heart of the process.

Note: Facing some problems in an adult learning group*

We are all faced with many problems in the course of our teaching of adults, and with experience we learn how to solve most of them. But even the most experienced teacher never learns how to solve all of them. So we need not be discouraged. But this suggests that it will be useful, both for our own sake as teachers as for our students' sake, to secure some line of communication outside the situation so that there is someone with whom we can talk the problem over.

The main point is to be sensitive to the existence of a problem. Once we are aware of this, the task of solution often becomes less difficult. Some people have this sensitivity from the start; others have to learn it the hard way. It would be a good thing, as a first step, if we can *decide where we stand on this issue of sensitivity*, whether we think we are or are not aware of how our group members are reacting to our teaching. But even if we are among those to whom such awareness comes easily, it will still be helpful for us to *arrange as many and as varied channels of feedback* as we can, so that we can keep ourselves informed of how well our student participants are doing and how they feel about aspects of the work.

A few of the more common situations that can arise are listed here, and some of the ways of dealing with them are suggested. The solution to any problem that works well on one occasion may not work equally well another time; each situation in adult education is unique. Thus the suggestions listed here are not meant to be prescriptive. In most cases there are several possible ways of coping with a problem, which need to be tested out at our discretion, so that eventually we can evolve our own ways of meeting such situations.

The primary attribute of the teacher of adults, above all, is *tact*. What is stated here briefly and on occasion baldly could be disastrous unless the execution of it fits into the normal pattern of our relationships with our student-learners. An artificial reaction based on a set of instructions in a teaching manual, bringing with it an abrupt change of classroom climate, could be ruinous for the work of the group. We thus need to choose a tactic that suits our own teaching style and adapt it; we must take our time over it.

---

* This section is based upon a paper first written by Dr Sam Lilley of Nottingham, but freely adapted here. The paper has been used in a modified form in the Nottingham University Tutors' Resource Kit.

Problems involving individual student participants

Persistent talkers

It is important not to let them wreck the group. Their behaviour can generate considerable anger amongst the other members, and this will rebound on
to us as teachers unless we are seen to take some steps to limit their impact
on the group.

To begin with, a gentle approach may succeed: 'Let's hear what the others
have to say first.' If that doesn't work, they may have to be taken on one side
and spoken to, either by ourselves or by one of the more respected participants.

If gentle tactics fail, slowly increasing firmness may be necessary. Take
advice before going too far along this route. 'You really must give the others
a fair chance' can lead on to a firm indication that, by monopolising the discussion, the over-talker is spoiling the enjoyment of everyone else. (We must
not forget, however, that they may have a following in the group.) Such
remarks could first be made privately, but after a time the group will expect
us as teacher and group leader to adopt a firm line in public. We risk losing
a group member, but this is usually a smaller risk than we think; and in any
case ruining a learning group is worse than losing one member.

The monomaniac

The person who raises essentially the same issue in every session is fortu-
nately relatively rare. A simple statement that they have already mentioned
the point in question and an appeal to stop is worth trying but unlikely to
succeed. Fairly harsh measures may become necessary at an earlier stage than
with the persistent talker. We can try to pre-empt the particular contribution;
when setting out the work to be done, we might end with the words that 'So-
and-so will no doubt say that . . .', summarising their point in perhaps a
quarter of the time they would take; we could even involve the person directly
– 'That's how you would put it, isn't it? – but allowing them little or no time
to develop the discussion by bringing in the rest of the group. One can go
further and prime other members of the group to speak up: 'We've heard that
often enough; let's talk of something else.' Sometimes we can even develop
our own contract with a monomaniac – give them a set time to present their
views on condition that they agree not to raise the point again. But they may
not keep the bargain, and a firmer line may be necessary in the end.

The mouse

A reticent member may refuse to be drawn into any discussion or group
activity. This needs great care and tact, for the causes of the reticence are

rarely clear. Unlike the cases above, the loss of a shy person as a result of tactlessly applied pressure would deny the whole purpose of the adult group.

We could perhaps try to persuade the member to talk outside of the group session – before the meeting starts, after it ends or during refreshments – to ourselves or to another participant. It may be possible to find out some opinions they hold, some skill or experience they possess; we can then try to guide the work of the group into these fields so that eventually they can fittingly (but never easily) make some contribution. Even then the hoped-for participation may not be forthcoming, and we may have to put words into their mouth: 'I was impressed with what so-and-so was saying to me . . .' We could then repeat the point, perhaps not quite accurately or with doubt expressed about some aspect of it; this may at last provoke an interjection. And once the ice is broken . . .

An alternative is to increase the contribution these members can make to the group by getting them to prepare a particular piece of work. It may then turn out that at some point this person is the only one with the relevant skill or knowledge to help forward the group's work. In this case, still using caution so that they do not feel too exposed, we can ask them directly to join in. It is useful to keep an eye on them (but not too obviously) as the programme continues; a frown or raised eyebrow, a drawn breath or a change in posture may indicate the one moment in the session (even perhaps in the whole course) when something is ready to burst out. We need then to abandon all else to make this happen if the student is to be freed to become a participant.

Sometimes the use of sub-groups will help such a student to participate. But some group members are so reticent that even the most experienced teacher is unable to extract a contribution from them during the whole programme. Because of this, we can never be sure that any progress is being made at all. Yet the person still may benefit from the course. Active participation by all the members is a desirable goal of all learning situations, but ideals are never fully attained.

More serious is the case of a whole group of reticent members, who may even sit together in silent sympathy. They may think of themselves as less skilful, less knowledgeable or slower thinkers than the others. Equally it could be our own fault for concentrating our attention on a few more congenial learners. Such a group needs careful attention, as we shall see below.

The alternative expert

One member may continually remind the group that they are more knowledgeable than us in some part of the subject. We are often asked by our student participants to teach on the limits of our subject; indeed, on occasion we are challenged on aspects of the subject about which we know little or nothing. In these circumstances, a person who asserts publicly that they know a good deal about some part of the subject can be looked upon by us and/or the rest of the group as an alternative expert.

This person is exceptional only in degree. Every group member knows something relevant to the subject that the teacher doesn't know; and they must all be given the opportunity to teach the others what they know. It is not always easy to discover what that something is; but if we can find it, every student participant can have their own teaching moment.

But for this particular person, the expert, there is usually no such problem. They often parade their special knowledge at every possible moment, perhaps with a display of more or less deference to our role as teacher. They may even deny our right to teach. We could find this threatening. We need to accept the situation – indeed, we can make them feel welcome, for they can be valuable teaching assistance. They almost certainly respect our general position, our expertise or experience, or they would stop coming to the group. In return we need to respect their expertise and involve them from time to time in the work of the group as teacher of either the whole or part of the group. Maybe they will show themselves knowledgeable but unskilled in teaching adults, in which case we can help them in this respect; and in doing so, we too will learn about teaching adults. Watching others teaching, and talking to them about their teaching, is an instructive experience.

It may be that the alternative expert comes to the group simply because it provides them with an easy platform to demonstrate their knowledge and skills. They are less concerned with the rest of the members learning something than with showing off. It is not easy to cope with this, for these people tend to be thick-skinned. One possible strategy is to formalise the situation as they would wish it to be for a short time. We could give them the opportunity to take over from us formally for a time. They may then learn that their knowledge, although deep, is too limited to sustain them over a lengthy period face to face with the student participants. It may be that the rest of the group will indicate their preference for us as teacher. Equally, they may not!

Problems concerning the working group

The mixed group

This group contains members of varied abilities and/or experience and/or knowledge. As we have seen, any group of adults will comprise a wide range in terms of age, existing knowledge, experience and willingness to learn from that experience, skills, attitudes and learning abilities. We may in time come to regard the mixed-ability situation as an advantage, a widening of the teaching opportunities open to us. But for the moment:

1 We do not need to feel that we have ourselves to do all the work of teaching. On carefully chosen occasions, we can ask those who know most or

have more verbal facility to explain a point to the ones who know almost nothing on the subject or are slower thinkers. We may be surprised how much the 'learned' will expose their own weaknesses – and set about remedying them; equally how much the weaker members can flourish. The group will become rather more homogeneous as time goes on.

2 On the other hand, we could teach a sub-group of the class. No group objects to a teacher who spends time now and again on an elementary explanation of some process or concept for those who need it, or another two or three minutes making a special point that only the most knowledgeable or skilled appreciate. It is surprising what can be done for the more advanced members of the group by means of a few well-chosen asides.

3 We may be able to satisfy the demands (or some of them) of the more advanced and well informed at some occasion outside of the group meeting. It is often possible to ask those who require some special 'bridging' provision to come a few minutes early or to stay behind for a short while.

4 Dividing the group into smaller groups in order to give each of them the special attention they need – provided the other members are engaged in meaningful tasks, either as individuals or in their own small group – is a useful strategy that paradoxically makes the entire group cohere more strongly. The use of sub-groups to maximise learning is a key element in the teacher's armoury. There are many kinds of sub-group, selected on different criteria: by ability (though the dangers of 'streaming' remain as true in adult education as in schooling), or mixed-ability groups working on different or the same assigned exercises. Sub-groups throw up their own structures, and we can help or hinder this by choosing or not choosing a leader/chairperson who may or may not be the same as the *rapporteur* (if one is needed). We need to experiment with various forms of sub-grouping.

5 Perhaps the most rewarding, but the most difficult, procedure is to adopt an unorthodox and original approach to the topic, to use materials that the knowledgeable have never seen before and that keep both beginner and more advanced interested. This requires a lot of time and resources, and it may be that the full-time adult teacher will be able to work out such approaches more fully than the part-time teacher. It would be useful for us to keep in touch with any full-time subject specialist we may know; they will probably have teaching material and/or methods that are new to us, which they may be only too glad to share.

6 The class/group meetings are not the only times available for learning to take place. The use of differential tasks (not the same work set for all participants like school homework) to be done individually between sessions helps to overcome the problems of disparate learning groups. We need to structure these carefully, and be prepared to give time to discussing this work with the participants.

In the end, however, all the members of the group start at different places and, using skills and aptitudes that vary markedly, end up at different places. Our objective is not to make all the learners alike, not to bring them all up to the same 'high' standard but to enable them to get the best out of themselves, each at their own level.

The duologue

A group may degenerate into a dialogue between the teacher and one member (or a very few). The danger is greatest when a participant has presented some piece of finished work for us or the group as a whole to evaluate. One possible answer is to get the fellow members to do their evaluation before we take part. But the teacher and the individual participant may be the only people present who have adequate knowledge of the subject under review, and it is natural for us to address our comments entirely to this one participant, which reinforces the exclusiveness of the situation. We need to remember that others are present also, to embrace them with our looks, to keep our eyes open for some slight change of expression or posture that will reveal the time when we can invite someone else to join in. Sometimes direct questions can be thrown out to the other members: 'What do you think about that?'

The mêlée

On occasion two or three topics get all mixed up. This arises (particularly in discussion groups) largely because members of the group, instead of listening to and addressing their attention to what has gone before, are anxious to deliver themselves of what they have prepared, while other group members may continue to concentrate on earlier subjects of group work. We cannot afford to let this go on too long; the intermingling of different material causes confusion and mis-learning. We may have to turn martinet for a short period and insist that the issues be sorted out so that each can be dealt with separately. To prevent people thinking that they are being cheated of what is their concern, we can make a list (perhaps on the blackboard, flipchart or overhead projector for all to see) of the different topics to be covered and tick them off one by one. The chances are that the subjects turn out to have more in common with each other than appeared at first sight.

The irrelevant topic

A question may come up at the wrong time. We may be in the middle of a carefully prepared demonstration or presentation, intended to develop a clear logical sequence, when suddenly a participant pops in with a question or comment that may be relevant but will divert attention away from the main point. Or it may be a question we intended to raise rather later on. Do we answer now or ask the participant to wait?

The act of teaching adults involves continual judgements on matters like this. Sometimes we get it right and sometimes wrong. We have to think on our feet.

The matter is relatively simple if the question reveals ignorance of something essential for the success of the demonstration or presentation; we should deal with that issue before going any further. We may feel inclined to do the same, even if the question is a hindrance to the group session, if the comment or question comes from one of the more retiring members who rarely makes a contribution. Sometimes the interruption will have less of an effect on our carefully prepared material than we think; at least there may be several strings to our answer that can lead back to the main topic.

On the other hand, we need not be too hesitant about asking members to wait until later for us to deal with their point. We can briefly explain at what stage in the session the matter will be handled and ask that it be postponed until then. Making a note of the matter or doing something to convince the questioner that the issue will not be evaded is useful; many students have had experience of education that is designed to avoid answering difficult questions and they may expect the same of us. We must be sure to deal with the matter in the end, perhaps with some recognition of the value of the participant having raised it at all.

The missing group

Sometimes only two people turn up: it happens to most of us occasionally. The first thing to do is to try to avoid it by persuading all members to indicate when they cannot be present. But it will still happen in groups of adult learners; bad weather, illness or a popular local event can interrupt even the most loyal attendance.

It may be possible to deal with some discrete topic that those present find useful and rewarding for their efforts but those who are absent will either not miss or can catch up on quickly. This is especially true if there is a high degree of continuity in the group's work and if to have a vital chunk of material missed by many of the learners would be harmful. We may be able to choose a topic that is not essential to the main line of the course, so that the two or three who are gathered together have a worthwhile learning experience. One useful activity is to spend part of the time getting to know the participants better – their interests, experiences, abilities and intentions. We may learn a lot about how the course is going on these occasions.

The missing problem

It is impossible to compile a complete catalogue of problems faced in teaching. New ones are always appearing. But some of the comments here may help us to identify these problems and to worry out some home-made solution to them. In many cases, it helps to find another teacher (or our supervisor/provider/organiser) or someone else in a similar position to swap experiences and advice. It always helps to talk things over.

Further reading

Belbin, R. M. (1980) *The Discovery Method in Training*. Sheffield: Manpower Services Commission.

Bligh, D. R. (1972) *What's the Use of Lectures?* Harmondsworth: Penguin.

Chickering, A. W. (ed.) (1981) *The Modern American College: Responding to the New Realities of Diverse Students and a Changing Society*. San Francisco, CA: Jossey Bass.

Griffin, C. (1983) *Curriculum Theory in Adult and Continuing Education*. Beckenham: Croom Helm.

Rogers, A. (1991b) *Teaching Methods in Extension*. Reading: Education for Development.

Rogers, J. (1984) *Adults in Education*. London: BBC Publications.

Stephens, M. D. and Roderick, G. W. (1971) *Teaching Techniques in Adult Education*. Newton Abbot: David and Charles.

Travers, R. M. W. (1964) *Introduction to Educational Research*. New York: Macmillan.

PAUSE FOR MORE THOUGHT

In the first part of this book we looked at the nature of the transactions taking place in the course of 'teaching adults', and at the parties involved, adult learners and teachers. We saw that there are two major problems for the teacher of adults:

- The wide range of experience, learning abilities and styles, and intentions that the members of the class or learning group possess.
- The tension between the need to define learning objectives clearly in order to achieve learning on the one hand, and the desire to respect and encourage the autonomy of the mature adult on the other.

In the second part of the book we saw that there are at least two ways in which these problems may be tackled:

- by the use of the learning group;
- by the use of a wide range of varied and active teaching–learning methods.

The remaining chapters are devoted to making our work more effective – overcoming obstacles, testing the value of our work and encouraging the student learners to take more and more control over their own learning processes.

10

BLOCKS TO LEARNING

What is stopping us . . . ?

Identifying the problem

At different times, everyone who has taught adults has come across the person who seems unable to learn something. A serious block appears to exist. We have all experienced this in ourselves as well, a failure to comprehend or master some aspect of the subject under consideration.

This chapter sets out to discuss the nature of these blocks to learning. Two introductory points are needed. First, all we can try to do here is to assess what is happening and, if possible, why. What is not always so easy to see is how to cope with each situation as it arises. This must be left to the individual judgement of each teacher in each setting – though the analysis itself may suggest ways of approaching the blockage. As with so much in adult education, there are no answers for universal application by all teachers, just a series of options to choose from, alternatives to try out.

The second point is that we lack firm evidence for an analysis of the situation under review. We are trying to assess what is 'really' happening rather than what the student participant *says* is happening. On occasion, the two may be the same. But more often, even when the learners are able to describe why they find themselves unable to learn something (and that is on the whole rare), they are unable or perhaps unwilling to give the true reason. One way of bridging this gap is for us to draw on our own experience to describe and explain the situation. This is a useful tool, provided we recognise the limitations of this process. For we are likely to be people who have been successful in our approach to the subject, not a failure; we are therefore unlikely to understand fully the problems that some of the learners will feel. Nevertheless, it is necessary for us to use our own insights in this field; and throughout this chapter, as elsewhere in the book, you will find the material of greater value when you test it against your own experience. To be an effective teacher of adults, we must learn to know ourselves.

It is important for us to remember that we are discussing here the blocks to *learning*. Patricia Cross in her study of *Adults as Learners* (1981) identified three main barriers which adults face: barriers which arise from the situation in which they find themselves; barriers which spring from the learning programmes themselves; and internal barriers, attitudes which the adults may possess towards themselves. But she is talking about 'barriers to participation', rather than barriers to learning once one is participating in adult education programmes. And although her three categories can be applied to the blocks to learning, as we shall see below, the primary focus to our discussion of barriers to learning must be centred on the personality barriers which prevent some adult student participants – who want to learn and who attend classes regularly – from learning.

The scope of the problem

Blocks to learning exist, and there are many reasons for them, the most important of which are personality factors. These range from what may be called emotional variables at one extreme to conceptual difficulties at the other extreme. At one end is the 'I-don't-want-to-learn' participant – not just the unmotivated but those who find the difficulties so great that they withdraw from learning. At the other end is the learner who tries most anxiously to grasp a particular process or idea but just cannot make it fit, remember it or understand how the various pieces of the subject go together. On the one hand, psychological factors prevent the acquisition of new skills or the assimilation of new knowledge; on the other, something perceived to be within the subject-matter itself or the way the new material relates to patterns of existing knowledge gets in the way. Both of these extremes spring from the same kind of cause in the end: personality barriers to change.

There are other reasons for the failure to learn, and we can dispose of these first. Some blocks to learning new skills and new concepts arise from *physical changes*; for example, declining dexterity or failing eyesight or hearing account for many futile learning experiments. More important and frequent are those immediate, and often temporary, *situational* causes; physical or contextual factors such as hunger, poor health, or tiredness or other preoccupations (money, family needs, work, shopping, etc.) may weigh on the minds of the learners. How many adult classes have been ruined for teacher or student participant because one of them has just recalled some errand left unfulfilled, some commitment uncompleted, and the mind is engaged in concocting excuses with which to meet the offended party? Other situational factors more specifically related to our classes include the room being too hot or too cold, too bright or too dark, overcrowded, smoky or poorly equipped (for instance, with uncomfortable seating), or where there are too many distractions that prevent concentration. There are also those blocks that spring from *bad relations* between the teacher and the learner or between learner and learner, or from the teacher's failure to communicate properly with the learner.

All of these, although not unimportant or rare, may be relatively easily remedied, once identified. The evidence is that these physical and contextual factors are hindrances rather than blocks. They seldom operate on their own but rather provide material for the other mechanisms to work on. Distractions alone rarely form a block to learning but come into play when other blocks begin to exert themselves. They are used by the learner to prevent learning, rather than preventing learning by themselves.

This is not of course to say that these situational barriers to learning are not important. They are. It is most important that we recognise that our adult participants are part of a particular socio-cultural context, and that their knowledge and values are rooted in and are continually being created by this environment. They are not psychological isolates divorced for a specific context; they are all social beings. And this context will be at one and the same time a help and a hindrance: it will often provide the cause of the learning need, but it will also provide many barriers to learning changes. It is from this context that our student participants will bring to the purposeful learning episode which we are building for and with them the knowledge and experience which they have accumulated over many years.

Such situational hindrances thus reinforce the personality blocks to which we need to turn our attention, those blocks to learning that exist for the alert motivated student participant, even in a context conducive to learning. Although they all spring from some sort of psychological and emotional 'hang-up', it is still useful to distinguish between those more concerned with pre-existent knowledge and those arising from personality factors.

Exercise
Before we go further, try to put down in the space below two 'blockages' that you have experienced, either as teacher or as learner. Amongst mine, for instance, are learning to draw and learning what goes on under the bonnet of a car; *I know* I can't learn either.

	Blocks	*Column 1*	*Column 2*
1			
2			

> *Query*
> In relation to the blocks you have identified above, can you
> determine whether they arise more from pre-existing knowledge or
> from personality factors (*column 1*)?

Pre-existing knowledge

We have seen that adult student participants know a good deal about what
they are studying, often more than they think they know. Students in a class
on medieval English history frequently assert that they know nothing about
the subject, but it is not very difficult to elicit from them a series of names
such as Robin Hood and Sherwood Forest, the Black Prince, Wat Tyler,
Chaucer and Wycliffe, the Black Death, as well as the clear markers of
Domesday Book, the Crusades and the Wars of the Roses. Most of them will
have visited a medieval parish church, if not a castle or monastery. Any view
of medieval history that omits to deal with these, to make sense of them in
an overall context, may prove unsatisfying to the participants. Indeed, these
topics provided by the group members can become the hooks on to which
most aspects of the course of study can be hung. The learners can see that
they have helped to construct the syllabus. The same is true of woodworking, keep fit, management courses and literacy classes. The learners will
already have some experience, direct or indirect, of these subjects.

Adult student participants have already invested emotional capital in
acquiring this knowledge and experience. They will expend much more in
defending the integrity of this knowledge, so new learning changes will sometimes be strenuously resisted. Thus a blockage arises from the *emotional
investment in knowledge* that we make. We all learn from some outside authority – a person or a book – to which we can give the title of 'a significant
other'. Any challenge to this learned material, to our existing knowledge,
implies either a challenge to our significant other (it may be mother, father,
teacher or some other respected authority) or a challenge to our self-judge-
ment (we *chose* to rely on that person, book, magazine or newspaper; it
seemed reasonable to us at the time) or to both. Two reactions are created.
In the first, by the use of 'withdrawal mechanisms' the challenged learners
will seek to defend their knowledge. In the second, through the employment
of 'ego-defence mechanisms', the learners will seek to defend their self-image.
We will discuss both of these below.

A second cause of such blockages is existing *prejudices*. These may be
defined as strongly held beliefs, perhaps based in part on knowledge, that we
are reluctant to examine in detail. Often this is because we suspect that they
are not firmly founded. It may also be that the fear of others prevents us from
exposing prejudices to analysis, for we may be forced to abandon stances we

have taken up in public. Prejudices are one form of what is called 'over-certainty', a state that results in stereotyped reactions. Racial, religious or ideological hostilities are the most conspicuous forms of prejudices; sexual, social or cultural preferences the most insidious.

A third cause of such blockages arises in those who are *habit-bound*. These have traditional patterns of thinking or ways of doing things, not merely from their search for security but also from an undue reverence for the past. Similarly, some people's *conformity needs* are excessively strong. Such people cling to existing ways and understandings as long as they perceive them to be the ways and views of the majority. Once more, emotional investments lie at the base of these reactions.

All these factors lead some of our student participants to resist learning changes. They cling to pre-existent knowledge and attitudes, and they find it difficult to assimilate new material or at least to make it harmonise with what is already there. So they adopt mechanisms, most commonly of withdrawal, in an attempt to preserve what they already possess.

Withdrawal mechanisms

There are many ways of withdrawing from a situation. The most obvious (not necessarily the most common) is physical withdrawal; the student participant stops coming to the group. More common are the following:

- *Compartmentalism* – the learners keep their knowledge in separate boxes; they create distinct patterns that don't touch each other but are drawn upon in different circumstances. This is a particular favourite of people who have been exposed for a long time to a formal educational system with its separate 'schools' of history, geography, maths, etc.; but others too engage in it.
- *Authoritary-ism* – the quotation of and excessive reverence for authorities. Some learners fall back on books (the *Encyclopaedia Britannica* syndrome) or even just seeing it in print – 'It must be true.' New knowledge is challenged if it lacks such authority. Others cite trusted people as the ultimate source of wisdom: 'If they say so, we can believe it.'
- *Reality-evasion* – daydreaming, lack of attention, is more likely to be a withdrawal mechanism than anything else. This can be tested, for the withdrawal mechanism is highly selective in its attention and perception. The student participants will notice everything that supports their existing patterns and just not hear whatever contradicts it.

Perceptive teachers will come to recognise other withdrawal mechanisms. Teachers are also selective in what they notice. We ourselves often ignore those things that contradict the views we hold about our adult students as well-meaning, highly motivated and intelligent friends – or alternatively as dull, reluctant learners. We should constantly examine ourselves to see what we are perceiving and what we are missing.

Unlearning

To grapple with this problem of the pre-existent knowledge, habits or attitudes of our student participants, we need to grapple with the notion of unlearning. It is sometimes said that for adults the process of unlearning is as important as the process of learning; that all participants in adult learning activities have much to unlearn as well as new material to learn. It is not possible for us to know in the case of every individual learner precisely where the new material conflicts with pre-existing patterns, but an awareness of the reactions of the learners to such new matter reveals much to the sensitive teacher.

The new material, to be properly learned, must enmesh with the older knowledge and not be left lying on top of the existing patterns, leaving them unchanged. This may mean not merely an exploration of the pre-existing knowledge itself but also of the way it was acquired. This is particularly important when dealing with the many long-standing myths with which all subjects, both skill-oriented and understanding-oriented, abound. Authoritative denials of traditional practices or other knowledge will be weighed against existing beliefs in which considerable emotional investment may have been made.

To illustrate: suppose that as teachers we think it important that the students learn the 'truth' about the narratives of the Christian Nativity. We will then run up against the traditional stories of the 'three kings' who came from the East to bring gifts to the infant. The existing information held by most of the student participants will be seen to be 'incorrect'. We can pursue a number of strategies:

- We can *tell* the learners that they were not kings and that there were probably not three of them. Such a statement will be assessed and may even be accepted out of respect for our expertise, but it will lie uneasily on top of the earlier acquired knowledge because it has not challenged the source of that information. Within three or four minutes, the participants will be talking of 'three kings' again.
- We can *show* them the narrative accounts in the New Testament that speak of 'certain magi' (soothsayers or wise men), not 'three' and not 'kings'. Such a reference will give cause for more serious reflection, and some will be convinced. Nevertheless, most of the student participants will within a relatively short time be talking once more in terms of 'three' and 'kings'. We will not have challenged the weight of tradition and the emotional atmosphere of childhood, families, Christmas festivities and the constant reinforcement by Christmas cards, carols and the like, all of which have created an attachment to the idea of three kings.

- The only successful way to bring about the new learning will be through a process of unlearning. This will involve seeing how the two ideas ('three' and 'kings') arose in the first place. Only as the learner *comes to see how* the description of the visitors in these narratives was altered will there be a major change in knowledge and attitudes – of how the statement in the Psalms that 'kings from the East shall bring gifts' was quoted in the primitive Christian church; of how the early representations of the magi in pictures and mosaics with tall head-dresses were taken by later interpreters to indicate royal imagery; of how the fact that there were three gifts led to an assumption that there were three travellers, etc. The students will thus understand the processes involved in the transformation of these stories, and their traditionally held views will become readjusted. They will see the constant reinforcement of incorrect knowledge for what it is, and when they themselves join again in references to 'three kings', they will hold a part of themselves back with an inner assertion that now they know better. The story will be seen to be what it is, a later myth, harmless but incorrect.

This is a trivial example, not one to be pressed too hard. It is not perhaps important to bring about this particular item of unlearning, any more than the correction of the traditional tales of Robin Hood and the sheriff of Nottingham may be important. But each of us at some stage will run across an area where an unlearning process will be necessary, some traditional but ineffective or even harmful process, skill or knowledge. It is not enough to make authoritative statements of facts or to give orders, for neither will overcome the weight of tradition combined with the practice of contemporaries. Rather the process is in most cases much the same as above. The most unsatisfactory and impermanent method of dealing with such incorrect views is one of new authority, laying new knowledge on top of the older learning without disturbing it or relating the new to the old. A better way is to examine the basis of the old (incorrect or undesired) knowledge and the newer (desired) knowledge; but this too will lead to conflict, authority against authority. The most effective unlearning process is not straight contradiction but the lengthier way of helping the learner to examine how the incorrect pattern came about and has been reinforced through long acceptance and use. Unlearning is a difficult and lengthy process, but an essential part of teaching adults.

Emotional factors

Sometimes there is no great range of existing knowledge to impede new learning, but still an inability or a refusal to learn exists. In these cases, another set of factors comes into play: emotional manifestations of negative self-concepts, some of them enduring (in which case they may be seen as long-term personality traits), others situationally controlled (which we may term emotional variables). The most important and the most common of these, especially for adults, is *anxiety*.

Anxiety

Anxiety is a characteristic of many adult learners. Most teachers of adults will face it in their student participants at some stage. It is a diverse phenomenon. It seems to consist of two main elements: fear of externally imposed requirements that are seen as a threat, and worries about the capacity to cope, about self-esteem.

There are many causes of anxiety. There may be an awareness of the process of ageing, of physical tiredness and declining powers of memory and concentration. There may be a negative self-image, too high a sense of need. There may be a fear of failing before the group; the exalting others as 'better' or 'better educated' than oneself:

> We were told we were going to have a free discussion and that we were all going to be expected to speak. That was all right for those who'd been at school more recently than me, but I'd been a mere housewife only a week before, and I made up my mind on the spot that wild horses wouldn't drag any discussion out of me. I *knew* I'd say something silly.
>
> (quoted in Rogers 1977: 34)

We must be careful of attributing such attitudes to all student participants in adult groups. The fear of disappointing someone (often the teacher, either as friend or as authority figure); a too low assessment of one's abilities, judgements and resources; a lack of trust in oneself; a sense that to admit need at all means that one is less than adult or that by becoming a student-learner one is rejecting the company of adults (based on the view that 'education' is for children, a process of initiation that in our case was badly done in the first place and thus we need to 'go back' to education, to engage in remedial adult education), even denying one's adult role – all of these can on occasion play a part in creating over-anxiety. On the whole, these persons see the cause of their 'failure' as themselves: 'Far from regarding themselves as casualties of an inadequate and ramshackle system, they see themselves as educational failures' (Rogers 1977: 50). Thus adult education is seen to be for failures, those who did poorly at school or who never took advantage of the initial education system and who must return to a system built on pupilage and dependency, and opposed to adulthood and responsibility.

Anxiety is not confined to 'second-chance' adult learners. It can exist in many other forms of adult learning, in both the formal and the non-formal sectors. Teachers selected to engage in courses on educational management, hospital administrators required to learn new skills or new approaches to their task, community workers coming to grips with new social trends, adults entering full-time certificated courses and so on – all of these can experience a sense of doubt as to whether they can cope with what is required of them. It may not take the extreme form of over-anxiety as described above, but it may well be present in some form. Anxiety becomes highest at times of evaluation: tests or examinations, submitting work to the judgement of the teacher or other members of the group. At this time, consciousness of what is perceived as the lack of educational skills is at its greatest: 'I can do this task but not that one'; 'I can discuss but I can't write.' Uncertainty about the standards to be used for assessing work done will add to such anxiety. For those who see education as instrumental, to achieve a set goal beyond the learning itself, there will be pressure against 'wasting time'.

Over-anxious adult learners tend not to trust themselves and thus turn to authority for guidance. As we have noticed, we can welcome anxiety as useful for motivation for certain tasks (page 67), especially for those calling for rote learning, persistence of application and the less difficult kinds of 'reception' learning. Anxiety can *help* performance, especially in a task where traditional answers pay off; after all, the anxiety in most cases could not have been too strong or the adult would never have come to the learning group. On the other hand, anxiety can impede even the mastery of new motor skills. It tends to interfere with and inhibit original thought. Tasks requiring some degree of personal judgement are thus harder for the over-anxious student participant than tasks demanding self-critical conformity to rules. Such over-anxiety tends to be higher when the learner is faced with intellectual or creative exercises, lower when faced with physical tasks. Anxiety inhibits complex learning tasks that are more dependent on improvised skills than on persistence.

Such anxiety may be expressed in a number of ways. Sometimes there are physical reactions – sweating, shaking and other signs of distress. More usually it will be confined to inner emotions which the learner seeks to hide. The individual, like the group, will take refuge in 'fight' or 'flight': attempts to avoid the testing situation by either absenting themselves physically (non-attendance) or mentally (daydreaming) or refusing to join in (see pages 171, 208).

What can we do about it?

Because there are so many different causes of anxiety, there are no simple answers. It may be tackled by trying to reduce the anxiety itself or by trying to reduce opposition to the learning tasks.

Some strategies will help. Perhaps we can cultivate an atmosphere in which the fact that one dares even to the point of looking foolish becomes acceptable. The use of the group, and especially of sub-groups, is helpful here. The use of sarcasm and ridicule is counter-productive: 'The adult tutor is there not to correct what the student says, because this denies his [*sic*] previous experience, views and beliefs, but to build up ways in which the students can evaluate their own opinions against those of the teacher and the rest of the group' (Rogers 1977). This is as true of skill-based courses as it is of information-processing courses. The learners need to be encouraged to experiment with new techniques and to evaluate the older practices against the new. Criticism, poor evaluations, signs of disapproval (the so-called 'chain-anxiety-producing sequence') will increase anxiety.

We can do more than just try to prevent the anxiety from growing. By managing the learning situation, we can help to reduce anxiety. The learning tasks can be broken up into smaller units to build up a sense of achievement. Carefully tailored rewards and reinforcements will be needed. Something of the fear-inducing 'novelty' of the new learning can be lessened, although some sense of novelty is often needed to key the learner up, to create expectations and awareness. The pace of work should be monitored and adjusted if necessary.

Above all, we should seek to build up a sense of confidence in the learner. Student participants who see in the teacher a sense of confidence and an encouragement to confidence, and who thus come to trust the teacher, in time also come to accept the teacher's assessment of their own ability to learn. If we believe that our student-learners with our help *can* cope with the learning tasks we have chosen and put clearly before them, and if we command their respect, most of the participants will come themselves to believe that they too can cope. It takes time but it can be done.

Positive aspects of anxiety

It sometimes gets overlooked that a certain amount of anxiety is desirable, for it will often motivate the learner. A series of graphs that appear in a number of books on education and learning illustrates this point. Figure 40a shows that maximum learning is achieved by a steady but relatively slow arousal of interest until high motivation is achieved; but excessive arousal so as to create too much anxiety will prevent learning.

Figure 40b suggests that too-quick arousal can achieve high performance in the short-term, but the subject will be underlearned and performance will soon fall off. It will prove impossible to maintain the level of interest and therefore the level of performance.

On the other hand, Fig. 40c indicates that it is possible to fail to arouse a student's interest, especially in easy subjects. Thus the material is apparently never learned properly at all.

In all three cases, once arousal has passed through the motivated stage to the stage of excessive anxiety, learning falls off sharply, and a block to learning occurs at this point.

Figure 40a

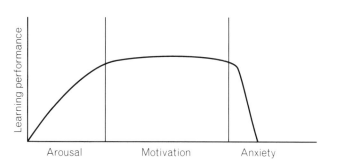

Figure 40b

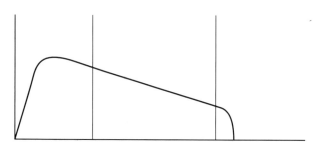

Figure 40c

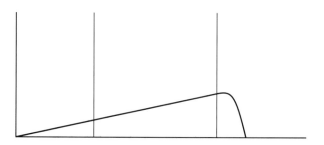

Sources of emotional difficulty

Emotional blocks other than anxiety may present themselves. Such a block may spring from the *fear of failing*, in the eyes of either the group or the teacher or indeed in one's own eyes, causing possible pain or shame. Such an individual will refuse to take risks. This is the characteristic of people who preserve a 'stiff upper lip', who consistently undervalue feelings and who use their emotional energies to hold back spontaneous reaction.

A second block may arise from a *reluctance to join in the methods of learning*. There may be several causes for this. One may be a reluctance to 'play' on the part of someone who is too serious, too academic in their approach, who fears to seem foolish. Activities such as buzz-groups are below their dignity. They are not willing to play around with problems or with concepts, to imagine, to experiment with the unusual.

Or it may spring from an 'impoverished fantasy life'. Such an individual asserts that the world of the senses is the real world; fantasies or play are unreal. They won't pretend, won't say, 'What if . . .?' They cannot work out the implications of a hypothesis because they are wondering all the time whether the hypothesis is true or not.

On the other hand, student participants who refuse to engage in the methods of learning may be running away from what they are sure will be inevitable frustration. Their thresholds are too low. They give up quickly in the face of obstacles. They try as hard as they can to avoid pain, discomfort or uncertainty. They will not practise or memorise, asserting that they know it will not be worth the effort.

A third and frequent personality block comes from the individual who takes too low a view of themselves, whose *'self-horizon' is too narrow*: 'I can't do it, I know I can't.' These people suffer from resource myopia, the failure to see resources to help them, either in their environment or in themselves; they undervalue both, especially themselves. Sometimes this may be due to sensory dullness – whether physical (bad eyesight or more frequently impaired hearing, for example) or psychological. The would-be learners make only partial contact with themselves and with their environment. The result is that their capacity and desire to explore the world become atrophied.

A further block can be seen in those who *fear the ambiguous*. These people avoid situations that lack clarity or where the probability of success is unknown. They will not 'try this' to see if it works, for they are convinced that, even if it does work, the reasons for success will remain unknown. They over-emphasise the unknown against the known, and so they won't set out to explore any part of the unknown.

Similar to these individuals are those who *fear disorder*, who dislike confusion and complexity, who have an excessive need for balance, order and symmetry. We all like to know where we are in any subject, to have signposts; but with these people it goes further than this. Their fear often leads to over-polarisation into opposites. They see everything in terms of black and white, good and evil. They thus fail to integrate the best from both sides of an argument. Role play for such student participants could become dangerous, for they may identify too closely with the case they are presenting.

Some student participants *fear to seem to influence others*. They don't want to appear too pushing or aggressive, and thus they hesitate to identify with new points of view.

There are other similar blocks to learning, but those listed above are probably the most common. Some of them can lead to other forms of blockage. Anxiety or too low a self-horizon can result in a failure to make any effort (most of us have met the student participant who sits on the edge of the group looking on with admiration as the other members master step after step of the subject) or conversely in trying to push too hard. In the latter case, the learner makes a more or less desperate attempt to keep up, to arrive at a solution. They become unwilling to let things 'incubate' or happen naturally. Too much effort sometimes springs from the same cause as too little effort.

There is a danger of exaggeration here. With all these various types of blockage present in every group of adult learners, and since we all to some extent share these characteristics, it may be wondered how any learning is done at all. But a good deal of learning does take place. The reason for itemising these blocks is not to deter the teacher but to remind ourselves that, when we meet a block to learning, it may well be caused by one of these factors.

Ego-defence mechanisms

Faced with a challenging situation like an adult education group, student participants with one of these characteristics tend to employ a range of ego-defence mechanisms in order to preserve their self-image. Such mechanisms may be defined as unwitting devices, unconscious distortions, subterfuges or self-deceptions that we all practise to some extent to maintain our conscious psychological equilibrium, to avoid mental pain, to keep up appearances to ourselves as well as to others when threatened by frustration, conflict or painful emotion.

There are a large number of such mechanisms. Some are aggressive in nature, others involve compromise or substitution. What follows is a brief annotated list intended for the teacher who wants to know what is going on in the group. Those who wish to learn more about the subject can turn to the standard works on psychology.

- *Fantasy* – not just random idling or daydreaming but escape from the situation in imagination even though physically the person remains present. In fantasy the participant gains alternative satisfaction; they fulfil themselves in imagination.
- *Compensation* – the group member turns to alternative activities (such as bizarre behaviour or costume) to make up for real or imagined inadequacies. If this leads to perpetual evasion of present problems and responsibilities, it will be over-compensation.
- *Identification* with others – the vicarious achievement of goals. This often happens in an adult class or group. One participant will join with another more successful one and bask in the reflection of the latter's glory though making no effort themselves. Sometimes identification can be with an imaginary 'hero' but normally it is with a real character, whether acquainted or not.
- *Projection* on to others of our own impulses and traits – we observe them in others or we attribute them to others. This usually takes the form of

criticism; we blame others for the faults that lie in us. Most adult class groups end up having a scapegoat. Sometimes it is possible to project the critical spirit on to others, to imagine that they are much more critical than in fact they are. Those who adopt this mechanism are always on the defensive against imaginary criticisms, always noticing slights and innuendoes, and hence are always taking offence.

- *Rationalisation* – the spontaneous giving of 'good' reasons. We find arguments to justify what we want to do or believe and even convince ourselves that these are the 'real' motives behind our actions or beliefs.
- *Repression* – selective forgetting according to the level of interest or displeasure associated with the technique or idea. Here again is a useful mental device that may prevent learning.
- *Sublimation* – a form of release, the diversion of frustrated energies into other (normal) channels of activity. In this, it differs from compensation. For an adult student participant, it may take the form of being particularly helpful in the group, performing certain chores and so on, in an attempt to avoid the more distasteful (i.e. active learning) work of the programme.
- There are others. *Displacement* is a process by which frustration or some other such emotion is turned away from the object that caused it and is vented on someone else. Supervisors reprimanded by their superiors have been known to 'take it out' on the people under their control; these in turn may express anger towards their families or other groups. Some teachers may vent the irritation caused by their student groups on others close to them, while others bring outside frustrations into the learning group. *Negativism* (not the same as indifference) sees every request as a threat that will ultimately lead to trouble and blame, and thus sees the appropriate response as 'No'. It is an extreme form of an uncooperative attitude designed to avoid difficulties. *Reaction formation* is another mechanism by which we concentrate on the opposite of what we really want to do but are rather ashamed that we want to do it – an excessive concern for cleanliness and tidiness or excessive generosity instead of a tendency towards untidiness or meanness.

We are likely to meet most of these ego-defence mechanisms at some stage or other. If you look again at your own blockages (page 206), you will probably be able to determine what withdrawal and/or defence mechanisms are employed in each case. In my own case (drawing and car maintenance) there is withdrawal; probably I set my horizons too low for both skills (I have been told so by colleagues who teach these subjects to adults; a certain art teacher still insists that anyone can learn drawing). In the case of the car I employ displacement, turning my frustration at my own failure and helplessness against the garage or the AA or anyone else in sight when the car won't work and I can't do a thing about it. Still I refuse to learn!

It is easier to describe 'blocks to learning' than to know what to do about them. Knowing what is happening is usually more than half the battle, and lines of approach may suggest themselves. But it is not always easy, when faced with student participants who persistently fail to learn, especially when this distresses them, to identify which of the many causes underlie the failure and precisely why the learners are seeking to defend themselves.

Query
In relation to the blocks you have identified above, can you identify any of the strategies which any of your student-learners have adopted (*column 2*)?

Changes in attitude

The introduction of learning changes into the area of attitudes is perhaps the most difficult task that faces the teacher of adults. In an oral rehydration therapy project in India, it was possible to teach mothers in certain villages that children plagued with diarrhoea should not be starved, the traditional remedy, as they will suffer from dehydration and ultimately die, but instead should be fed with a mixture of water, sugar and salt. But it was not so easy to persuade them to follow this in practice; it went against their family and community traditions, what they had learned from the past and what others around them were doing and expected all members of the village to do. There was a block to learning new attitudes, not new knowledge.

Modifications of attitude are the hardest change of all. The following points may help:

- Identify as clearly as possible precisely what the attitude is that is preventing learning changes and what are the most important pressures against making such changes, not just what the student-learner says they are.
- An adequate basis of new or revised knowledge is necessary for any attitudinal change. Later threats to the new attitudes will be resisted in proportion as the new knowledge is firmly based and internalised. Such new knowledge should not appear to threaten the learners but to help them.
- The amount of change called for should not be so great that the learner rejects it outright as calling for too radical a reappraisal of thinking and behaving. It should build on existing life patterns, not oppose them. (But equally it should not be presented as insignificant or trivial; no effort to change will then be made.)
- The learners should be left to draw their own conclusions from the material learned in this context, not exhorted to change their attitudes and practice.
- The new material should come from a source regarded as trustworthy and

attractive (this will reflect on the teacher). The main mode of learning is what is often called 'human modelling'.

- The use of a learning group to create a climate in which such changes can be brought about is often effective. A public display of new attitudes helps to promote more permanent changes. It is largely a matter of commitment to new ways of thinking and behaving, and commitment to a group can assist in this.
- Role play, through which the participants play out the parts of those who hold the new desired attitudes and perhaps also those who hold in an extreme form the undesired negative attitude, can also be useful, though it needs to be used carefully.

Each teacher of adults needs to face every situation as a unique event, requiring a new assessment and perhaps new methods. What will work with one group may not work with another.

Conclusion

We suggested at the start of this chapter that many student participants put a good deal of emotional investment into defending their existing patterns of knowledge, attitudes and behaviour. Attempts to build up new patterns, to introduce learning changes, may result in strong emotional reactions. The teacher must tread carefully. And we have also suggested that all our student participants are part of a specific socio-cultural context. We need to help them to identify and to build upon the motivators and resources and the support networks and mechanisms in that environment; just as we need with them to identify the demotivators and to take action to weaken their effect on the student-learners.

Further reading

Gagné, R. M. (1975) *Essentials of Learning for Instruction*. Hinsdale, IL: Dryden Press.

Gibbs, G., Morgan, A. and Taylor, E. (1982) Why students don't learn, *Institutional Research Review*, 1(10).

Gross, R. D. (1987) *Psychology: The Science of Mind and Behaviour*. London: Hodder and Stoughton.

Tennant, M. (1988) *Psychology and Adult Learning*. London: Routledge.

11
EVALUATION

How can we tell . . . ?

The need for evaluation

Like earlier sections of this book, this chapter is intended to raise questions rather than to propose firm answers. The approach to evaluation here is a practical one; the intention is to make conscious what most of us do much of the time as part of the process of teaching. It is often assumed that the need for and the means of evaluation are self-evident, but if it were, teachers would be better at doing it and would be able to see themselves doing it, more often and more effectively. Evaluation is one of the more difficult skills required of the teacher, and we need to work at it consciously. There are different possible strategies involved, and our task is to choose between them, to decide for ourselves our own preferred way of working.

Along with this should go a willingness to change what we (and our student participants) are doing. There is no point in evaluating the teaching–learning situation if we are unwilling to change course. Evaluation will be effective only if we are prepared to alter or even scrap our existing programme when we detect something wrong and begin again.

A distinction also needs to be drawn between evaluation and assessment. *Assessment* is the collection of data on which we base our evaluation. It is descriptive and objective; if anyone else were to do it, they would come up with much the same findings. *Evaluation* on the other hand is a process of making personalised judgements, decisions about achievements, about expectations, about the effectiveness and value of what we are doing. It involves notions of 'good' and 'bad' teaching and learning, of worth. It is based on our own ideology.

Why evaluate?

Evaluation is necessary for at least three reasons:

- To improve our performance as teachers. Questions of quality, of account-ability, of protecting our 'customers', of being effective are important not just for the providers and organisers but also for our student participants and for ourselves. We must believe in what we are doing and that we are doing it well, in order to do it well.
- To plan new strategies, make choices, establish priorities; to determine where we are in the teaching–learning process at present and what to do next; to identify helps and hindrances and decide what to do about them.
- To learn: to assess how much progress has been made, in which direction and how much farther there is to go. Evaluation is an essential part of learning.

Two main forms of evaluation have been identified by writers on this subject: *formative* – the ongoing evaluation that is inherent in the learning process itself and leads to learning changes; and *summative* – evaluation that takes place at different times, particularly at the end of the programme of learning, to see how far we have got. But these are not in fact two distinct processes, only one. If a summative evaluation undertaken at the end of a course (a teacher's report, for instance) is used to plan new programmes and new approaches, then it becomes a formative one. It is the way evaluation is used that distinguishes it. If it looks only backwards and reviews what has been done, it is summative; if in addition it looks forward to, and influences, new procedures, it is formative. The latter is more productive; evaluation judgements should lead to change. But there is also a time for the former.

Who evaluates?

We can also distinguish between *external* and occasional evaluation, prac-tised by the organiser of the programme or some inspector or external vali-dating body, and *internal*, more regular evaluation, practised by the teacher in the course of the teaching programme.

The *organiser* will be assessing how the programme objectives are being met. Are we getting in our groups the right kind of student-learners, the ones the programme is primarily intended for, those we feel to be in most need? Are they learning the right things? Are the courses meeting their needs and intentions? Are the programmes on offer reflecting the selectivity-, compet-itiveness- and competency-based criteria of the existing educational system, or are they offering a different (non-selective, non-competitive and effort-based) ethos? In addition, at a time of static or dwindling resources, the providers' concern will be with matters of quality control. They need to determine whether the resources they have at their disposal are being used most effectively and, in certain circumstances, to establish priorities. To do all this, they will need criteria to determine whether some courses are better than others and to plan accordingly.

The *teachers* also evaluate their work in order to plan. They are concerned with whether they are being effective as teachers; whether the objectives they have set are the right ones and at the right level, as well as whether they are being met. They need to assess progress, match between intentions (objectives) and outcomes (the results of the teaching–learning process), to measure change, appraise efforts, identify new needs and assess strengths and weaknesses. They will wish to learn whether the short-term goals and the tasks they have laid before the group have been achieved and whether they are of the kind that will contribute towards the desired learning changes. They need to test whether the learners are ready to move on to the next stage or not. They will want to see clearly the *intended* programme of learning, the *implemented* programme (which may be different from what was intended for various reasons) and whether that again differs from the *received* programme.

Both organiser and teacher, then, evaluate for much the same reason, for their own learning and to plan changes. But teachers also build evaluation into the teaching–learning process for the learners' sake. They use evaluation for (extrinsic) motivation (although not all of the participants need this). What is more, an ongoing programme of evaluation is a necessary part of the learning process and becomes part of the work of the whole group.

So thirdly the *learners* themselves evaluate in the course of learning. Evaluation is an essential tool for developing new skills, knowledge and understanding. Hitting a tennis ball against a line on a wall in a practice session brings about no learning changes by itself (though it may strengthen the muscles). What is needed is a series of judgements: 'That was too high'; modification; 'That was too low'; modification; 'That was about right'; repetition; 'That was good'; once more; and so on. Only by such an evaluative process will learning changes take place. Trial-and-error learning particularly is based on evaluation, but most other kinds of learning also rely on this process for effective changes. The learners then engage in formative evaluation in order to learn. They will also pursue summative self-evaluation for motivation: assessing their own progress and performance, rekindling their enthusiasm for the learning goals in the light of their achievements (what is called ipsative evaluation).

It is likely – though not inevitable and probably not desirable – that the evaluation by the teacher and by the outside body (usually organiser) will not be the same, for their objectives differ to a certain degree (even though those of the organiser are subsumed in those of the teacher). It is also likely – and almost certainly undesirable – that the evaluation by the teacher and by the learner will be different. A hierarchy of evaluation thus emerges and should be developed more consciously, the organisers and inspectors (where they exist) should encourage the teachers to evaluate, and they in their turn should encourage the student participants to engage in evaluation. Since evaluation is largely a skill, the teachers need to teach the learners how to evaluate; they should demonstrate the process. Evaluation is one of those exercises that need to be practised jointly between teacher and student participant rather than be taught by exhortation.

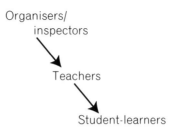

Organisers/
inspectors

Teachers

Student-learners

Evaluate what?

There are many different tools of evaluation. One of the more useful ones which may be used for any formative evaluation of adult learning programmes is the appropriately named SWOT approach: to assess the *strengths* and the *weaknesses* of the programme or class and to assess the *opportunities* which it opens and which may or may not have been taken up; also the *threats* which will hamper the effectiveness of the programme and which need to be addressed if the goals of the learning programme are to be achieved. This approach has specific advantages in that it encourages us to look beyond the normal assessment of strengths and weaknesses to explore other possibilities and the risks faced in the programme.

In evaluating our adult education activities, there is one overriding concern – whether the learners are learning or not. That must be the eventual standard by which our programmes need to be judged. In order to assess this, we may look at three main elements: goal achievement, teaching processes, and student attainments.

1 Goal achievement

The learning objectives need to be submitted to evaluation in two main ways: Are they the right ones? How far are they being met? We need to identify clearly the intentions of the programme of learning and to submit these to some form of judgement. Perhaps we take for granted that the objectives of our courses – to learn a craft or other skill, to study literature and so on – are the right ones, self-justifying. But these assumptions need to be examined in depth. Is the learning primarily concerned with personal growth, or with socialisation and social change, or with vocational advancement? Whose goals are they, ours or those of the student participants? We also need to assess how far these intentions are being achieved, whether the programme of learning is proving effective. Throughout, we must ask whether the student participants are learning in a particular area, even when this learning is seen as a means of achieving some goal that lies behind the learning.

Even if the goal is to pass an examination or to create a work of art for oneself, the means to the satisfactory attainment of these goals is student learning.

2 *Teaching processes*

The entire process by which the teacher creates the learning opportunity (planning skills as well as powers of exposition) needs to be evaluated. Once again the main concern is with the learner rather than the teacher; the purpose of effective teaching is student learning. The question is less whether we are teaching well than whether the student has been well motivated. There is not much point, as we have remarked before, in the teacher teaching if the learner isn't learning. Evaluation of our own teaching thus includes the process of feedback.

3 *Student-learner attainments*

At the heart of the evaluation process there lies the question of student learning. Are the learners learning? How much and what are they learning? What form of learning are they engaged in: is it product or process, to handle tools or to produce a table to a set standard? What is the quality and level of their learning? How well is the material learned? Have their skills of learning increased during the programme? These and many other similar questions occur in the process of thinking about the evaluation of our work as teachers of adults.

One of the issues here lies with the concept of progress in learning. If ignorance is seen to be deprivation, then progress will be seen in terms of acquisition – of new skills, knowledge, understanding and attitudes. 'Progress' is usually viewed as advancement along a straight line of development. But there is not always a straight line of progress in learning.

An essential part of this evaluation will be with the attitudinal development of the student participants – with how much additional confidence, how much increased motivation have arisen from the teaching–learning programme. This aspect is often omitted from the evaluation process which concentrates more on increased knowledge and more highly developed skills; but the assurance and enhanced self-image of the students, their willingness to continue to study, their increased interest are all outcomes which need to be evaluated.

And finally we will need to look for the unexpected outcomes, the impact of our teaching–learning programmes. Some of this may have to be done some time after the course has finished – what is sometimes called *post hoc* or postscript evaluation. Experience indicates that at times, whereas the learning objectives of a programme may have been achieved, the longer-term impact of one or other course could be negative (Rogers 1992).

Evaluation methods

Exercise
Before starting this section, look at the course which you are taking as your case study and try to determine how you plan to evaluate it – what indicators will you look for. I suggest that you write them down here:

How to evaluate?

Student learning is the main focus of our process of evaluation. But there is no single right way of evaluating this; we have to decide for ourselves how to do it. Obviously we need to ask a series of questions, and determining what some of these should be is relatively simple. It is more difficult to come to some agreement on the criteria by which to judge the answers.

Over the years, organisers and providers have used a number of criteria to assess the effectiveness of their programmes and to establish the relative merits of their courses. Some argue (on *a priori* grounds) that longer courses are better than shorter ones (by no means always true) or that those taught by well-qualified teachers are better than those taught by less well-qualified staff (again not always true). They thus judge their programmes in terms of the numbers of longer courses or by the qualifications of the teachers used.

1 Satisfaction indicators

Others rely more heavily on satisfaction indicators such as

- indicated demand – requests from prospective student participants, individually or through organisations, on which the programme is built and which are taken to indicate that it must be meeting needs;
- effective demand – the numbers of student-learners attracted to particular classes; the size of the group is sometimes taken as a means of assessing the value of a course;
- follow-on – whether an extension of the learning situation is requested and taken up; a course is deemed successful if the learners request more of the same;

- follow-up – whether the learners continue to study on their own or pass into new programmes, whether they practise their new skills, read more, etc.;
- attendance figures – in terms of both regularity of attendance and low numbers of drop-outs;
- verbal or written comments by the student participants – both approval and complaints, indicating the learners' sense of success or dissatisfaction.

Teachers, too, often use such popularity or satisfaction indicators to help evaluate their work. But we need to examine them more closely to see whether such popularity signals truly indicate that effective learning is taking place.

2 Contextual preconditions

Among the factors that contribute towards the effectiveness of the learning process are those relating to the context within which the teaching takes place. These too are the concern of evaluation by both organiser and teacher. Since part of the task of evaluation is the identification of the good and bad influences that affect the results of our teaching, we need to consider carefully the *setting* (the room, furniture, temperature, lighting, teaching aids) to see whether it is conducive to the student participants' learning and to remedy any hindrances it contains. The *climate* also needs examination, both that of the institution within which the course is set and that of the learning group itself. There is little hope of creating effective learning changes in the direction of greater self-confidence and self-determination if the whole ethos of the institution is opposed to this or if the class denies the learner any opportunity to exercise such qualities. Overt and covert pressures for or against the goals are important elements in the process of teaching adults, and need evaluation.

3 Criteria from teaching

These two elements in the evaluative process, satisfaction indicators and signs of a conducive context, although valuable, say little about whether the student participants are learning or not. For this, other ranges of criteria can be drawn up, both by organisers concerned with the quality of the programmes they provide and teachers concerned about the effectiveness of their work. These criteria are based on what happens during the teaching–learning experience, and sometimes consist of a description of what happens, moment by moment, an analysis in terms of events and learning episodes. Some attempts have gone beyond this, trying to identify those processes that need to be reinforced and those needing to be corrected or nullified.

1 Some evaluators have looked to the *emotional climate* and *management controls* of the class (see pages 164–6) for their indicators. These are

perhaps more properly the preconditions of learning; they do not necessarily indicate whether learning is taking place. However they should
contribute to the criteria by which we can assess teaching–learning effectiveness.

2 Another kind of evaluation is based on an analysis of what educational
events occur during any teaching session. Thus some have recorded the
number of *learning events* taking place and of what kind they are. (One
such scheme divides these events into acts of memorisation, acts of divergent and convergent thinking, and acts of evaluative thinking.) Others
have concentrated on the logic of teaching and of the language used in
teaching; episodes have been listed such as defining, reporting and desig-
nating. These techniques however are more readily practised by others
than by the teachers themselves; you cannot easily use them on your own
group except by watching yourself teach with the use of a video-recorder.
(It is well worth doing this, if you can get hold of the equipment; but if
not, you can visit other classes and see other teachers at work, and in this
case it is valuable to have in mind what you are looking for.)

3 More useful for the practising teacher is the analysis of the number and
kinds of *transactions* that take place during any teaching session: transactions between teacher and learner, and between learner and learner. The
participation of the student-learner in the work (activities) of the group is
seen as one indicator that learning is taking place. If the teacher talks for
a long time, only one kind of transaction is taking place; questions on the
other hand comprise more transactions. The most frequently cited analysis of these transactions is that by Flanders, which records events every
three seconds, but once again teachers usually need to rely on what they
can deduce from their own teaching, and sophisticated techniques are
probably not appropriate.

4 Others have concentrated on *types of method* used in the class and the
involvement of the student participants in their own learning. The use of
'approved' teaching–learning methods such as demonstration or discussion is frequently felt to lead inevitably to learning. But it is not always
easy to see how the teacher can test, at the end of each such occasion, how
much and what kind of learning has taken place by the use of these
methods. A substantial amount of subjective impression will add itself to
our evaluation; we will *feel* good about the teaching session. But a reliance
on particular teaching methods will not always lead to learning and may
introduce an element of artificiality into the experience.

4 *Teacher and learner*

An analysis of what goes on during the teaching session can tell us about
ourselves and about the learners, and may throw light on whether learning
is taking place.

The first part of this analysis relates to our *performance* as teacher. Such an analysis will centre upon our subject expertise and skills of presentation and communication. Evidence of preparation, both of the subject-matter and of the modes of teaching; awareness of the student-learners; the clarity with which the goals of learning are defined; the structure of the learning episode – its level, pace of learning, relevance to the learner and to the task in hand – and the clear signposting of each step of the learning process are all capable of assessment. Our personal style of teaching (self-projection, confidence, voice level, powers of organisation, the rapport built up with the learners, the development of interaction and feedback), the methods used, the involvement of the learners in the processes, and the creation of feedback and evaluation procedures can all be recorded on a positive–negative scale. Positive recordings are those which it is believed will produce an occasion conducive to learning. This is perhaps as far as we can go along this line of enquiry.

Secondly the range and nature of *student activity* can be recorded as part of the evaluative process. The nature of the group, the kinds of interaction between members, the range of expectations and intentions they declare and the clarity of their goals, the kind of work they do in each session and between sessions, the questions they ask (as signs that they are grappling with the new material), the involvement of the learners in evaluating themselves – positive recordings in each of these areas are thought to be indicators that learning is taking place. At each stage, judgements need to be made: as to whether the activity in which the participant is engaged really aims 'at the *improvement* and development of knowledge, understanding and skill and not merely at its exercise'. In the end a description of the programme of work is not in itself an adequate means of assessing effectiveness, but a programme in which the learners are active is more likely to lead to learning changes than one in which they are passive recipients of information and instruction.

5 Performance testing

Involvement by the learners in the learning activities does not always reveal the *kind* of learning taking place, even if it can be relied upon to indicate that some form of learning changes are taking place. We noted (pages 127–8) the two types of learning (inner learning and the behavioural expressions of that learning, the distinction expressed in the terms 'public' and 'private' effects of our teaching) and the discussion as to whether all 'private' outcomes can and should express themselves in behavioural (performance) terms. *Behavioural changes* and performance targets are easier to assess than inner changes in understanding, values and attitudes, and this fact will influence the procedures of assessment and evaluation we adopt. Part of the process of evaluation then is to interpret behavioural patterns and to create a range of performance situations in order to see how the more private learning changes are expressed.

We need to identify or create certain activities (making something, or writing, or speaking, say) that in themselves express the desired learning, in order to assess whether progress is being made and what kind of learning change is being achieved. But once again we need to remind ourselves of a number of caveats:

- These situations should be real ones, not artificial; there is little point in asking adult student-learners to engage in false activities that they will never engage in again once the course is over.
- The primary purpose is to evaluate the hidden depths (expressive objectives) that lie beneath these competency-based activities.
- Outside influences may hinder or prevent the exercise of the desired function. Activities (including words) do not always reflect inner learning changes and they rarely reflect their nature. But they are often the only way we can evaluate the learning changes of others.

6 Examinations

Despite the hesitations of many teachers in adult education, examinations are used with adults to evaluate student learning, and there are signs that their use is increasing. The variety of such so-called objective tests (usually subject based) is also increasing. They range from the very formal (standardised testing) to the very informal: written examinations (unseen, open-book, pre-set or home based), tests, essays (whether structured or subjective; that is, devoted to whatever the learner wishes to write about), practicals, observation of exercises, oral tests, questions, discussion, assignments, projects and so on. They tend to test the end product of the learning, the competencies attained; and their effect on the learning process is usually short-term.

The problems of marking examinations, of norm and criterion referencing (that is, whether each exam is to be marked against a 'normal' distribution pattern of success and failure, say 5 per cent top grade, 20 per cent second, 50 per cent third, etc.; or against an objective standard of competence that is supposed to exist somewhere outside of the examiner) and of whether the learners are thinking for themselves are well known. Their accompaniments – the prejudices of the examiners in relation to particular learners, the problem of extrinsic rewards rather than intrinsic motivation, the increase in competitiveness and selectivity, feelings of anxiety, failure and injustice, the distortion of the curriculum and of the pace of learning, the fact that many exams are set and marked by people unknown to the learners so that the aim comes to be to defeat the examiner rather than to learn – are again well known. They have led to a widespread concern to seek ways to replace élitist and selective examinations with other forms of evaluation; to replace prizes with goals that all may achieve. One of the most significant modern developments is the marathon run, which all may enter and all may win in their own terms because the participants choose their own standard and determine their own attainments; frequently they set themselves against themselves alone and assess their own attainments. Modern processes of evaluation are seeking similar ways of helping student participants to assess their own learning progress.

Nevertheless we may not dismiss such formal methods of evaluation entirely, for they can be formative as well as summative in their nature. Internal tests may be as much a means of new learning as of assessment. Sometimes they are intended to be solely summative, leading to the evaluation of attainment levels and on occasion to the award of certificates of competency. There may be a place for these in some forms of adult education, but a number of factors limit their usefulness:

- The problem of how to evaluate progress made as distinct from levels of attainment. Some adult learners, starting from a base lower than that of others in their group, make more rapid progress but remain well behind the attainment levels of the rest. The way to reward such effort and advances while retaining the prescribed or desired attainment levels is problematic.
- Adult learners not only start at very different points; they also choose different goals for themselves. The ends and intentions of adult learners are not homogeneous.
- There are no age-related criteria for adult learners as there are for many younger people.

7 End product

It remains a fact that the most frequent means of assessment and evaluation in adult education is the quality of the end product, be it a piece of writing, the ability to engage in a series of exercises, a fabricated article or role-play exercise completed to the satisfaction of the teacher, who is for this purpose the assessor. These, as we have seen, are not to be judged solely on their own but according to certain criteria attached to the performance of behavioural objectives: the level, the purpose for which it is being done, the conditions under which the actions are being performed, and so on (pages 130–1). Any evaluation will need to include some clarification of these conditions as well as a definition of the activity itself.

The only fully satisfactory mode of assessment as to whether the learners are learning the right things and at the right level is the performance of the student participants after the end of each stage of the learning programme. Do they act in such a way as to reveal increased confidence, in whatever field

Figure 41 An evaluation schedule: suggested headings
(Try this out on the course you listed above, page xi)

Objectives   • their nature   • the clarity with which they are perceived
Context   • the milieu/setting   • the climate
Teacher   • subject competency   • performance as teacher   • materials used
Student learners   • activities in group   • activities as individual learners
Level of performance   • the finished product
Unexpected outcome   • positive   • negative
Indicators of satisfaction   • whether goals have been/are being attained
Assessment of success or failure   • and reasons

of learning they are engaged in? Do they exercise the new skills better and/or more often? Do they reveal new understandings and new knowledge in what they say and do? Are they continuing to learn in directions of their own choice? Do they show signs of being satisfied with their own performance in their chosen field or of striving towards further improvement? The ultimate evaluation of the success or failure of our teaching will be seen in the exercise of the new skills, knowledge and understandings and of new attitudes towards themselves and the world around them. It is a question of whether our adult students reveal in their behaviour signs of increased adulthood and maturity, of development of their talents, greater autonomy and a sounder sense of perspective.

This is not easy, especially as most teachers of adults lose contact with their student participants soon after the end of the course or programme. The possibility of delayed learning (we know that it takes time for feelings, creative approaches and understandings to emerge) means that we can never be sure, in the case of seeming failures, that our work will not eventually bear fruit. Nor can we be sure that the learning of those with whom we seem to have been most successful will be permanent. For true evaluation ought to address itself not only to what the learners *can* do but to what they *do* do subsequently.

Does this mean that summative evaluation is impossible for the teacher of adults? The answer must be no. But it does mean

- that formative evaluation is more important in teaching adults than summative;
- that our summative evaluation will always be tentative; we can never know for sure.

Some teachers of adults will find this unsatisfactory; but we will often have to be content to cast our bread upon the waters in the expectation that it will (may?) return to us after many days. Perhaps the most rewarding aspect of the evaluation of adult learning are those signs of satisfaction that so many adults reveal in their relations with their teachers. The student participants are after all the best judges of whether they are getting what they feel they need.

Further reading

Charnley, A. H. and Jones, H. A. (1979) *Concept of Success in Adult Literacy*. Cambridge: Huntington.

Clark, N. and McCaffrey, J. (1979) *Demystifying Evaluation*. New York: World Education.

Flanders, N. A. (1970) *Analyzing Teaching Behavior*. Reading, MA: Addison-Wesley Pub. C.

Guba, E. and Lincoln, E. S. (1981) *Effective Evaluation*. San Francisco, CA: Jossey Bass.

Rowntree, D. (1987) *Assessing Students*. London: Kogan Page.

Ruddock, R. (1981) *Evaluation: A Consideration of Principles and Methods*. Manchester: Manchester University Press.

12

Participation

Can we all join in . . . ?

Involvement in the process

Learning is active

We have seen that, for learning to be effective, the student participants in our groups need to be active; they must be fully involved in the learning processes. The teacher teaches; the learners do the learning. Jennifer Rogers once said that for us as teachers to say that we taught but that the students didn't learn was as ridiculous as saying, 'I sold him a car but he didn't buy it.' Teaching adults is not a question of 'selling' anything. Rather it is a matter of setting up a programme of activities, study and practice, and encouraging and enabling the student participants to join in. They do the work and arrive at the goals. The teacher cannot introduce the learning changes; only the learners can do this.

It is surprising how often we forget this simple truth; how often teachers concentrate on what they are doing rather than on what the student participants are doing; how often we think that learning is dependent for its effectiveness on our activity (the way we present knowledge or processes, our skills of communication, our demonstrations and visual aids and so on). Any book of course that deals with teaching adults runs the danger of compounding this error by concentrating upon the activities of the teacher rather than on those of the student-learners. So right at the end, especially when we have just been considering evaluation, a task most teachers see as theirs alone, it is necessary to spell out once more that unless learners are active they will not learn.

It is necessary for the student-learners to be active in their own learning for a number of reasons. First for motivation: they need to achieve something regularly in order to build up and maintain a sense of success.

Summative activities, assessments as to how much we have completed, how far we have got and how much further we need to approach the goal, are essential for keeping going at the learning tasks. Secondly, for learning itself, the introduction, acceptance and internalising of the learning changes: formative activities, assessments as to whether we are on the right lines, trying out whether this is or is not the right way to go about it, reflecting critically whether these are the right responses or not – all of these activities and judgements are involved in the process of learning itself.

Learning is lifelong

There is a further reason why the student-learners should be active, and that is the need to encourage them to continue purposeful and structured learning once our particular programme is over. Learning continues throughout life; it is a necessary part of life itself, not just a preparation. We need to continue to learn because we cannot learn at the start all that we shall need during our path through life. Not only is there not enough time, but also many things will be unforeseen, and in any case many things will not make sense until we are actively engaged with them. Some time ago the question of exorcism arose in relation to many parts of the Christian church, and most of the clergy who found themselves faced with this subject had to learn about it from scratch. Their initial training made no contribution to their understanding in this area. Even if the subject had been included in the curriculum of the theological colleges, it would not have made as much sense or been treated with the same regard as it was when these ministers were faced with the question in real life. The same is true, time and again. It is even true of teaching adults; we need to learn how to do it while we do it.

We all learn as part of our occupation, whatever that might be. We learn as part of our social roles and relationships, as we either enter new ones or reinterpret existing ones. And we learn anew as we enter new phases of self-development, as we acquire new interests or discover new talents within ourselves. The ultimate goal of all this learning is enhanced adulthood, greater maturity and self-development, a fuller sense of perspective, and increased autonomy, responsibility for ourselves and perhaps for others. The final aim of learning is liberation, self-determination, freedom.

Sometimes such lifelong learning processes take on a special character; they become purposeful learning episodes. For a time we set out to learn something in a structured way, to acquire a new skill or a new understanding in order to meet some situation in life. Most of our adult learners engage in our programmes precisely for this reason; it is part of their ongoing learning activities, and will continue once our course is over. This means that the way we conduct our adult learning should contribute towards the goal of all learning: liberation. Our aims are to enable the learners to enhance their own adulthood, to maximise the range of choices before the learners, to increase their control over aspects of their own lives, environment and their own learning.

Teaching for freedom

The education we create for the student-learners should build upon these more structured natural learning episodes rather than contradict them. This gives us not only the goals of our teaching of adults but also our subjects and our methods. The way we select the content of our programmes and the methods we use should both foster the adulthood of the learners. They should assist the development of the learners as individuals, encourage the development of perspectives and provide opportunities for the exercise of autonomy. All education needs to contribute to continued learning and strengthen the independent learning habits of the participants.

This means breaking the traditional dependency lying beneath so much current education. Anything we do that leads the student-learners to become dependent upon ourselves as teachers will be denying their adulthood. We teachers must work to make ourselves redundant in the process of creating discriminating learners. This can be achieved only through active learning methods in our adult learning groups.

But it is not just a matter of constructing exercises for the participants to try during the course. Rather it is the encouragement of the student-learners to join in all parts of the process, planning as well as demonstrating and instructing. They need to join in determining what they should be able to do and what they should know about. To quote Albert Mansbridge (1920): 'The initiative must lie with the students. They must say how, why, what or when they wish to study.'

Adult student-learners can join in the planning of the course, the stages of learning, the steps by which the skills and knowledge are built up, areas that most teachers guard carefully to themselves. They can contribute to setting the goals, for they have their own intentions in joining our learning groups, and it is best, if we wish to encourage autonomy and independence, to start from these intentions rather than to impose our own. They can help in constructing the learning schedule, the methods/content part of the course, the sequence of events and activities, for they all have their own skills of learning. They can also share in the process of evaluation; they will often watch more closely than the teacher what is happening in the group. Adult learners *can* then contribute to all parts of the teaching–learning process.

Exercise

In the course you have chosen for this work (see page xi), what parts of the decision-making have the student-learners participated in?

Such insights have led providers and teachers of adults to experiment with different forms of learning groups for adults. Some of these are very exciting – experiential learning programmes, confidence-building, self-exploration, self-programming groups (most recently with unemployed workers but earlier with many other types of participant), weight-watchers, Alcoholics Anonymous, group therapy and self-awareness programmes, writing circles, social action groups (especially local community and residents' groups), quality circles and so on. The variety of groups is great and the range of activities wide. Even in more traditional classes where the presence of a recognised teacher-figure is accepted, experiments with different forms of learner involvement in all the stages of constructing the activities have been conducted; deciding what shall be learned, how it will be studied and what shall be done with the learning changes at the end of the programme are all matters for the group and not for the teacher alone.

Sharing, not serving

The learners and knowledge

But it can go further than this. Adult learners can create knowledge. This truth has come to be recognised in some new forms of teaching adults that have sprung up recently: self-learning groups, community action, research study groups and project study groups which may even publish their find-ings (Rogers 1995). The archaeology class that under supervision explores an area and excavates new sites; the natural history group that records the flora and fauna or surveys the geology of its own region; the residents' group that investigates the schooling, housing or development needs of its own community; the village community that conducts its own needs survey – all of these create knowledge. Many of them seek to give that new knowledge back to the community from whence it came, through exhibitions, publi-cations and other activities. In the process new insights into the varied kinds of knowing have been produced, a new relationship between learner and knowledge has come about.

It is important for us as teachers of adults to appreciate this. Knowledge is not the preserve of the few, the educated, to be doled out in small parcels to our student participants. It is something all of us can share in creating and discovering, which we will all view from our own particular perspective.

The teacher and knowledge

This calls for a radical change in the role of the teacher. Teachers and organ-isers nearly always do too much for their students; they work too much on their own. They exclude (often without realising it) the student-learners from many parts of the task. The teacher (and/or the provider) chooses the subject and the content; the teacher chooses the goals, the pace of learning, the level of the course; the teacher chooses the methods and evaluates the results.

All of this is done naturally, for it springs from a deep-rooted set of attitudes towards the learners. Some of us tend to see the learners as handicapped by being deprived of skills and knowledge, in which case those who possess the ability and the knowledge should give it; the learners need 'input'. Some of us also tend to believe that the student-learners are not capable of taking control of their own learning, that they cannot act on their own. There is a sense of the superiority of the teacher arising from the traditional world of education, a world that sees being 'learned' as the desired goal of all education, a state of attainment that the student-learner might, by great effort, ultimately reach. There is in this attitude a view of education as a one-way process, the transfer of knowledge and expertise, the imparting of some good.

A reappraisal of the roles of both teacher and learners will affect all parts of the teaching–learning opportunity. If the teacher abandons the attitude of 'I'll tell you' but instead says 'I'll help you to work it out', the whole curriculum will change. If the teacher abandons the attitude of 'I'll tell you' but instead says 'I'll help you to engage in a series of learning activities', the whole body of teaching methods will change.

Such a reorientation of the relationships between teacher, student-learner and knowledge will seek to cast aside attitudes based on hierarchies of knowing. There will be no more room for saying, 'I know what you should learn'; no more placing of theoretical knowledge higher than practical or experiential knowledge; no more insistence that what the soil chemist knows about mud is superior to what the child who plays with mud or the builder who makes bricks knows. Such attitudes of the learned demean experience and lay unhealthy stress on accumulated practice or book knowledge. A new relationship between learning and learner will give value to all views (not just those of the academic), will see the application as well as the general principle, and will admit on occasion, 'I don't know' or 'I don't see it like that.'

If we reject what I call 'the arrogance of the learned', the 'deficit and input' model of learning, we must equally avoid the opposite extreme, what may be called the 'pooling of ignorance', the rejection of the help of any teacher, the refusal to admit that the experience of the qualified and experienced teacher has worth. Some new insights, some introduction to the processes of finding out, some input is necessary to achieve transferability of skills and knowledge.

Any process of teaching adults that introduces divisions and despises the views and activities of others is unacceptable. Teachers must not only be able to admit that they have much to learn from their students, but must seek to strengthen rather than weaken the different elements brought into the learning situation by all the participants. It is a process of sharing, of valuing each other, of 'two-way learning'.

Teaching seen as 'informing' will be one-way and dependency-creating;

it will not be education (freeing). Clearly some information-gathering is necessary as part of the learning process, but the new knowledge does not need to be and should not be provided by the teacher alone. Compared with 'informing', training in skills can be liberating. It can make the learners free to exercise their newly won learning as and when they wish. But training on its own too can be binding, especially when it sets out to demonstrate the 'right' way to do something without considering that there are likely to be circumstances in which the 'right' way might well be wrong! It is not enough to teach people how to do something or other without encouraging them to consider the social and political factors involved in this activity and the structures of society that control access to these resources. Only by doing this wider task will the participants be able to grow towards a freer way of life.

How do we do this?

Easier said than done. We can talk about 'teaching on equal terms' or even about being the servant of the learners, and we can see how it applies in some contexts. Social action groups that choose their own leader, women's studies circles and community development programmes will operate on such a basis more easily than will dressmaking and advanced engineering classes.

We each need to explore these changed attitudes and the changed relationships between learner, teacher and knowledge for ourselves. Perhaps the key, when we have come to put the student-learner first rather than the teacher, is the need to listen more and to talk less. This book is, as we saw right at the beginning, not a good example of what I mean. It is by nature one-way, though I have tried to encourage you to use your experience on the material it contains and to test the views it expresses for yourself. But it seeks to encourage the development of a listening society rather than the talking (or even shouting) society in which so many of us live. The maintenance of pluralism rather than uniformity, the valuing of the experience, knowledge and insights of others, and the search to strengthen these rather than weaken them, are basic to all approaches to teaching adults, if we truly respect their adulthood.

Those outside and those inside?

Perhaps more fundamental is the view that teaching adults is not a process of instructing others but of enabling them to get a voice; not a process of bringing them into society (our society) but of helping them to play a fuller part in the society of which they are already full members. In a country like Bangladesh where those who are functionally non-literate form nearly 70 per cent of the total population, a view of literacy that speaks of 'bringing the illiterates into society' treats the majority as inferior and will hardly lead to active learning. They are already part of our society, and our task is to help them to lead a fuller life, to join in controlling their society.

If we see our work as part of this process, if we seek to share with equals rather than to instruct our inferiors, then we must be concerned about those who are *not* in our learning groups as much as with those who are. If we teach gardening, it will concern us that there are some who have gardens who apparently do not wish to learn more about this aspect of life; it should also be important to us to consider why some people have no gardens at all. If we teach health studies, we shall be concerned that those who are not in reach of our programmes may have opportunities for their needs to be met as well.

The question of participation is not just a matter of what the student-learners in our classes and learning groups do in the process of learning. It is also about getting others to take advantage of the learning opportunities on offer. This will lead us to experiment with new formats of classes and groups, with new times, with new approaches to the subject-matter that will be more appropriate to different groups of learners, with restructuring our contents and methods, to try to overcome the barriers that still exist in all societies.

There are two parts to this. On the one hand there is the provision of programmes to meet the needs of existing and new participants. We need to become more aware of the barriers we put up to participation, not only to those not in our learning groups but also to those who are, and seek to reduce them. We can play our part in increasing provision, creating new learning opportunities to meet the needs of those who do not attend. (Archbishop William Temple is reputed to have said that the Christian church was an organisation that existed for the sake of those who were *not* its members; teachers of adults will often share much of the same concern.)

On the other hand increased provision does not always lead to greatly increased participation. The barriers of attitudes (the 'it's-not-for-me' syndrome) will remain. It is up to us as privileged people and experts and teachers to address ourselves to the problem of overcoming the sense of exclusion that we have created in many of our fellow human beings. Then we shall be truly concerned for participation.

Further reading

Cross, K. P. (1981) *Adults as Learners: Increasing Participation and Facilitating Learning*. San Francisco, CA: Jossey Bass.

Flanders, N. A. (1970) *Analyzing Teaching Behavior*. Reading, MA: Addison-Wesley Pub. Co.

Gibson, A. J. (1981) *People Power*. Harmondsworth: Penguin.

Illich, I. (1973) *De-Schooling Society*. Harmondsworth: Penguin.

Lovett, T. (1982) *Adult Education, Community Development and the Working Class*. Nottingham: University of Nottingham.

Midwinter, E. (1975) *Education and the Community*. London: Allen and Unwin.

Rogers, J. (1976) *Right to Learn: The Case for Adult Equality*. London: Arrow.

Epilogue

Hanging on the wall of a small hut in one of the crowded suburbs of Madras, the offices of the Committee for Development Research and Action, are the following verses, which say it all:

Go to the people
Live among them
Learn from them
    Love them
Start with what they know
Build on what they have

But of the best leaders
When their task is accomplished
    Their work is done
The people all remark
'We have done it ourselves'.

BIBLIOGRAPHY

ACACE (1979) *Towards Continuing Education*. Leicester: ACACE.

Ackoff, R. L. (1978) *The Art of Problem-Solving*. New York: Wiley.

Alexander, Sir William (1975) *Adult Education and the Challenge of Change*. Edinburgh: Scottish Education Department.

Ball, C. (1991) *Learning Pays: the Role of Post-compulsory Education and Training*. London: Royal Society of Arts.

Belbin, R. M. (1980) *The Discovery Method in Training*. Sheffield: Manpower Services Commission.

Berne, E. (1970) *Games People Play*. Harmondsworth: Penguin.

Bloom, B. S.(1965) *Taxonomy of Educational Objectives*. London: Longman.

Boshier, R. (1989) Participant motivation, in C. Titmus (ed.) *Lifelong Education for Adults: an International Handbook*. Oxford: Pergamon.

Brookfield, S. (1983) *Adult Learners, Adult Education and the Community*. Milton Keynes: Open University Press.

Brookfield, S. D. (1986) *Understanding and Facilitating Adult Learning*. Milton Keynes: Open University Press.

Bruner, J. S. (1974) *Toward a Theory of Instruction*. Cambridge, MA: Harvard University Press.

Chickering, A. W. (ed.) (1981) *The Modern American College: Responding to the New Realities of Diverse Students and a Changing Society*. San Francisco, CA: Jossey Bass.

Christensen, R. and Hansen, A. T. (eds) (1987) *Teaching and the Case Method*. Boston, MA: Harvard Business School.

Claxton, Guy (1984) *Live and Learn*. London: Harper and Row.

Cross, K. P. (1981) *Adults as Learners: Increasing Participation and Facilitating Learning*. San Francisco, CA: Jossey Bass.

Davies, P. (ed.) (1995) *Adults in Higher Education: International Perspectives in Access and Participation*. London: Jessica Kingsley.

Department of Education, Ireland (1984) *Lifelong Learning: Report of the Adult Education Commission for the Republic of Ireland*. Dublin: Department of Education.

Dewey, J. (1933) *How We Think*. London: D. C. Heath.

Dewey, J. (1938) *Experience and Education*. New York: Macmillan.

Dudley, E. (1993) *The Critical Villager*. London: Routledge.

Egan, K. (1986) *Individual Development and the Curriculum*. London: Hutchinson.

Eisner, E. W. (1985) *The Art of Educational Evaluation*. London: Falmer.

Elsdon, K. (1975) *Training for Adult Education*. Nottingham: University of Nottingham.

Erikson, E. (1965) *Childhood and Society*. Harmondsworth: Penguin.

Freire, P. (1972) *Pedagogy of the Oppressed*. Harmondsworth: Penguin.

Gagné, R. M. (1972) Domains of Learning, *Interchange*, 3(1): 1–8.

Gagné, R. M. (1975) *The Conditions of Learning*. New York: Holt, Rinehart and Winston.

Griffin, C. (1983) *Curriculum Theory in Adult and Continuing Education*. Beckenham: Croom Helm.

Habermas, J. (1978) *Knowledge and Human Interest*. London: Heinemann.

Harris, T. (1973) *I'm OK, You're OK*. London: Pan.

Havighurst, R. J. (1952) *Development Tasks and Education*. New York: McKay.

Henriques, J. (1984) *Changing the Subject: Psychology, Social Regulation and Subjectivity*. London: Methuen.

Herzberg, F. (1972) *The Motivation to Work*. Chichester: Wiley.

Honey, P. and Mumford, A. (1986) *Manual of Learning Styles*. London: Peter Honey.

Houle, C. O. (1961) *The Inquiring Mind: a Study of the Adult who Continues to Learn*. Madison, WI: University of Wisconsin Press.

ISCED (1975) *International Standard Classification of Educational Data*. Paris: UNESCO.

Kelly, G. A. (1955) *Psychology of Personal Constructs*, 2 vols. New York: McGraw-Hill.

Kidd, J. R. (1973) *How Adults Learn*. New York: Association Press.

Knowles, M. S. (1990) *The Adult Learner: a Neglected Species*. Houston, TX: Gulf.

Kolb, D. A. (1976) *Learning Style Inventory Technical Manual*. Boston, MA: McBer.

Kolb, D. A. (1984) *Experiential Learning: Experience as the Source of Learning and Development*. Englewood Cliffs, NJ: Prentice-Hall.

Laing, R. D. (1972) *Knots*. Harmondsworth: Penguin.

Leagans, P. (1971) *Behavioral Change in Agriculture*. Ithaca, NY: Cornell University Press.

LEIF (1990): Erno Lehtinen, From superficial learning to true expertise: education challenge of the future, *Life and Education in Finland*, 2(90): 14.

Lewin, K. (1935) *A Dynamic Theory of Personality*. New York: McGraw-Hill.

Lucas, A. M. (1983) Scientific literacy and informal learning, *Studies in Science Education*, 10.

McClintock, C. G. (1972) *Experimental Social Psychology*. New York: Holt, Rinehart and Winston.

McGregor, D. (1960) *The Human Side of Enterprise*. New York: McGraw-Hill.

McGregor, D. (1967) *The Professional Manager*. New York: McGraw-Hill.

Mansbridge, A. (1920) *Adventure in Working Class Education*. London: Longmans Green.

Maslow, A. H. (1968) *Towards a Psychology of Being*. New York: Van Nostrand.

Mezirow, J. (1981) A critical theory of adult learning and education, *Adult Education*, 32: 3–24.

Neugarten, B. L. (1977) Personality and aging, in J. E. Birren and K. W. Schaie (eds) *Handbook of the Psychology of Aging*. New York: Van Nostrand Reinhold.

NIACE (1970) *Survey of Provision*. Leicester: National Institute of Adult (Continuing) Education.

OECD (1977) *Learning Opportunities for Adults*. Paris: OECD.

Rahman, Md. Anisur (1993) *People's Self-Development: Perspectives on Participatory Action Research*. London: Zed.

Rogers, A. (1977) *The Spirit and the Form: Essays by and in honour of Harold Wiltshire*. Nottingham: University of Nottingham.

Rogers, A. (1980) *Knowledge and the People: the Role of the University in Adult and Continuing Education*. Londonderry: New University of Ulster.

Rogers, A. (1991a) *Teaching Adults in Extension*. Reading: Education for Development.

Rogers, A. (1991b) *Teaching Methods in Extension*. Reading: Education for Development.

Rogers, A. (1992) *Adults Learning for Development*. London: Cassell, and Reading: Education for Development.

Rogers, A. (1993) Adult learning maps and the teaching process, *Studies in the Education of Adults*, 22(2): 199–220.

Rogers, A. (1995) Participatory research in local history, *Journal of Regional and Local Studies*, 15(1): 1–14.

Rogers, C. (1974) *On Becoming a Person*. London: Constable.

Rogers, J. (1969) *Teaching on Equal Terms*. London: BBC Publications.

Rogers, J. (1976) *Right to Learn: the Case for Adult Equality*. London: Arrow.

Rogers, J. (1984) *Adults in Education*. London: BBC Publications.

Rogers, J. (1989) *Adults Learning*. Milton Keynes: Open University Press.

Rotter, J. B. (1982) *The Development and Applications of Social Learning Theory*. New York: Praeger.

Schein, E. H. and Kommers, D. W. (1972) *Professional Education*. New York: McGraw-Hill.

Schön, D. A. (1983) *The Reflective Practitioner: How Professionals Think in Action*. New York: Basic Books.

Sheehy, G. (1976) *Passages: Predictable Crises of Adult Life*. New York: Dutton.

Stephens, M. D. and Roderick, G. W. (1971) *Teaching Techniques in Adult Education*. Newton Abbot: David and Charles.

Strategy Report (1980) *Continuing Education in Northern Ireland: Strategy for Development*. Belfast: Northern Ireland Council for Continuing Education.

Thompson, J. L. (ed.) (1980) *Adult Education for a Change*. London: Hutchinson.

Tight, M. (ed.) (1983) *Education for Adults*. Vol. 1: *Adult Learning and Education*; Vol. 2: *Opportunities for Adult Education*. Beckenham: Croom Helm.

Travers, R. M. W. (1964) *Introduction to Educational Research*. New York: Macmillan.

UNESCO (1975a) *ISCED: International Standard Classification of Educational Data*. Paris: UNESCO.

UNESCO (1975b) *Educational Radio and Television*. Paris: UNESCO.

UNESCO (1976) *Nairobi: Recommendations on the Development of Adult Education: Declaration of Nairobi Conference*. Paris: UNESCO.
Whitehead, A. N. (1959) *The Aims of Education*. New York: Macmillan.
Wood, J. (1974) *How Do You Feel?*. Englewood Cliffs, NJ: Prentice-Hall.

INDEX

LOCAL EDUCATION
COMMUNITY, CONVERSATION, PRAXIS

Mark K. Smith

Drawing upon the experiences of adult and community educators, youth and community workers, Mark Smith examines the practice of educators who build up ways of working with local networks and cultures. Shops, launderettes, streets, bars, cafes and people's houses are the settings for much of their work and when they do appear in schools and colleges, they are most likely to be found in corridors, eating areas and student common rooms. Their work is not organized by subject, syllabi or lessons, it is about conversation and community, a commitment to local democracy and self-organization and community, a commitment to local democracy and self-organization, and is often unpredictable and risky.

The author offers a rigorous analysis of the subtle and difficult activity of intervening in other people's lives, or conversing with purpose, and of engaging with people to broaden opportunity and to effect change in their lives and communities.

Contents

Introduction – Being local – Being an educator – Engaging in conversation – Thinking about direction – Structuring the work – Embedding practice – Reflecting-in-action – Fostering community, conversation and praxis – References - Index.

208pp   0 335 19274 2 (Paperback)   0 335 19275 0 (Hardback)